LONG TIME APPROACHING
An Incomplete Memoir

Glenn Martin lives in Sydney, although he lived in the bush on the far north coast of New South Wales for two decades. He has been a teacher at high schools and tertiary institutions, a manager of community services organisations, and a commentator on management, business ethics, employment law, and training and development. He has been the editor of publications for management and training professionals and an instructional designer for online learning. He is the author of over twenty books.

LONG TIME APPROACHING
An Incomplete Memoir

Glenn Martin

G.P. Martin Publishing

Published 2023 by G.P. Martin Publishing
Website: www.glennmartin.com.au
Contact: info@glennmartin.com.au

Copyright © Glenn Martin 2023
All rights reserved. No part of this publication may be reproduced or transmitted in any form or by any process without the prior written permission of the publisher, except for the inclusion of brief quotations for a review.
Glenn Martin asserts his moral rights as the author of this book.

Book layout and cover design by the author
Typeset in Sitka 11 pt
Printed by Lulu.com

Front cover image by the author. Bamboo glade at Crystal Castle, Mullumbimby NSW.

ISBN: 978 0 6488433 7 5 (pbk.)

A catalogue record for this book is available from the National Library of Australia

For family and friends,
and those who love our striving
for attainment, connection and harmony.

Contents

Foreword 1
1 Beginning 2
2 Childhood 3
    Things I know 4
3 God 4
4 1968 9
5 War 14
6 Army 17
7 Utopia 21
8 Poet 23
9 My leg 24
10 Hospital 26
11 Hitch-hiking 28
12 Psychiatric nurse 31
13 Queensland 36
14 Kindness 37
15 Not belonging 40
    Things I know 41
16 Hippie 41
17 Teacher 50
    Things I know 54
18 Horseshoe Creek 54
19 Betrayed 61
20 Dream 64
21 Divorce 65
22 Father 66

23 Restabilising 67
24 Kyogle stories 70
    Things I know 72
25 Adult education 72
26 Youth worker 76
27 Lady 2 80
28 Skills 84
    Things I know 85
29 William Irwin Thompson 85
30 Council 87
31 Challenge 93
32 Lessons 97
33 A breakdown 100
34 Lady 3 103
35 An intimidator 105
36 Teaching again 107
37 University again 108
38 Beardless 112
39 Career 113
    Things I know 114
40 BBus(Hons) 115
41 Driving 119
42 100+ job applications 120
43 Sydney 123
44 Separation 125
45 Apprenticeship 127
46 Poetry collections 133

47 Bliss..137
    Things I know 138
48 Writing a story...139
49 I Ching..142
50 Leadership (1) 146
51 Dirty business 148
52 Tribunal.. 151
53 Leadership (2) 152
54 Contracting..155
55 Drinking..158
56 Visiting Greenacre...159
57 Maturity.. 161
58 Concerts..169
    Things I know 171
59 Santana.. 171
60 Nashville...175
61 Memoir...176
    Things I know 181
62 Attempted PhD... 181
63 Family history 184
64 Travel to Asia 188
65 Vietnam 191
66 New Zealand...193
67 A new book..194
    Things I know 196
68 Tane Mahuta 196
69 Napier...198

70 Echidna	199
Things I know	201
71 Going to Woodford	202
72 New Year's Day	205
73 I Ching reading	206
74 The three muses	207
75 Kate	208
76 The Lettering House	210
77 Bob Hawke	211
78 Woodford talk	212
79 Chai	213
Things I know	214
80 Fire Ceremony	214
81 Nostalgia	216
Things I know	217
82 Soup and moonlight	217
83 A death	219
84 Another death	221
85 Professional staff	221
86 College	224
87 Four pillars	227
88 Staying home	229
89 Library	232
90 Career progression	233
91 A public role	235
92 Magazine editor	238
93 Academia	239

94 Young, Living, Firm Ground 240
95 Death of a publication 241
96 Travel to England and Ireland 243
    Things I know 245
97 Ireland and Cork 246
98 About Cornwall 247
99 Railway interlude 248
100 Cornwall and London 249
101 Office decorations 251
102 Disengaging 252
103 Four pillars: Competence 253
104 Morality 256
105 Beauty 256
106 Love 257
    Things I know 258
107 Love and marriage and me 258
108 Finish 259
Stories 261
    The Language Lesson 261
    Dancing with Intent 264
    Postcards from Woodford 267
    Love and marriage and me 270
Other books by Glenn Martin 274

Foreword

A foreword to this book is unnecessary. The book is what it is: you will get the idea. I am saying it is a memoir because it is "a record of events, a history treating of matters from the personal knowledge of the writer" (Shorter Oxford English Dictionary, 1962). It has no semblance of fiction or fictional overlay.

In some instances, I chose not to use names, and I have not used made-up names. Where I wished to hide the names of persons or organisations, I have simply left their names out. In some instances, for simplicity and clarity, I resorted to the device, "Lady 1" et cetera. This is my story, not a vendetta or an exposé.

As a memoir, the book is incomplete. Firstly, this is necessary because the book could have become vast, and there is a certain point where enough is enough. One must "Leave the past alone and be happy with what you have." The book is also incomplete because I have chosen to leave some things out. There were many reasons for this – enough reasons to fill a book. Suffice to say, not everything needs to be said.

Is this book my story? Yes and no. It is my story in the sense that it tells many of the significant events and episodes of my life. However, I have written around twenty other books, many of which deal with specific episodes or themes in my life. Not wishing to duplicate what I have said in those books, I have referred to them here. In that sense, this book is a doorway into many other of my stories, and it is incomplete without them.

This book includes a section of photos from my life, and there is a section of "stories" at the end (articles, essays, poems).

Enjoy.

1 Beginning

I could say this is another attempt to weave a thread through my difficult years, doomed relationships and fragmentary attempts at a career path where, by turns, I served communities, ran from them, wrote essays on ethics and universal spirit, tried to be a good man, practised teaching, and then built walls around so I could listen again for the words that needed to be said.

Clouds and thunder bring life. The seedling emerges to sway and lean, then to stiffen and green. Sprouting is everywhere, abundant and enthused, fresh and thick. No need to go far: the place of striving is here. It is sufficient; it is more than enough for now. The seed will grow into its kind, but what it will look like, only time will give of its secrets.

Noble one considers his principles. Life sucks in air, already triumphant against the windy, broad-scale tide of decay, of tearing things down, of wearing them out like a ragged shirt. In the midst, there is the seed's mild song.

Of course, there is the dream of plenty and ease. The king looks over the ripened harvest, deeply content – there will be enough for all. He will direct his strength wisely and fend off over-indulgence. Thus, his capacities will expand and the people will build on their meagre comforts, embellishing.

Meanwhile there is a path to be trod, and it is much slower, stumbling through the first ignorant steps, the gruelling practice and hapless mistakes, the wounds, and the stretches in time that seem to be exile or worse, stagnant.

2 Childhood

This is what a childhood at the fringe of Sydney could look like in the 1950s. I had unvoiced desires and I was ambivalent, hovering at the fringe, wanting to belong, and not wanting to, simultaneously. Every time my voice came to words, it chipped against the mob, resisting the edifice of my neighbourhood, the world as I was supposed to receive it. I recognise now that it was the belligerence of the world that I was not enamoured with. Home was a refuge, but the world was warning me that I would have to toughen up if I was to get on in it.

There were books. Very soon, as soon as possible after kindergarten, there were books. So much so that in First Class, at the end of April, the teacher and the Assistant Infants Principal decided that I should be promoted to Second Class. So I was walked across the playground to the new class, tentative but sufficiently confident, trusting that they must know what was best for me.

The new teacher decided that I could read well enough, and allowed me to sit outside for the reading lesson. I could choose a book myself from the shelf at the front of the room. I read many books; they were short. I remember the teacher as quietly affectionate. At the end of the year, she gave me a present, a book which she brought to me from her home. My mother was a little embarrassed when I showed her, but I had accepted the book with surprise and gratitude. I read the book until I knew all the words and all the story.

It signified to me that being able to read was to be treasured. I had no sense of competitiveness about this. It did not matter to me that other pupils had not received a book from the teacher. It was not a public event. I remember that it was a bigger book than the ones I had read from the front shelf in the classroom. It was a long story, and there was a dark part of the story in the middle that was a little frightening. I had to go through this. I had to make sure I came out each time, safely. After this, I was going into Primary School, which was a male domain. I took the gift of reading with me.

Things I know
Everything in nature tends towards the fulfilment of its potential. Later, I learned that Aristotle had said this. However, it hardly mattered. It was true anyway.

3 God

I went to Sunday School. Children need to belong, and I needed to belong. It wasn't really a choice. There was no question about it; it was like breathing. We learned from the Bible. All the stories were holy. One week we learned the story about Abraham taking his son up on the mountain. The son didn't know it, but his father was going to sacrifice him. At the last minute, God speaks and tells Abraham it won't be necessary. He has proved his faith.

It was a holy story, but I couldn't accept it. I pondered it all the time I was walking home. I didn't talk about it. I knew that this would be to question the whole fabric of the church. Indeed, not only the local weatherboard church, but the entire church all over. I had been through that stage where you write down your address as the full address – house number, street name, suburb, city, state, country, the Earth, the solar system, the galaxy and the whole universe. So I knew that to question what the reverend said at the local church had deep and long implications, and there were many leaders in the vast hierarchy who would demolish my questions – viciously, snidely, heavy-handedly, high-handedly – and they would not answer my logic.

However, it was a problem. This God had told Abraham to kill his own son as a sacrifice to Him. And this God was the Creator and Lord of all creation, the Ultimate Father, so there was no higher authority. What kind of father would sacrifice his own son, supposedly for the sake of the Father of all Fathers? What kind of a God would ask that? The question sat very uncomfortably. The people at church said that the fact that God had told Abraham he didn't have to go through with it proved that He was merciful, but I thought differently.

The fact that God had asked Abraham to do it indicated that it was considered to be an appropriate command. Some of the older people at the church tried to explain that this was meant to show how exalted God was, that He was more important than anything and everyone, so He was worthy of any sacrifice, even your own child. I didn't say anything, but I still couldn't get over my repugnance.

When I got older, and some people in the church were getting more educated – one of them had started theological college – the argument shifted. We learned that there was a distinction between the Old and New Testaments. Some of the things in the Old Testament no longer applied, because the New Testament had brought a new order, through Jesus. Presumably the new order meant that you could no longer be asked to sacrifice your child. You didn't even have to approach it like it was a test of faith where you would be let off at the last minute.

As the years passed, and my own education took root in my life, I took the path of questioning the Bible rather than harbouring resentment against a monstrous God. I eventually made progress with this dilemma. When I was young, the ministers and the other church leaders, particularly the Sunday School leaders, were people of simple faith and confined thoughts about their religion. Their faith was expressed in singing the hymns and simple songs, and reciting the stories and not questioning anything. My mother, who seldom went to church, also told me I shouldn't think too much; it would only cause me grief.

In my late teenage years, I discovered bookshops. At first, I had discovered libraries, which were important because I had no money. As a family we had very little money, enough to do the necessary things – food, clothes and education. The library was the first doorway. There were books there that addressed the questions I was having and which offered different perspectives that challenged and extended my thinking. I realised I had embarked on a process whose end I did not know.

Progress with the dilemma of the appalling stories in the Old Testament eventually came, when I was about twenty-one (around 1971). It was in a bookshop in the city. I think that it was not a Christian bookshop, but a bookshop that had a section on religion. The title of the book was clear enough: *The Authority of the Bible*. It was written by C.H. Dodd. I bought it. I was starting to get the feel for what you do when you pick up a book. You turn immediately to the back cover.

There was the most wonderful promise on the back cover: "No one can read this book without feeling that he has been brought into a spacious world in which, while he must walk with reverence, he can move with exhilarating freedom." And I wished that the book would be able to do that. Would it answer the questions that had plagued me in secret for all of my growing years?

Next, I looked at the chapter headings, and comfortingly, they were laid out in terms of the Old Testament and the New Testament. I read that book avidly, and then read parts of it again. I still have the book, in what is now a considerable personal library. I also took stock of who C.H. Dodd was. I didn't have a category for him. The Christian books that I was familiar with were all devotional. None of them spoke to questioning minds. Dodd was different. For a start, he was old. He was not a shining young man who was a great advertisement for the church. When books had got fancier in the 1960s and acquired coloured covers, suddenly all the authors became handsome.

Dodd was born in 1884. The few Christian authors I was familiar with were probably born in the 1930s. Dodd was educated at Oxford and was ordained. His life's work was to do with biblical commentary, and he worked on a new translation of the Bible.

I felt that as a young, ignorant questioner, Dodd was probably a good place to start, although I was sure that most people I knew would not know of him, and would probably question his position in the church. A Sydney suburb was a long way from the cloisters of the English church establishment.

I was interested in crossing boundaries, and finding my own place to stand. I have now found that Dodd died in 1973, not long after I discovered him. *The Authority of the Bible* had been first published in 1929, and the edition I bought was released in 1971. I pondered about what he said for a year or more. The idea of authority resonated with me. Why do we accept things as being true, or as being the foundation for the decisions we take? It seemed a rather fundamental question.

I bought and read three more of Dodd's books. The latest one was published in 1970: *The Founder of Christianity*. One of the reviews on the back cover suggested that it might play "a powerful part in the revival of a positive and intelligent Christianity". At the time, this was an attractive proposition. I had moved from my local church to a new, shop-front church-alternative that considered itself to be radical. It attracted many good thinkers and lively souls, keen to revive Christian faith and practice.

The organisation, the House of the New world, had its own newspaper, and I found a place for myself on its editorial committee, for I wanted to write – well, I wanted to think and write. They gave me opportunities to do so. I wrote about contemporary society and my dissatisfaction with it. I wrote about authority and experience, and authority and freedom. I had been studying existential philosophy at university, so I felt that I had things to say that might be helpful to other unsatisfied souls.

Two things are of interest to me now: the first is that my articles were published at all, and given prominence. I still have copies of some of the newspapers. I even have copies of the articles in their initial, hand-written form. The other surprise is that I still largely agree with what I wrote. I am not outraged, or too embarrassed with myself.

"I was six years old and I realised I had to do what the teacher told me. I was thirteen and heard myself saying that all Europeans were dirty. Didn't that sound just like my mother? I was sixteen and taking seriously the sermons preached at the local church. And besides, didn't that book I read say, 'It would be presumptuous to question what the Church has accepted for 2,000 years'?

"But by then I was eighteen and went to university. Karl Marx said 'Religion is the opiate of the masses'. It was in the curriculum for Marxist Philosophy. Nineteen, and the *Nation Review* said that the government, the Vietnam War, expressways, high-rise buildings, supermarkets and the price of meat were all a capitalist plot. And everyone was saying that sex and marihuana were the two badges of the free. And then I was twenty and the Vice Chancellor of the university said "Come unto me all you who are heavy-laden. Give me your minds and I will give you security and a house and a two-car garage.

"The context in which we find ourselves incorporates many authorities which compete for our allegiance."

After a few pages, I ended by saying: "Whether it is the question of God or whether it is the question of other beliefs and behaviour, the quest for authority is the quest for hypotheses that are adequate to account for our experience, and which in the first place acknowledge the validity of our experience. It is so easy to make authority your truth rather than truth your authority."

I could argue with the phrasing of the final thought, but there is substance there that I recognise and accept. But the seeds of leaving Christian congregations had already been laid. Perhaps it was more about the form of the church rather than the content of its message. When I faded away from membership, I felt I was broadening, not rejecting an inner truth. There was a big, wide world beyond Christianity, other types of spirituality, and I felt that some of it was likely to also be worthy of respect, attention, perhaps even affection and devotion.

4 1968

In 1968, the world seemed to turn on its axis. Students in Australia were demonstrating against their universities. It wasn't isolated to one university; it was widespread. Students overseas were likewise demonstrating and rioting, for example, in the U.S. and France. The Soviet Union was crushing Czechoslovakia, the Vietnam War was grinding on. Martin Luther King was killed; so was J.F. Kennedy's brother, Robert. Gough Whitlam was coming to prominence, although it would be four more years before he became Prime Minister. The U.S. was preparing to launch a rocket to the moon with astronauts on-board. John Lennon had paired up with Yoko Ono, and the Seekers had become the Australians of the Year.

Faith in the Vietnam War was failing, because the war was no longer at a distance: it was on television. I could say of these years that I was disoriented because my father had died suddenly in March 1967 when I was in the last year of high school. You wouldn't know it by looking at my school reports for that year: "Glenn is an excellent student and deserves his results" (Dux of the Year, and first in several subjects). But there is no dismissing the intensity of events in 1968, both in Sydney and in the wider world. Who was I to unpick the threads of my turmoil?

I have written about my father's death elsewhere. In the poetry book, *Love and Armour* (2007), there is a poem, "A dead man", which is about my father, and there are notes about my father's death later in the book: pp. 49-55.

I used to go to The Domain in Sydney on Sunday afternoons, often. In those days it was a ferment of opinions and causes, and brash, loud-mouthed firebrands who attracted hundreds of people to listen. In classic fashion they stood on soap boxes and shouted without microphones to whoever gathered around. I was myself in ferment, listening to see if anyone would make sense, something that I could integrate into my developing mind.

The spectre looming over young men at this time was conscription into the army. Since 1962 the Australian government had committed troops to fighting in Vietnam, and the number was steadily growing. In 1964 the *National Service Act* had passed, requiring some 20-year-old males to serve in the Army for a period of two years. The selection was, in true Australian fashion, through a lottery, following which young men were sent a letter of notification.

Predictably, for those of little faith, the *Defence Act* was amended in 1965 (when I was fifteen) to provide that conscripts could serve overseas. It was one of the things that the government said it would never do, and I would have preferred not to grow up cynical. Australia managed to get all the way through the First World War without succumbing to conscription. It had a form of military training for young men, but it did not extend to sending conscripted men overseas. And conscription was firmly rejected twice, in referendums.

In World War Two, conscription was introduced early in the war, but again, it did not allow the government to send conscripted soldiers overseas. They could serve in Australia and Papua New Guinea. I felt that a lot of Australian history had been overturned to make it possible to send me to fight in Vietnam. I had two levels of conflict: I was not sure that I believed in going to war and fighting (that is, killing people) anyway, and I was not sure that the Vietnamese people were our enemies.

Nowadays, I could just say all the arguments are old. Some people would be willing to continue with the argument about the threat of the Communists, and credit Australia, the Unites States and New Zealand with stopping the spread. In 1970 I knew that Vietnam had had a complicated colonial past which included the French; not much more than that, but enough to know it was not a simple case of Communist marauders steaming down through Vietnam as if all the countries were Dominoes.

I was also influenced by the nature of the war the Americans fought. Even in the First World War, the old idea of noble soldiers fighting gallantly was gone. It was, instead, a mutual slaughter of soldiers with industrially produced weapons. The second World War confirmed this, and added its own mother-of-all industrial weapons, the A-Bomb. But the general avidity for the war was matched by the readiness of leaders on all sides to raise their sons up to the slaughter. In Vietnam the strategy was taken to the next step: if we can't find the Vietcong in the jungles, we will blow the jungles up, burn them down and poison them with Agent Orange.

The leaders, of course, avow that they will not take the means of destruction any further. And then the soldiers come home and we expect them to be well-adjusted, and to take up normal lives and not hurt anyone anymore. There is no healing for such men (and women); there is only hope, and much of that in vain.

However, layered over this animated discussion that was occurring everywhere – excited by fear, anxiety and nationalistic fervour – was the thinking that came out of Christianity about loving one's enemies. I had separated myself from the church sufficiently, at least emotionally, to know that when Jesus had said to "Bless them that hurt you", He didn't have half a thought aimed at reconciling his philosophy with a state-sponsored institution that would provide blessings for favourable wars.

I was young, I was surrounded by radical thinking, by thousands of young people who were wilder than me and who were ready to demand their version of justice and freedom. It seemed wrong to be lining up with a war that was supported by such crazy, extreme Anti-Communism that no freedom was possible in our own society. Yet, 1968 was perhaps the first time it had been possible to examine these questions.

I left high school at the end of 1967. Midway through the next year, I went back for a visit. I expected to speak to a few teachers, that's all. And I did. But then the Principal, Mr Wright, saw me and called me up to his office. He had always been quiet, even aloof. Even though I had been the School Captain, I didn't know him well. I laughed at the idea that I could be in trouble! But he shook my hand and called me into his office and shut the door. Then, after a few minutes of pleasant chat he became serious. He looked straight at me and said, "Glenn, what's going on out there?"

He meant university, but there was also a wider thrust to his question, meaning, the whole of society. I was stunned. I had been asking myself the same question, but what did I know? I was only eighteen. Anything could have been happening before I came along, and anything could happen now. And then I felt sympathy for him. He had been a decent School Principal – honourable and fair, not swept up by mean, crazy or pompous people – and he was nearing the end of his career.

I said that the protests were mostly the expression of anger and frustration about political decisions that had been made to follow foreign powers (that is, America), and about some of the academics who had curricula that hadn't been refreshed for thirty years, and that they didn't expect their students to think about the course material, just to accept it blindly. I thought I was treading close to the line, but I was no longer a school student, so I could exercise some freedom. I said that today, students expect to think about things. Mindful of the anxiety he was expressing, I said I thought much of it would settle down. Many of the protesters would finish their degrees and go off and get jobs.

Sadly, I agreed with what I said, although my reasoning was different. Perhaps Mr Wright thought it was timely that he was approaching retirement. In fact, a couple of years later he died – a heart attack. The same way my father had died last year. I did think that most university students would complete their degrees and get jobs, and mortgages. They would live the elevated life they had trained for. Their supposed ideals would prove to be expendable.

Perhaps, in articulating my impromptu speech for Mr Wright, I had articulated my own position by omission – I would be one of the few who did not complete his degree, and would not enter into the workaday workforce. I would be an outsider. That visit to the school happened first, in 1968. So it was after that that I went to a concert at the University of New South Wales. I was still a student there, studying engineering; I completed two out of four years – successfully. My mother had trained me to try not to leave a mess behind me.

I didn't go to many concerts. I studied my subjects and I read theology. I was not a screaming, fawning, drunken groupie. I was more temperate. But I went to see Tully at the Roundhouse at the University of New South Wales. It was a three-hour concert, and everybody was sitting on the floor. I just sat and listened, mesmerised. It was a full band, with occasional vocals by one man, and a saxophone, clarinet and flute played by another man. I did not take drugs at this time, and I was fully sober. The music took me to far places. It shook the daytime world out of its nest, and created something exalted, extraordinarily beautiful.

Years later – forty years – I learned that Richard Lockwood, the reed player, had given up the spotlight after Tully, and just played music. He had discovered Meher Baba. I heard that he felt that he had achieved bliss, which was the same as boundless love, so what was there to strive to do? He said the words that night: "There is a paradise of perfect silence, not far from here, or you, or there. Through the doorway of life and death it lies, and before. We will all still be here when we are all there."

I love that story. It makes me think that I was not foolish that night; I did hear something that was peerless. But, at the same time, I felt that I had to live my life, even if it turned out to be difficult. And I did not know this life. I was trawling around, picking up clues.

5 War

I went to see a man that I had met down at The Domain. He was not vociferous. He only ever had five to ten people gathered around, who were somewhat interested, that is, unless they were taunting him or trying to attack him. But he wasn't the kind of man who attracted a boisterous audience; they soon left. He had a few copies of a pamphlet which consisted of a cover that was deep red, and a single sheet of paper inside, printed both sides. The cover just said "The 'Royal' Road to Peace". It was a royal red. His message was that Jesus was a man of peace. So, I could ask him about war?

Indeed, the man did have something to say. He did not shy away from the question, or tell me empty things that would not help me. That was why I went to his home later. He said, "I have a book at home on this very question. I will give it to you." I did not think there was any danger in going to his home and besides, I was young; I was meant to be adventurous and do unfamiliar things.

His house was in Glebe. It was set up for church, with a circle of chairs in the biggest room. The ceilings were thirteen-feet-high. I was from the suburbs, where all the houses were new and the ceilings were generally eight-feet-six-inches high. I was learning many different things. I didn't know Glebe at all. I could see that most of the houses were close together and old. I knew my parents had lived in the inner suburbs when they were young, so I guessed there was some connection, if I were to go back a generation or two.

The man showed me the book, *War and the Gospel* by Jean Lasserre, published in 1962 in London. Lasserre was a Minister of the French Reformed Church. I hadn't known about French people not being Catholic. How much did I not know, or not even know about?

The man wouldn't take any money for the book. I think he felt that I needed it, and I did. Nor did he invite me to church. I think he felt that that was irrelevant to our purpose in meeting.

When I look through the book now, I see my pencil markings, so I had been brave enough to take ownership of the book and mark passages in it. I was still notionally in the Church of England church. What had my church had to say about serving in the army and going to fight a war? One suggestion had been to continue to love our enemies, even as we were shooting them. I had despaired at the mental convolutions necessary to achieve that.

Lasserre's book quoted someone in a Christian Church who had put forward this argument, then Lasserre said he was outraged, that this would destroy body, mind and soul. Love had to be manifest in action. I was still looking towards the prospect of conscription. I know many people can accept the social framework. If they are told that it's necessary to join the army and fight a war, they will do so, and do their best. They will do it for their country, and for their fellow citizens, for their family, their neighbourhood. They will do it for their neighbouring countries.

However, in England, where Lasserre's book was published, the 1950s had brought fear of the A-Bomb and the H-Bomb, of the idea that there would be no point in anyone fighting the next war because the Big Bombs would put an end to everything. Australia was a bit further away, and its main threat was the hordes of Yellow People. I thought that there always had to be a fear or a threat.

I felt as if I had come into this world at the end of untold years of sorry history, and that history was rolling on, eager to repeat itself. I didn't want to be part of it. It was also clear that to be part of it all, you had to stop thinking and just accept your part in it. Nor are you allowed to say this, because you have to pretend that you are able to think whatever you like. And I didn't want to fight in the streets, whereas some of the protesters did. They wanted to get angry and assert that that it was righteous anger. They said this is how things got changed. They didn't seem to mind if they hurt people. They would say, "They deserved it", or, "It helped achieve the purpose."

There was still a lot of that sentiment at school among the more maladjusted teachers. The cane was still part of the repertoire, and pain was supposed to be beneficial: "Teach them a lesson!" And if that's the way of it, then everyone has to be in it, even if they don't believe it. Those difficult times had not changed yet. If nothing else, it was a last-stop resort. The new ways might start here and there, but they were accused of being weak, and leaving teachers, and all hierarchy, defenceless. But the thinking that had started was ethical thought: if violence is wrong in school then it is wrong in parenting. If it is wrong in one context, then it is probably wrong in another.

It took years for all the thoughts to coalesce. In the meantime, rules and relationships were rough, with unfortunate zones of ambiguity. In my milieu, some people thought it was alright to protest with violence when the behaviour protested about was violent. I stopped Engineering and moved to the University of Sydney and started a Bachelor of Arts. Accordingly, I did a course in Psychology. I wanted to look at the motivations of people who were involved in violent protests. However, I got waylaid because it was the heyday of Behavioural Psychology, and the only behaviour we learnt much about was rats, mice and pigeons.

It got my attention. Why did professors study such asinine subject matter and pretend it illuminated the human mind, all the while ignoring much more worthy matters? They were serious people. They expected silence in their lectures – rapt attention. However, I got my revenge. Twenty-five years later I went back to university. I had not finished the Bachelor of Arts, and I left it alone. After half a career, I went to Southern Cross University in Lismore to study a Bachelor of Business.

It was an odd course, drawn mostly out of the Law School and a little bit out of Education, with some new material about Business and Human Resource Management, but I liked the range of subject matter. I felt that the legal subjects would be useful (they were). However, there was one subject in first year that I would not be able to bring myself to do: Psychology.

I looked at the requirements for Advanced Credit so that I would not have to do it. I looked at the syllabus and some of the same appalling content on Behaviourism was still in there. The study guide said that you had to have done the subject in the previous seven years. For me it was twenty-five. But I was not going to be beaten. All these years I had carried around with me, from place to place, up and down the east coast of Australia, all my lecture notes and essays, as well as my transcripts.

I spent an afternoon gathering it all together and took it into the university, along with my argument for credit. The lecturer kept the package for three days, then he rang me up and asked me to come in. I think he weighed up the fact that it is usually useless to force someone to study a subject they don't want to. I had got a Pass with Credit originally, so, even though it was a long time ago, I couldn't do much better now. I think he also weighed up the fact that it's best not to discourage a forty-seven-year-old who has come back to university after twenty-five years to do a Bachelor of Business in the brand-new university's brand-new Business course.

That was my revenge – not to have to do the subject again, although there was another part to my revenge as well. When I took the notes back home, I lit a fire in the backyard and burned them. I very much enjoyed that fire.

6 Army

Perhaps all that did happen at Sydney University was that my attention got distracted. Did I stay distracted for twenty-five years? That's one possibility. But in some ways, my time at Sydney University was already an aftermath. I may have been trying to gather some sense of self together, but I had already won, and I had already been beaten. I had to address the question of the army while I was still at the University of New South Wales. There was no one else to do it. My father couldn't advise me. He was gone. What could he have done anyway? He couldn't change my circumstances, and he couldn't make me want to go into the army.

I doubt if my father would have wanted me to go into the army. He had not been in the army in the Second World War, and I never felt that he had any attraction towards the army. He had supposedly been in a protected industry during the war. I have pieced together stray facts that indicate he worked for Pinkertons, the glass makers, who made equipment for the war. I believe he was a storeman. After the war he became a painter there, but that didn't happen until after the war.

He got married before the war (1935), and they had two children – this was before the family I was born into. But in 1943, his wife died – young, of a heart attack. Her sister and her husband helped to look after the children. They must have been lonely days for my father at the factory. It must have seemed as if everyone was just enduring another day and hoping for a better future. So, I don't think he would have thought about me in the army with any joy. The wartime was just part of his dark years.

It was after the war when dad met mum and they got married and moved to Greenacre to build a new house. I accepted the achievement of that, and the comparative comfort of living it brought. At the same time, I did not like it there. But where did I want to be? Not really anywhere. I wanted to be looking at everything. It didn't really matter where I was. I wanted to write, and that was about understanding what I could see. At the time it was books that were extending my understanding of what I could see.

No, I wasn't planning on becoming a travel guide. I wanted to write, and that was in my head. Nowadays it is different. You can write publicly anywhere. I read a response to a song on Youtube: "i am fourteen and i am trying to write stories, as much as i can. i wanna be a writer in the future. i listened to your songs in 2018 for the first time. from that day, whenever i stuck and don't know what to write in my stories, i come here. your songs are inspiring me, thank you for that. a teenage girl from turkey."

No, I didn't think my writing would be stories like that, but I liked the flailing enthusiasm and the dogged pursuit.

Perhaps it was my father's death that shook my hinges a little, and the fact that I just needed to "soldier on". But who is to say? A lot of things were happening, in and around my life. I felt that I had had a narrow escape from a very bad decision, thinking that I would become an engineer when I just wanted to write and think. But I had done it: departed from the University of New South Wales with a clean set of heels, and I had segued myself into a teaching course at Sydney University, for teaching mathematics. That was an easy jump, and I was already halfway finished. I would be out teaching the following year. I started the Bachelor of Arts at the same time; it would take me a bit longer.

I knew these were small steps, and no goal was visible. Across the plains, nothing was to be seen. The clouds swarmed in and mist descended. Perhaps there was something hidden, but I was reduced to watching my feet plod. I still had many obstacles to contend with. I could see no way other.

I relented about the army. I don't think dad would have counselled me differently. Joining the University Regiment meant that I could keep going at university, in exchange for nights at Parade and occasional weekends at camps. More importantly, it meant that I could not be sent to Vietnam. While it felt like escaping to take this route, it was legitimate, and it meant that I did not have to resolve the questions in my head. They were now merely theoretical.

I made sure that I always looked presentable, and my shoes were always well-shined. Other boys scorned me for taking such care. But I knew the value of invisibility. It keeps you out of trouble. I was amazed at the change in personality that came over some lecturers when they donned a uniform, if they were officers. They became bombastic. Some were cartoon extremes. I had to take it seriously for the sake of keeping the harshness at a distance and avoiding attack.

The army experience made me think seriously of escapism. I know that it is unhealthy for a person, but it was the last place on earth I wanted to be. I had to work at maintaining inner calm all the time. But, my experience was no worse than most other young men there. Perhaps the worst experience was a mock battle where our group (company?) were instructed to attack a mock Vietcong camp. We had engaged in running, arm-waving movements, sprawling and weapon-brandishing, but not to the murderous extent required by the commander of the scene. He castigated us and demanded that we re-enact the scene with convincing demeanour.

In that hapless, deficient way, I managed to pass eighteen months of service. Our requirement was to serve twenty-four months. At the end of the eighteen months, the numbers for the allotted birthdays had been drawn out of the barrel. As it happened, this was a lottery I did not win. My number was not drawn out, and I did not have to serve any longer. Nominally we had to serve another six months, but the Regiment had discovered it was too difficult to enforce the regulation, so they allowed us to return our gear and finish up. I had no shame in doing this.

My resolution of the question of pacifism did not occur. And it is different when the question is not academic. People can sit in the pub all day and argue about questions, but you can tell when it doesn't really matter. In the early days of Australia's commitment of troops to Vietnam, I had a cousin about my age whose new husband had been called up. He received six weeks' training and then was sent straight to Vietnam, in an Engineers Corp. He was there approximately six weeks when he was out on the road on patrol and his jeep was blown up. He was twenty-one.

My cousin's young life was shrouded in grief. I don't argue that a whole war can be decided on the basis of a single death, that seems to mix different elements together, but it did mean for me that the question was not academic. I had to weigh the arguments for the war against the cost of a person whom I knew, whose wedding I had been to just a few weeks earlier.

Afterwards it seems surreal. Vietnamese refugees came here to live, and we accepted the reality of their plight. Australian tourists go there to visit and enjoy (as have I).

7 Utopia

The questions, of course, scurried on. If you saw yourself as a citizen who would simply be a soldier for a while, and not ask questions, whatever it meant doing, it was okay, or at least consistent. My position was not consistent, because I did not see myself that way. I saw myself on the fringe. I had taken a job teaching because I was on a three-year bond. It simply put off the question of career for three years. I looked normal, apart from my hair growing longer.

However, I was thinking about people who were living in non-conventional, alternative ways. It was lifestyle that came to the fore now, not so much religion, theology or beliefs. They seemed arcane and irrelevant.

If I was looking now at my thinking at this time, I would focus on the concept of utopia. At that time, utopian thoughts seemed like the promise of something better, new beginnings where everything had been rethought and remade. Real changes – a world without war, greed, power. The old and the corrupt cleared away. There were many utopian influences. The movie, *Easy Rider*, had been released, which dealt tolerantly, even indulgently, with the hippy commune farm. Many radical groups had started up in society, related to everything imaginable – political groupings, food cooperatives, eastern religious affiliations.

I remember that Peter Fonda said years later that he had only said one thing in the movie that he didn't believe. When they were on the hippy farm, and the people were sowing seeds by hand, and the whole possibility looked extremely fragile, Peter's character said: "You're gonna make it."

He told the interviewer later, "No, I didn't believe that statement at the time." And we know he was talking about a broader field than the field depicted in the movie scene; he was talking about the future of hippies and the hippy farm movement.

I am sure there were failures, but I also know there were some long-term successes in America, and in Australia also – and other places too, such as Findhorn in Scotland. There was an alternative movement. I didn't see myself as a leader. I suppose I saw the communes as an example of what was possible, what they proved.

America was a long way away. It carried another land's dreaming. But I got sustenance from that dreaming. I couldn't enact it. I was still living at home, and I felt that my mother depended on me being there. I listened to music, I studied, I thought about what was possible.

I thought about moving out of home and moving in with friends. Many people my age, and younger, were doing that. It seemed like something I needed to learn. But I told my mother I was thinking about it and her reaction was electric. She didn't argue; she just stopped talking and became bleak. She didn't talk for a week. Meanwhile I was in utter darkness. My proposal was unable to be borne. It wasn't something she could even discuss. I could have forced the point, but I didn't see the benefits of that. Anger lives long and it doesn't die easily. I was a little worried that I might never get to leave home, but it was not urgent. After a week, I said to mum, "I'll stay home. I don't need to leave at the moment."

I just put the question off the table. There was no point in being angry about it. I had been going to set up house with two or three other young guys, but another time would come. It would be okay.

8 Poet

I wrote poetry throughout these years, although not a huge amount. I was, after all, teaching full-time, studying at university (still doing a Bachelor of Arts degree), and being involved in other groups. I had a motorcycle and I learned my way around Sydney. It was liberating. Life was full.

I didn't try to get this poetry published. There was one period when I tried, before I was about twenty, but to little avail, so I left it alone. I had established that I was not going to be a writer or poet in any public sense. That didn't stop me from writing.

I see the clumsiness now in the poems, but they show some sentiments I am still sympathetic to: "the only responsibility is to keep growing, which is to revoke our baptism into futility again and again."

As a poet I surveyed the array of young acolytes around me and cast a critical eye, conscious of my own vulnerability to criticism: "Raw youth, at once bitter and intense, but setting his questions at the possibilities, raw youth assuming the posture of prophet."

As a poet I said, "Yes, I am a judge, and I keep my eye open for the occasional prophet, but to the rest I am merely a professional cynic. Not that the choice is mine. Still, in a few years, I shall be past my dangerous stage, and people will merely call me a dreamer. Just a few years, and I shall be as harmless as any park bench-sitter who just hasn't learned that things are getting better all the time."

At one point I stared into the future, asking "How is it going to be? Forty-two and a study of my own, comfortably walled in with books? That room should stand, happily, forever. I will be the one who waits around until the right word can be said and then moves on, still falling in love, perhaps, and having too many scruples to confess it, or a feeling for the ridiculous."

I said, "It will be alright, not that it has to be, simply that living is a possibility. I am living close to the source, where reaching out is easy. How is it going to be? Forty-two and the light strong and defiant in my eyes."

In the last poem I wrote in this period, I said, "I have already come to where I'm going."

9 My leg

Six days later I was knocked off my motorcycle and my leg was smashed up. I have talked about this elsewhere, so I don't want to do it again (in my poetry book, *Volume 3: That Was Then*, in the introduction to Section 4, there is an account). It was a dramatic event. For a time it looked as if I might lose the lower half of my right leg. I went in to have the operation and the gas gangrene, remarkably, had gone. The orthopaedic doctor was perplexed but pleased, and sent for the plastic surgeon the same day. The crisis had been averted somehow. About eight centimetres of my fibula was discarded, too messy to reassemble, and my right leg has become accustomed to its deficiency. It works/walks proficiently. I don't engage in too much running.

I always thought there was a lesson in the motorcycle accident. I had, in the days before the accident, come to a crossroads, amusing though the metaphor may be. I was being urged to become a full-time, live-in supporter at the shop-front church. It had been a few months since my mother's meltdown at my suggestion that I would move out. I thought that she was more amenable to the idea now. And this would be an opportunity to be fully involved in the work of the organisation. And of course, I had much to give.

In truth, I was not so close to a decision to move out. I was not quite so sure that my mother was ready for it, and I harboured reservations about becoming that much a part of an organisation.

There would be no room for nuance or subtlety; you would have to be an ardent supporter, that's all.

So, I was momentarily becalmed, not that I shared that with anyone. I would make up my own mind. When I was hit by the car (tootling down the street, minding my own business), it was as if I had been pushed in a certain direction. I was not to be subsumed as a street worker into some kind of Christian garrison station.

I spent several months in hospital. I had visitors but I didn't have a great deal of closeness with anyone. People had their own business to attend to. Then again, why should anyone have made me the centre of their world? I realised that I was on the fringe of their world, and in my view, that was okay. I had one faithful friend who brought me music every week: cassette tapes of current groups and albums, all well-chosen. Renewed weekly, about a dozen at a time. That was the best gift I got from anyone in hospital.

There is a point when the young man who was hit by a car is no longer an object of attention. The surgeries for skin grafts continue, but the healing is slow. People drop off, time falls into limbo. There was nothing I could do except read. I had little desire to summon up a project; it would only be make-believe, for the entertainment of myself or others. I know that people do things like this. I know that people share in the make-believe. I know that people get wary if you seem to be doing nothing. They worry that you are or will become depressed.

There was probably a sense in which I could be described as mildly depressed, but there needs to be time to think about things. I was used to sitting thinking. Often, I sat with a book in front of me so that it would look like I was reading. When you sit and think, you can allow things to come into focus. You can see what place they assume, and how everything else sits in relation to each other, although it's not that prescribed. You don't need conclusions, or at least, not ones that you could relay to anyone else.

I thought about the collision, the one between me living at home with my mother and me living as part of the Christian urgency corp. I just let them drift apart again. No one ever said a word. Sometimes words are not needed.

10 Hospital

I made a visit to a courthouse. It had been three months since the accident, and the police had asked me to appear and give a statement about the accident. The driver of the kombie van had been driving towards me when he suddenly veered in front of me to go into a laneway on my left. It was as if I wasn't there. I wasn't doing anything untoward. I was in my correct lane, I was travelling at modest speed, evenly. When I realised that the van was going to keep coming, it wasn't going to return to its lane, I tried to veer off towards the left to get around him, but he was too close. He clipped me, and I ended up smashing into the back of a parked car. That's all I remember, except that I was aware that the kombie van had stopped in the laneway, and a woman was kneeling beside me, holding a tourniquet around my leg. Apparently she was a nurse.

When I arrived at the courthouse, a young man with long brown hair came up to me. It was easy to know who I was. My right leg was in plaster and bandages and I was on crutches. He asked me if I would change my evidence, and say that I was on the wrong side of the road, because he had already lost points off his licence and he didn't want to lose his licence. I was stunned into silence. When I gave my evidence, I gave it as it happened. I didn't say anything about the young man's attempt to make me change my evidence to his advantage.

I thought about that when I was sitting in hospital. I didn't make it into anything. I didn't feed it with anger, I didn't plan retaliation, I didn't harbour sorrow. I just wondered about what that young man had felt it necessary or acceptable to do. I wondered whether he knew that I had nearly lost my leg.

One day, during autumn, the sun was shining and for once, the nurses weren't busy. Some patients had gone home today. One of the nurses came to me and asked, "Would you like to go outside today?"

I didn't know what she meant. I was trussed up in a bed. The skin grafts had started, and I had skin running from my left hip to my left wrist. That is hard to describe. A deep layer of skin had been peeled off my hip, but still attached along one end at my groin. Then it had been rolled up and sewn up to make a tube. The end of the tube was sewn onto my left wrist, which had been opened up to take it. The point was to generate a blood flow through the skin, so that it could eventually be sewn onto my right shin. You could say it was macabre.

What the nurses were proposing was that they would wheel my whole bed out onto the verandah for an hour or two. I was dumbfounded, but "Yes" I nodded. I had not thought of this at all.

It was one of those simple things, the young nurses wheeling the bed towards the door in joyous enthusiasm, but having a mind to the other sick and sombre patients in the ward; the older matron standing at her desk and doing a fine job of looking stern, and me, trussed up, dangerously exposed to the public eye, and still unaware of what was really happening.

When the bed was in place on the verandah, I looked up and found myself in a courtyard of the hospital, two floors up from the ground. The sky was blue all over, unimpeded by a single cloud, and a full, tree-shaped tree stood right in front of me, as green as could be. The sun was warm. I had not realised it had been so long since I had seen the sun. I think it was around ten weeks. I felt tears in my eyes, a flood of emotion coming up. Grateful for everything.

"What did I do today? I went out and saw the sun. It was a lovely day."

Always there was the devil chasing, eager to get to the end of this contest: the skin against the leg. Other people had found these operations difficult. The Plastic Nurses had taken me to see one of them. He was a mechanic who had been blown up in a garage because of petrol fumes. His skin was a mess. Parts of it they had tried to do with small postage-stamp-sized pieces of skin, which worked, more or less. In one place they had tried a pedicle skin graft, the same technique as mine, but it was not going well. The nurses thought that I might be able to offer hope and encouragement to him.

I tried. How does one try to offer hope? But I did. I caught that moment in his eyes of grand despair and I held it. The same devil had tried for me. I keep on the path. The nurses were quiet when we left. We each have to try, each one of us.

After I came out of hospital, I came back to mum's house, and everything had changed. I had to find my way back into work, and social engagement. But it wasn't as if I was a unit of social functioning to be re-primed for interaction. I was a lot further away, looking back in. My connections had all broken. I wasn't teaching at the same school anymore. Besides, I was nearly at the end of my three-year bond. Would I stay anyway? Why was I teaching? I had never intended to.

In hospital, a man who came to see me suggested that I should write while I was lying there in bed. This merely annoyed me. He was suggesting that I write for my own amusement, not that there was any purpose or merit or interest in my writing. I admit that my ego was slightly dented. When I was put face to face with myself as a writer, I couldn't stand the scrutiny. I was just like the teenager on Youtube: "I wanna be a writer!"

11 Hitch-hiking

By the time Christmas came I was back on my feet – no plaster, no bandages, and just a walking stick to boost my confidence. I went to Tasmania and went hitch-hiking by myself – up the middle from Hobart, then across to the east coast and back down to Hobart. It was the time of the fight about Tasmania's wilderness, so there were loaded trucks on the road all the time, roaring up the highway with freshly felled trees for the mills. They were trying to get out as much as they could, in the expectation that logging would be stopped.

Sometimes I would be picked up by an old Tasmanian man in a car he had owned for years. This day, the man didn't ask me what I was doing there. He was just content to take me to some place I wanted to go along the road. He slowed down to observe an eagle coming over the brow of the hill, and he let me off just down from the shopping centre. After this he disappeared like a painting. I would work out where I was staying and be thankful for the fine weather. It was another day given.

I did keep a diary. And I did meet other young people, as you do when you are hitch-hiking. I watched and listened to the play among them over several days. Even without a plan, things take shape and eventuate. I could have been a part of it, but I wanted to watch, this time around. I was just coming back in, and the writing was me seeing if it even made any sense to write things down, especially things that were unplanned. I kept that diary in the box with other things I had written, and it stayed there for years. I put it in a book I wrote in 2020. The book was about Tasmania, so it seemed fitting: *The Quilt Approach: A Tasmanian Patchwork*.

I went onto the committee for the newspaper at the House of the New World, and I wrote articles. But it didn't seem like a tight group. The others were different to me, I was different to them, and the people outside the committee seemed to have different expectations for the newspaper too – what it should be in the public eye, and that was another set of influences. It didn't seem coherent. Beyond this, I felt that I was going to blow up and leave, not in anger, but as an effusion that could not contain itself. I thought of that story of Jesus about the new wine not being able to be contained by old skins.

I made a number of decisions in the first few months of the new year (it was 1974). They were certainly bold. Were they rash?

I don't think so. Time was just catching up. I finished my three-year bond as a teacher and I left teaching. I decided to go back to university full-time. I was halfway through a Bachelor of Arts degree at Sydney University. I was studying Philosophy and Education. Did I have a plan? No; these were just the next steps on the road.

I had left home, not alone, and my mother was more accepting. I had left with a lady. She had a copy of the Tully album. It was like a sign. She also had a copy of Santana's *Caravanserai* and two albums by Yes: *Fragile* and *Close to the Edge*. Music was a high road to a good place. It seemed to substitute for mountains of knowledge about all aspects of life, if but for a short time, and it left an ache that seemed to be necessary.

Wasn't this good – a relationship? Perhaps. Was it wonderful? Was it passionate? Maybe. It's hard when it all eventually fell to bits, because, you think, when did that start, and why? Or, whose fault was it? Now it is simply pointless. Maybe I didn't know how to be happy. Maybe I was troubled because of the motorcycle accident and all the operations. Maybe I was still out of balance because my father had died when I was sixteen. Speculations.

And maybe the world was falling apart, and this was just a small part of that. Maybe I couldn't work out a constructive place for myself in this world. Maybe it would have been easier if I had been just a flying piece of fragile body after the bad guys had blown the man off his motorcycle in *Easy Rider*. I didn't usually allow dark thoughts like that to arise. And besides, my lady was pregnant. I had never resisted the idea of parenthood; I knew it would happen one day, and I knew I would be very happy to be a father.

The pregnancy meant making some changes. It was a version of growing up, I suppose, taking responsibility. I had to let university go and get a job. I wasn't sorry about university. My stocktake of it was this: I was doing two subjects – Education II and Philosophy III. The Philosophy Department had broken apart and we now had three quasi-departments – the Traditionalists, the Marxists and the Existentialists.

The Traditionalists were the ones who would prefer it if you just thought up different examples for their arguments about the truth, that is, if you refrained from really thinking. The Marxists were angry, and in their cosy little corner of the quadrangle they were spewing out hatred towards Capitalists and the upper middle class everywhere. How long would it be before they were upper middle class themselves? And the Existentialists represented a philosophy of despair and self-centred meaninglessness, proving that this is possible. I was feeling that there had to be a fourth school, but I didn't think anyone would thank me for suggesting it.

That left Education. The students of this school had overthrown the lecturers and were deciding how to devise and teach courses themselves. They didn't seem to have much idea about what should be taught, or how, which was not surprising as they hadn't passed university themselves. That is a throw-away comment, but the situation deserved it. I wasn't against their efforts to explore, but they were not more entitled or qualified than I to do that, and if I decided to do that, I would do it at home, or as part of a higher degree. It was a misuse of the university context to do it there, and a pretension to its status.

What was the difference between me and these other students? There was some kind of effrontery they had that I didn't have. Was I too working class? The important thing to know was that it was a good time to go and get a job.

12 Psychiatric nurse

There was a time near the end of high school when I had boundless curiosity. I would have liked to have gone to university and studied everything. I found knowledge exhilarating. Now I realised that knowledge came freighted. It wasn't innocent and empowering; it was hitched up to wagons already. It was used to entrench those in positions of power, or it was angry protesting knowledge. It was carried like weapons or paraded like smug conceit. It was frequently used for deceit.

In those days of serious decision, I often found myself sitting, sitting in the sun with a cup of tea before I had to decide to traipse off to university for another onslaught of righteous philosophy. I remembered, "There is a sound of perfect silence, not far from me, or you, or there." It seemed bounteous, that silence.

I signed off from the hapless university courses and left. It was twenty-five years later when I suddenly realised that it would be appropriate to return to a campus and obtain a degree. It was not over yet. Music had its own comment to make. The first time I walked onto a university campus, at the University of New South Wales in February 1968 to start an engineering degree, The Doors band were playing on a loudspeaker. When I walked onto the campus in Lismore in 1993 to start a Bachelor of Business degree, The Doors were again playing on a loudspeaker, the same album, and I remembered this. "My goodness!" I thought. "Time has stood still for twenty-five years."

I got a job as a psychiatric nurse at Parramatta Psychiatric Centre. Someone had said, "You learn a lot about a society by the way it treats its mentally vulnerable people." I knew of some fellow students at high school who had gone to work in psychiatric centres. I didn't know why they had done so, apart from the attraction to a job that was not ordinary nine to five. A post-school qualification wasn't necessary. They offered study on the job.

The shifts were irregular, so the times off work were likewise irregular, and the pay was alright. It didn't seem to involve too many heavy-handed supervisors. But what was the work like? Well, it appeared that you could relate to some of the patients without too much trouble, and you didn't have to do heavy things like lifting people.

My mother was not happy. She said, "You've got a teaching qualification. You should be using it. You're wasting yourself." But that's all she said. She could have argued with me; she didn't. I wonder if she was letting me take my own course because of the accident and all the time I had spent in hospital. Did she think I would get whatever it was out of my system and then settle down to teaching? Perhaps. But I had misfired long before. In many ways I was just like the students I had seen at university. I had a devastating critique of all manner of subjects, whether it was church, religious beliefs, a school at the university, education in general, or modern capitalist society as a whole.

Would everything be alright if I could go back to the beginning? I had the idea that things are okay at the beginning. Babies, rustic lifestyles, villages where there was still personal involvement and nurturing, not distant rationality. But human affairs are not clean and tidy. When you arrive, things are already messed up. What do you do then? Usually, people try to wrest control back.

In the psychiatric centre, the managers had already wrested control back. Control was not in question. There was a diverse range of drugs to ensure control. Patients were for the most part subdued. The old psychiatric nurses told stories of the days after World War II, when they had started work, and seeing patients tied to every post in the quadrangle all day. Trousers were soiled, screams were loud. Danger was imminent. The drugs were better now, they said.

I stayed there six months, long enough to see what happened: what staff understood from their patients' behaviour, what staff and doctors were trying to do, and what kinds of situations they thought were satisfactory. I did not see a great deal of overt malice, although I did see some. Some people have a way of weaving malice into the way they work, as if work were a forum for the exercise of their spite.

I thought there were a great deal of careless assumptions about the truth of things. There was a simple way to deal with people – the drugs made that all too easy, and they introduced a kind of deadness to the atmosphere, as if something were being stifled. There was no upward path, no return to life, just becoming more accustomed to deadness. Compliant behaviour was its perfect partner. It was strange how quickly patients learned the latter. Was it a sentence for life? I suspected so. I saw some instances where the family had worked out the outcome they wanted from the patient, understood in terms of power and compliance, and had obviously obtained the support of the staff to this end.

Now, someone might ask me what I mean by that, but I have nothing to say. I can't fix it, I couldn't fix it, it's all too big. The perspective of the staff and the doctors, the perspective of the institution and the government, is of social control and order. They have arguments. I lasted six months. When it came to Christmas, I found a job teaching in Queensland, and I left with my wife and new child.

My mother never told me that my father's mother had been put into a mental institution, and that she had never come out. She had died there, aged seventy-five, having been taken in at the age of thirty-eight. My father had been young at the time, only seven. If I had known that, I probably would not have gone to work in the psychiatric centre. It seems too insensitive. I was being observational and critical, but it was actually a family matter.

It was 1920 when Mrs Elizabeth Martin, wife of William Thomas Martin, had a breakdown. There were seven children, the youngest of them just five months old. She had tried to drink sheep dip, and she wasn't in a coping state of mind. She went into Callan Park Mental Asylum. The situation did not improve. Gradually the children were sent off to other relatives to be looked after. In 1930, when Bloomfield Hospital was built out at Orange, many of the patients were transferred there from Callan Park, as was she. It is unlikely that Elizabeth's husband or children saw her again.

That situation was like a slow bomb. I didn't know until I started delving into family history after I was sixty, and then it took a few years more. It affected everything retrospectively, like whether or not I would have gone to work in a psychiatric centre. Now, there are patients that I remember, no, not even remember, just that I have an impression of an old woman who kept to herself, who muttered a lot, and I didn't understand what she was muttering about or why. She was inoffensive and she just shuffled along with the group, and I imagined she must have a family somewhere.

Eventually mum told me what I needed to know about my father's mother, so that I could pursue it. She knew I was exploring the family's history. It became more and more extensive over the years. I don't know what her feelings were about it, but she resisted less as time went by. I think she thought if I was persistent, I deserved to be able to find out. I know what many people in her generation thought: "These young people just like to dive straight into all the misery. It would be better to let it die." I think she thought that if the knowledge of a bad thing could die with her, then it would be a good death. That was the sacrifice she would make.

But I have dug up the story. It is there anyway. It's in the circumstances of Elizabeth's death, being at Bloomfield Hospital at Orange, while her husband's was at Lidcombe Hospital. It's in the fact that he was buried at Woronora but I couldn't find her there. She has a plaque in the wall at the Crematorium at Orange. I know, from having read the hospital's records, that Norm Martin was the only family member to attend his mother's funeral at Orange. Norm was the eldest child. My father was the fourth, although the second died at birth, so dad was really the third.

I wonder whether perhaps I really knew this story at the time, but I'd forgotten it, or forgotten the words of it. Maybe I had heard the story somehow, when I was very young, how children half-remember things that adults say late at night. So, perhaps I was really insensitive and just felt I had a right to do what I wanted. Regardless, it was with some relief that I left at Christmas for Queensland. I know it looked like I was coming back into the workforce, teaching, but really, I was running a long way away. Mackay was halfway up the coast of Queensland and I was sure the laws were different and the reality was different.

13 Queensland

I wanted to get away. I had read the *Time* magazine article about the Club of Rome's report into the state of the planet. It had come out in 1972. The news was comprehensively bad: we were heading for a catastrophe. We didn't seem to be managing the planet very well. All the power that we had, we just used it to consume more materials – as much as we could. The greed and excess were breath-taking, the lust to take, to expend. It seemed impossible for people as a society to be moderate or modest. Leaving Sydney was an expression of my wish to be out of the stream of it. If I was powerless to change it, at least I could stay out of it. I would go somewhere far away.

However, I wasn't happy in Mackay. It was far away from the worst excesses of the big city, which was welcome, but it was backward in ways that I thought were unnecessary. I thought their ideas about teaching and learning were more about adhering to a set of conventions than about having any insight into the teaching/learning process. Most of the teachers weren't interested in the processes of learning and change. To be fair, I suppose they realised they were living in a tropical town, close to the ocean and the islands. Fishing and recreation were of more importance than theories of learning.

There was quite a cohort of young teachers, and many of them came from distant places. The Department was finding it difficult to find teachers. In our staff we had teachers from elsewhere in Australia, New Zealand, the United States and the United Kingdom. They were all interesting people. Ernst came from London, but his father was German and his mother was Irish. He taught English and he had a caustic tongue when he chose.

He told us of an argument he had had with the principal. Ernst had changed a practice (it was something that his class normally did) and the principal had objected. It had obviously been like two heads butting horns. The principal delivered his climax: "But we've always done it this way."

And Ernst gave his immediate rebuttal: "You can do the same thing thirty times, but it could just mean that you've done the wrong thing thirty times."

14 Kindness

Despite the camaraderie of other young teachers, I still felt that I was an outsider, and it would be best to step carefully. People here were supportive of those they deemed to be compatriots, but they could be savage with outsiders. I kept myself low. I also had to acknowledge forms of friendliness. I was not done with operations on my leg, and I had to take a week off school to fly down to Sydney for an operation. That went well enough.

On my return, I was at home for a couple of days, and the school principal came around to our home and personally delivered my pay cheque. This was in the time when there were no credit cards. If you ran out of cash, you simply didn't have any money until next payday. I had planned for my trip to Sydney, so money was not at crisis point, but I was quite taken by the thoughtfulness of the principal. Sometimes life is simple and wholesome. Whatever thoughts I had about backward approaches to teaching, I had to give credit for basic humanity.

I had another instance of kindness, too. On a weekend, we had gone on a trip outside of town. Perhaps we had visited another teacher in the countryside. In the usual fuss of getting things packed into the car again – baby's stroller, spare clothes, nappies – I had actually left my wallet on the roof of the car. I did not realise this until we had arrived back home, when, of course, the wallet was no longer there. This was a disaster. We had no spare sources of money.

Less than an hour later, before I had decided what course of action to take, a car pulled up out front, and a man came to the door. He asked me my name, and when I told him, he held out my wallet to me. I was shocked. It was such a huge relief. I wanted to give him some money, but he said, no. It's just something you do for a fellow human being. We are all in need sometimes. And then he was gone. So, in a short space of time, I had two instances of human kindness. It was a sober reminder about letting high ideas slide into an absence of warmth.

There was an easy, relaxed aspect to life in Mackay, an effect of the constant heat and the sea breezes. But one would have to settle down to life at that level. Life for most people revolved around beer and barbecues, and they would have to be persuaded that that was the norm for you too. I see it differently now. A person can stay in a place and acquire their own persona. And they can be whatever they want to be (within reason). They don't have to belong to the main group. If they are clear enough and firm enough about who they are, they can stand on solid ground.

I didn't want to be an outsider here. I wanted to be somewhere where I could be part of something good that was going on. I wanted to belong to something positive. I didn't think this would be religious anymore, but it would be about living in an alternative way. In the meantime, another baby came along, another girl. All the threads of life continued; no great triumphs or tragedies occurred. We had the need for small, daily joys and in goodly measure it was so. I read *Earth Garden* magazine and created my largest vegetable garden to date, taking over most of the backyard lawn. It was productive and it pleased me.

What was I doing? Was I trying to grow all our own food? No, it was just a gesture. Was I making a spiritual statement in the face of the over-developed planet? Well, yes, I suppose I was, but I was not being grandiose. Was I training in order to prepare to garden on much larger scale? Yes, I felt that I was, although my plans were not clear. And I liked being able to pick vegetables and bring them in for a meal. They were fresh and healthy, and I had had little experience of that in my life. Also, it was a much better lifestyle than going down to the hotel on Saturday afternoon and drinking.

After eighteen months of this exile, we left. We did not go back to Sydney. I had no desire to return there, and there was nothing I could have thought of to do there. Having lived in a regional town, I was ready to live in the bush. In Mackay it had been quiet; well, the background was quiet, whereas in the city there was always a background of buzz. At two a.m. in Mackay there was one sound: the drone of a propellor plane on its way north. I supposed it was the aeroplane taking newspapers and mail to Cairns. It had a steady, faithful drone to the engine, as if it could be counted on to fulfil its task dutifully. And it summed up the settled-ness of Mackay, as if, for all its faults, it could be relied upon to continue. But I wanted to be doing more.

The hard edge of Mackay was that these were the Joh Bjelke-Petersen years. He was the Premier, and in my eyes, he was both crazy and corrupt. He painted all his acts with a conservative Christian veneer, but to me it was a crude, sleazy charade. Charades are invariably made worse because the people using them come to believe in them themselves. And it suited most people not to question it. But there was a savage side to all of this, an underbelly of violence behind all the easy hospitality. The attitude made for a very polarised society. I wasn't interested in having to fight such battles. I wanted to garden and live an "alternative lifestyle": that was the best language I had for what I wanted to do. Clearly, it meant leaving Queensland.

The tenor of the society was summed up one weekend when we were coming back from out of town. On the broad, four-lane entrance road into Mackay we found ourselves behind a large, dirty four-wheel-drive with a trailer and cage on the back of it. In the cage was a wounded boar, which had obviously been captured by the men. What they planned to do with it I don't know, but it was a chilling sight. It was standing there, sullen, head down, with blood flecked over its body from various wounds. One imagined the exultation of the men in the vehicle. They were savouring their slow journey down the road as a lap of triumph. But not for me.

15 Not belonging

I had no illusions about my prowess as a teacher. The inspector who examined me at Mackay commented that I seemed to have little commitment to my career. It was true: I didn't see me teaching in the long term. It had been a short-term plan: how to get from being an engineering student to being in the professional paid workforce in the shortest possible time. Teaching had been the way to go. I don't deny that I had toyed with the idea of being a teacher when I was in primary school, but I wasn't swamped with ideas about careers. My father was a painter, my mother was a dressmaker.

Yet, perhaps I could have become a teacher. I liked the idea of teaching, and I liked students. But I was steered into teaching mathematics only, and my interests were much broader. And I think I was too much of a student myself to ever settle as a teacher. And I wonder about that phase of life, the mid-twenties. Perhaps it's not the time to be thinking about your career. I was busy with a wife and family and a house, and wondering about the community I was in, or was leaving. I didn't really have a career plan, or rather, I was against having a career plan.

Was I someone who had failed as a writer and failed as a teacher and didn't know what else to do? Was I going to be a warrior in the alternative society somewhere? I had cut myself off from all the groups I had been associated with, and all my connections were temporary. Partly it was a quandary about not wanting to do anything structured, and on the other hand, having to earn money. I could work in a garden all day and it would come to look beautiful and the vegetables would pour off there bounteously. What if we found a place where I could do that?

There was a sense of urgency, and also an acceptance that there were multiple perspectives. I had to avoid being a simpleton. I couldn't become a radical who was unable to mingle in society, someone who was rigid, doctrinaire and self-righteous. I didn't know where we would go or where we would end up. However, although I am not greatly courageous at geographical adventures, we packed up and left Queensland with a loaded station-wagon and a trailer, and a truckload of furniture sent onto storage in northern New South Wales.

Things I know

I have already come to where I'm going. I had put it into words a few years ago. It is very powerful to put something into words. There is no logic to it, it is simply a truth that you know to be true. Perhaps, also, it could be true in different ways.

16 Hippie

We spent several weeks wandering around in the car, camping here and there, visiting hippie farms we had heard about. We were not "between here and there", we were simply on the loose. Who knew where we would end up? But neither of us was made for the road, so time was leaning on us. There were options.

We ended up on a multiple occupancy property west of Lismore. I think the persuasive factor was that it was actually conservative socially. It consisted of separate households, not one big living family. It was, you could say, disorganised, but most such places were, and you could say that was necessary, given what the multiple occupancies were reacting against. I had come recently from teaching, so I understood what power structures and domination looked like, so I understood the desire for freedom and relaxation of rules.

It was a loose congregation of people: a family with a ten-year-old boy and a one-year-old girl, the parents had both been art teachers; a young guy who was quite independent, he had worked as a gardener; a family consisting of a relaxed Vietnam veteran, his Indonesian wife and three young children; a young couple who were Swiss: she was pregnant and worked in health. There were others who were involved in the property but were not here at the moment.

There was a loose vision of what the place would become. It was a large, bushy block of 600 acres along the top of a ridge, but running all the way down to the creek on the other side. There were a few clearings, and a rough road that went all the way through the block. Two surrounding blocks had also been bought up by alternative settlers. The intention was to kick off all the cows and let the bush regenerate, and just keep some clearings for gardens and housing.

There was no religious aspect to the group. I didn't mind; I couldn't imagine what kind of "religious aspect" would be amenable. Mostly, I thought, they would be doctrinaire and authoritarian. The group in *Easy Rider* had seemed to have settled on a form that expressed devotion and gratitude without too much intrusive theology, but that was a bit much to hope for. Nor had I seen any groups where any set of practices had been settled on. I had looked into yoga before I left Sydney, but from a book, not from a group of people that I knew of.

We moved onto the property, choosing our own spot in a clearing. We were allowed to do this; there was little discussion, and I don't think the group had discussed what criteria would be wise to apply to people deciding on places to live. Everywhere was difficult in the sense that water was not available around most of the property. Once you were settled in a spot, you could instal tanks. So, we began by carrying water in forty-four-gallon drums. With two girls in nappies, that was arduous, working out arrangements for washing.

There is little to be said about this enterprise. I was determined but unwise. We spent several months there, trying to make headway. I bought a rainwater tank; I bought a slow-combustion stove. I started building a shed, I bought two goats. I started a garden. This was not my first garden, and this one was a good size, but as I said, we had no captive water, so I had to be sparing with watering it. Fortunately, the rain was kind that year – moderate and spaced out regularly. In fact, after we left, we visited for several months and picked vegetables.

It was a long way to where we were camped, right up on top of the ridge, looking back towards the east coast. There were times when I just sat there, say, in the afternoon, and watched and listened. I thought about my life growing up in Sydney, I thought about how claustrophobic I had been starting to feel about Sydney, and I felt that I was far enough away now. It was quiet; even the bush was without sound for much of the day. In the middle of the night, a long way from any town, there was the heavy drone of a single aeroplane on its way somewhere from one place to another, a regular pattern, just as there had been in Mackay. I found it reassuring, without knowing why.

One day, as I was walking back up the road towards our camp, alone, just me and the wilderness all around, all the way to the horizon, I heard a sudden ear-splitting roar. And at that moment, far below me, a jet plane (an F111) hurtled down the valley, following the contours, not much higher than the tree-line. It is eery to see an aeroplane in the air travelling at high speed, but actually below you. The sound I heard was the plane breaking the sound barrier. It was deafening. It also meant that I didn't hear it until the plane had already passed me. Here I was, as far as I thought I could be from modern society, and it had paid me a visit. But I felt peaceful about this. It made me think that I did not need to go further away, because there was no point.

However, I recognised that my wife was finding the place isolated and the conditions too primitive. We didn't mix a lot with the other people, and I don't think that she felt she had much in common with them. That's a big question, isn't it? Do you have something in common with the people around you? And what kind of a place would you have to be in to feel that way? Sadly, I felt that she would prefer to live in suburbia. Still, it raised an interesting standard: was my life better than suburbia? In what way?

The deeper question was whether we were basically incompatible. She left, saying she was taking the girls to visit her parents. Being up on the mountain alone was in part scary, because I wasn't sure if my marriage was falling apart, and in part a feeling of vastness that I was at home in. I wanted the road to go along smoothly, and it wasn't. I had to compromise if I wanted to keep the family intact. I never contemplated living without the girls, but a life in the suburbs with a normal job was too distant from me now. A life of conformity with the old world was something I had rejected soundly.

What was I after? Had I been expecting the multiple occupancy to establish a robust alternative way of life, where we could be both happy and proud? Could that group of people have built a stable, functioning community with ideals? Could I have led the people to such a goal? But I didn't want to lead. It was the stage of life where I had to confront such questions and find my place. The most solid sense of spirit I felt was through magazines like *Earth Garden*, that offered an alternative to either suburbia or doom.

There were clearly people "out there" who did not expect to conquer the world, but who were not going to sink into mindless obscurity. They were building knowledge and experience about how to live modestly and close to the earth, not minding that hosts of others might think this foolish. That was forming in my mind as a noble aspiration, something worthwhile aiming for. There was no point in going to university and getting a degree, or several degrees. That was merely to climb up a well-trodden path, not to carve out a new path: one is not allowed to do that. The noble ideal was to carve out the path you wanted to go, and felt you should go, not looking for approval from others.

The man who had been in Vietnam was sympathetic. He could see that I would not last on the mountain with my family. He had a genuinely relaxed attitude to life. He didn't set rigid standards for himself, but nor was he foolish or dissipated. His children seemed to be happy. He suggested that I drive over to Kyogle and have a look. I might find it amenable, and I could find a farmhouse there to live in that wouldn't be very expensive. Kyogle hadn't really been "discovered" and it probably never would be.

I drove the Land Rover into Kyogle. It was on the other side of the mountain range. From the lookout coming from Cawongla, you looked down into the upper reaches of the Richmond River valley. It was all farmland, rolling hills and mostly dairy cows. Up in the hills they still logged timber, but it seemed to be a steady occupation rather than a bloodthirsty lust to consume everything in sight.

Alan Cunningham had first looked into this valley from the north in June 1828. He was the colony's Botanical Collector, and he was on an expedition to find a track from the Darling Downs to Moreton Bay, so that the wool clip could be delivered to a port. He passed through the mountains at the head of the Richmond River, calling it Richmond Gap. This was along the border with Queensland, near Mount Lindesay. In the years to come, the area was settled with cattle stations, and then dairy cows moved in before the end of the 1800s.

Kyogle was not trendy like the areas near the coast. It was nowhere near the surf, so it did not have the complementary oceanic ambience. Kyogle was still just country, more well-known for cowboys and timber-getters for whom it was not positioned in relation to fashion. There were still people living in Kyogle who had not seen the ocean, because they had never had any reason to travel to the coast. People with long hair were tolerated because there were so few of them and because they knew it was best to keep a low profile.

Some of the young, long-haired people had actually become part of the community because the few farms that were available for sale were not in high demand and they were cheap. A young man who was a pharmacist in town and who had inherited the pharmacy from his father, also owned a cattle property ten miles west of the town. He had an old couple living there to look after the place. The man looked after the cattle on the property. There was a second house as well. The story was, it had been hauled there from down the road about twenty-five years ago. A team of oxen had hauled it. It was set up with water via a tank and a pump from the creek, and the electricity was connected. It was also right next to the road, which didn't matter, because it was right near the end of the road.

I wandered into the real estate agents once I was in town. It seemed like the next thing to do. The young man there told me all about the house for rent. It had been empty for a couple of months. It seemed like people didn't come asking all that often. I wondered what had been happening before I arrived, But later, I realised that life is always happening in a country town. They are never waiting for life to happen. It is full, and of interest. That, I realised, is what a community is, not suburbia where life is mechanised. What is the difference? I could smell the difference. I was probably not so good at describing it.

So, my wife and children came back, and we became part of Kyogle, a community that had enough through-flow of people to remain fresh, but not so much that it became a transit lounge with no soul of its own, a strain that some of the towns near the coast suffered.

The pharmacist was friendly. He was curious about where we had been living. He was curious about young people with long hair. His shop in town was a tight ship. All the employees were attractive young women with smart, prim uniforms. There was a suggestion of James Bond about the place. There was just enough of a hint that it left you wondering what went on when the doors were closed. John had a girlfriend. We discovered that they had been boyfriend and girlfriend for years. She was a kindergarten teacher at the Catholic school. She was also the leader of the town's troupe of marching girls.

There were many things I had to assimilate, things that I might previously have scorned, at a comfortable distance. But here, these things were part of the continuum of life. Years later, I wrote a history of the school. One of the sayings of the "Kyogle kids" back in the war years, was "Kyogle kids can do anything!" I came to see that the people of this town saw themselves as a continuation of those kids, with that deep faith in their capacity to handle whatever life threw their way. I was somewhat humbled and awed.

I saw some old photos of Kyogle, from the 1950s. Obviously the 1950s was the peak period of Kyogle's history. The photo showed Kyogle on a market day; the main street was crammed with cars. Dairy farming had been the main industry then, family farms, before farms began to be consolidated and capital-intensive – "Get big or get out!" Most people had lived through the war years. There was a residue of that feeling that they had helped bring the country through the war. All the women knew work. They had helped keep dairy farms going, including milking cows by hand, and kept households together. And many of them were members of the Country Women's Association. They were charitable, but they brooked no nonsense.

Many of the men had been to war, and had gone back to farms afterwards, or to newly formed farms. I was sitting in a strange place, not part of any group, yet not so far removed from the local people, it seemed. They saw me as my former occupation, a schoolteacher, and in this society, that was quite a respectable thing. I had a wife and two children, so I seemed quite normal. In some ways, being a schoolteacher was moderate, not extreme, whereas being a farmer or timber-getter led to the assumption that you had particular points of view about most questions in life.

Yet I was not a schoolteacher. I was long-haired and unemployed, and I didn't want to go back. And I was hurt from our failure to "make a go of it" at the multiple occupancy, and I had to accept that I had been unrealistic to expect my wife to survive there. I didn't know where I fit in or how to survive financially. It was possible to survive for a while on the dole.

One weekend, the pharmacist and his girlfriend said they wanted to visit the place where we had been. They had a four-wheel drive and they would take us all. I was curious about the place. I had not been there for several weeks. I still had a vegetable garden there. My wife was not enthusiastic, but she was nevertheless curious enough to want to come. It was quite a drive, right to the top of the ridge. It was a long way; the four-wheel-drive was in low-range, just crawling up the steepness slowly.

The pharmacist and his girl were impressed. The day was clear and the view was grand, forests all around. The attraction of the place was evident, but so too was its isolation. The garden belied its neglect. The rain had continued to fall regularly. There were plenty of vegetables for all. On the drive back to Kyogle, the pharmacist said he had access to a tractor-mounted rotary hoe, and he could dig up half an acre for me. Maybe there was enough old wire and posts around for me to put a fence up around the ploughed soil and make a garden. I gratefully accepted his offer. He turned up the following weekend with shiny new machinery, and in half an hour a patch of ground had been ploughed.

The old guy next door was gruff but helpful, and he sorted out some old barbed wire for me, and posts that weren't being used. I dug all the holes by hand and put the wire around the patch. It was the biggest garden I had had yet. This year I wasn't working, meaning, I didn't have a job and I wasn't looking for one, so I tended that garden every day. It was a cold place in winter, down to minus seven degrees with heavy frost, but by 9:30 in the morning it was already warming up, so it was a garden that grew well.

I spent a day or two a week driving around looking for grass for mulch. I was reading books on organic gardening and testing out the ideas. I even had a hose set up so I could water accurately and as needed. I had a protected spot for seedlings. It became a beautiful, fertile garden. I had a wide variety of vegetables, even things I had never heard of before, like kohl rabi, sorrel and English spinach. And in a small way I became part of the community of Norco customers, rubbing shoulders with other people who were doing something practical, not just talking about concepts. We looked for seeds and seedlings, we bought tools and materials, we looked at what each other was buying.

When spring came, I learned that there was a local agricultural show, that had been running since 1910. Maybe I could enter some vegetables in the show? As far as I could see, I was eligible. I suppose it was my way of saying I wanted to become part of this community now. I didn't really know who I was in relationship to this place, but I was here, and it seemed, I was staying.

It was exciting. Such a simple thing – grow some vegetables, select some categories to enter, pick the vegetables, wash them, and drive them in to the show. Fill in an entry form for each category you are entering. Pay the fee. See what happens.

It was the 1977 show. And I won prizes! The show was in October, so my vegetables reflected the fact that I had had a good winter garden. I won prizes in five categories: first prize for a small cabbage, first prize for a bunch of three large beetroots, first prize for a collection of seasoning herbs, green, second prize for a bunch of eschallots, and second prize for a collection of vegetables of twelve or more varieties. My collection of vegetables included silver beet that was so tall it came up to my waist.

My name was spelled correctly on most of the certificates. It was wry validation. I guess many people wouldn't notice or care, but my name is my name. It matters a little bit. I heard one man complaining that someone "from out of town" had entered the competition (meaning me), but I also heard another farmer laughing that some people never liked to have any competition. I detected good humour in this town.

I had a good year. It was a year of enjoying simple things – family, household, garden, embedding my everyday skills around the house and yard, getting to know some people in town. I was even getting used to not being a university student, and not having the goal of getting a degree and perhaps a professional or academic career. It had been a while since I had been at university, but for the first time since then I was doing nothing. I wasn't used to doing nothing. I usually had somewhere to go every day, myriad chores and obligations, and the weight of study.

Nevertheless, I felt it was time to take another step. Towards what? My hippie dream, if it could be called that, had collapsed. Was I sorry? Perhaps not too much. Part of that dream had been about community, and I hadn't felt I had been part of a great community. That was that. It was good to be in Kyogle, west of the McKellar Range where we had been part of the multiple occupancy, but distant from it. We were even west of Kyogle, another ten miles out on a rough road with no through traffic. It felt distant, but calm. It wasn't caught up in any events. From our house, there was only a bush track that went way out through the hills and eventually ended up on the road to Toonumbar Dam, a dam that had been built for farmers in 1971. (So, actually not long before we arrived here.)

17 Teacher

Time to take another step. I was thinking that I should get a job, and wondering casually about what that might be. There was a local newspaper serving Kyogle and Casino that came out twice a week – Wednesdays and Saturdays. It had local news – stories about people in the community and about farming – and classified advertising. Casino had a meatworks, its main industry. I used to read just about all of the newspaper. I was learning about the local community, and besides, I had nothing to do except tend my garden.

It was the Wednesday paper that I was reading, and I had got to the classified advertisements, and I used to read them all. You never know what you will find. There were a few employment advertisements, but not many, and they were only jobs like shop assistant or welder. I ended up reading the "Wanted" advertisements. It was odd what people advertised for. This time, there was an advertisement for a teacher of technical drawing. "Ability to teach maths may be an advantage." And a phone number.

How odd, I thought. Who would put an advertisement in the newspaper like that? And who would possibly read it? But I had! I had the suspicion that the advertisement was directed precisely at me, as if someone was looking over my shoulder!

I had taught mathematics, but never technical drawing or technics, which I understood to be a mixture of woodwork and metalwork. But, given how the advertisement went close to targeting me: it might as well have said, "Glenn Martin of Wyndham Creek", I would give the number a call. I wasn't working at the moment, so I could contemplate a new job. I rang the number. The person turned out to be the principal of St Mary's, a junior Catholic high school in Casino, which was twenty kilometres south of Kyogle. She invited me for an interview.

At the interview, Sister Anne wasn't put off by the fact that I had long hair, or that I was not a Catholic. She liked my experience with teaching mathematics, and she wasn't perturbed by my lack of experience in technics. What seemed to weigh in my favour was my two years studying engineering at the University of New South Wales. That was unexpected. She said that the subject of technical drawing was part of technics, and my engineering studies seemed to point in that direction. She was reassuring.

The school was new. It had been created just the previous year and it was co-educational. It even seemed to be in my favour that I had been to a co-educational high school. Strathfield South High School had been a new school, opened just two years before I had arrived. I had had a choice: either that, or a selective boys' high school. I had not wished to attend a boys' high school. It didn't matter to me that I wouldn't be studying with the "academically superior" students. I was following my own path; the course would be the same. I didn't need to be with the "best" students. I thought that a boys' school would favour the boys who were tough and who liked the rough-and-tumble of football. I didn't.

It seemed that Sister Anne was looking for a teacher who had experience of being in a co-educational environment. For me, that was a given. Finally, the grounds of the job were presented. It wasn't a permanent job. I would be temporarily replacing a teacher who had been diagnosed with cancer. He was having treatment. In a Catholic environment, he apparently felt that a miracle was in the offing. Subtly, Sister Anne inferred that she did not share his optimism. There are times when optimism does not stand on solid ground, and one might intuit this.

It was a precarious issue for a nun to broach with a long-haired stranger whom she might best deal with at arm's length. But she was not that much older than me and it was her first appointment and she wanted to exercise her position with trust. Perhaps she was more trusting with me than the circumstances warranted. But I was the person at whom the advertisement had been directed. I was also elevated above my circumstances. Moreover, it came close to my own life when she talked about a person facing death, and the possibility of a miracle. I had walked in those waters and I had a story to tell.

I did not tell the story that day, but I felt it was in the air. I said I would do the temporary job if she wanted me to, and I would be glad to leave again if the teacher recovered. She told me that the thinking around the school was linked with Vatican II, which I understood to be a new wave of reform that had swept through the Catholic Church world-wide, which cultivated social works and the building of community, rather than emphasising ritual and authority. That was the extent of my knowledge. It seemed to fit with my own desire for community.

I began teaching mathematics and I talked with the teacher who looked after manual arts, now called technics. The curriculum was still being developed, and even the rooms were still being constructed. The parish priest had promised a grant of money to buy equipment for the rooms, and the two of us were to be responsible for planning and implementing all of that. But at the moment, things were on hold because of the teacher who was sick.

All the pupils were from twelve to sixteen years old, boys and girls. Most of them came from Casino, but some of them came from Kyogle. Even the daughter of the real estate agent who had been the leasing agent for the house where I was living at Wyndham Creek. I was happy to be back in the classroom, and I was comfortable teaching mathematics. I could tell that Sister Anne just wanted me to keep things calm and peaceful in the classroom. She was thinking about what the children might be thinking about having a teacher who might be dying. In a Catholic school, this raises all the questions about death – why does God allow fatal diseases?

The conversations I had with Sister Anne were in one sense discreet and innocent, and in another sense wide open. She did not intrude into my personal religion, beliefs or practices, and nor did I disclose. But I had experienced times in my life when things were suddenly okay, without any reason for that to be, and I carried that with me. I could not have explained that, and I didn't. Sometimes a pupil would ask me an angular question about the teacher who was off sick, but all that was important was for this moment to be okay, for us to know that it was okay. I didn't try for the right words, because I no longer thought that the right words existed. They always failed, and in the end deflected us from the present.

In the event, the teacher died, and I think my first event as a permanent teacher at the school was to attend his funeral. It is difficult to say; memory can be hazy about such things. But I remember being amongst the pupils at the funeral, as one of their teachers, not feeling alien about not being a Catholic, nor feeling overwhelmed by death. I was attending an honouring of life and death as an aware human, accepting of my inadequacies, accepting that I was not the master of the universe.

Oddly, all this took place with a traditional Irish priest at the helm, Father Relihan. The nuns and brothers at the school seemed to be diametrically opposite to him. They were new; he was old. His mental perspective seemed to be rural Ireland a century earlier, that he was attempting to keep alive in a meatworks town in Australia. I heard that he used to go back to Ireland every couple of years, to visit family, and probably, to freshen up his accent. He seemed to carry a lot of weight around the town, which was strongly Catholic. It was an odd place for me to be, yet here I was, and apparently accepted by both teachers and pupils.

Things I know

There are some things you know, even if you don't know how you know that you know, and even if this is not true much of the time. What does one do in such an environment but learn how to relax a little bit more?

18 Horseshoe Creek

Later that year I received a sum of money. It was in settlement of the court case that related to the motorcycle accident and my injuries. Now I was in a position to purchase a property, and it was going to be somewhere around Kyogle. It wasn't going to be a share in a multiple-occupancy. I would buy it and own it myself. I had looked at properties all around the far north coast. A lot of it was not amenable, especially closer to the coast. New settlers were arriving in the region. Already, growing popularity had pushed prices up. I had looked at ten acres of steep land with no proper dwelling, no real water, and most of it covered with lantana, but with a price tag of more money than I now had.

I had looked at open bushland with an old house on it that was so horrible I would have driven a bulldozer straight through the middle of it. And I didn't really know what I was looking for. In the end, my wife and I sat down with a piece of paper and wrote down everything we wanted – Essential and Desirable. We needed a liveable house, we needed water, we needed access to the road that was not too difficult. We wanted electricity, we wanted bush, we even wanted a yard for a goat, although that was unlikely.

And instead of looking for five or ten acres, we wrote down "The biggest property you've got for this price". On a Saturday morning, I went in to see the real estate agent we knew and told him I was looking for a property. We wanted to stay in Kyogle. I gave him an idea of our needs and wants. I wasn't expecting this to lead to any revelation, but the agent was suddenly galvanised, as if he had just had an idea. He grabbed his coat and said, "Come with me. There's a place I want to show you."

I had this idea that a real estate agent's work was all left-brain logical: x properties with y-characteristics, and x possible clients with y-features and assets. One did one's best to match one up with the other. But now it seemed so much more swirly than that. These features could mean different things to different people. There was the swirliness of how happiness was possible in a given set of circumstances, and the genius was in the possibilities the agent could see in how that might work for a particular person or family.

I drove out with the agent and had a look. In terms of list-matching, the place had everything on our list, which included a yard that would be suitable for a goat. In terms of access, water, electricity, bush, whatever we had tried to think about, it was there. Beyond that, it was just lovely and welcoming. I went back to town with the agent and I went home and picked up my wife and the two girls, and we went straight out there together to inspect it. We wandered around for hours, including down to the creek, which was just twenty metres down from the house, with fresh running water and a swimmable pool.

The house, I found out later, had been built in 1935. The place had been a dairy farm since about 1905. There was a solid dairy building up behind the house. Electricity had come quite late to the valley, about 1961. It had ceased being a dairy farm about ten years ago, and the property now ran only a few head of cattle. It consisted of 310 acres, most of it steep hills and gullies, tree-covered, and about five acres more or less cleared. Perfect. I was not anticipating becoming a modern-day farmer, but I did want space to play. Who knows, perhaps I could start a herb farm?

My wife's concern had been about living primitively, so it satisfied her that the house was solid, decent and comfortable. The place belonged to a couple who had farmed there since 1950, the year I was born. They had brought up four children there. The children would have been about our ages. The couple lived in town now, but they still obviously had affection for this place. When we met at the house for the handover of the key, the farmer and his wife both had tears in their eyes. It took a while to realise the extent of what that meant.

I couldn't have thought of a better set of circumstances. I thought of the other house, the one that I would have cheerfully driven a bulldozer through, and thought how fortunate we were. We were to enter a house that had been filled with love, and we were to keep it going. Perhaps that had been what I had been looking for: to be the continuation of something that was worthwhile. I thought of the John Denver song, "Rocky Mountain High", where he talks about "coming home to a place he'd never been before". Perhaps that is our deepest desire.

When we were growing up, life was never seen as a continuation of the past, but as something that had to start out new. We were thrust towards the future from a past that was fearful and had ceased – the Second World War, the Depression – with nothing remaining. We were to live in new houses, with new furniture, new decorations, new appliances, new toys, new clothes. Our jobs would be new, to live in a modern world. But we never knew why this was necessary, or where the old world had gone. And once you have something that is new, you realise, even the very next day, that it is no longer new, so it could have already become discreditable, and you don't know why. You never knew at what point an artifact became old and unworthy, replaceable.

Worse, there were still some things around that were deemed to be worthy, and you didn't know why that was so either. I knew that I liked our new house, which was an old house, much older than me. I had no aspirations to live in a new house; it would have lacked something. I was more comfortable having a past, as long as I felt that it had been a good past. I didn't mind modernising, as long as I wasn't simply trying to eliminate the past. Everything in nature tends towards the fulfilment of its potential. The effort spent in modernising should be an effort spent in bringing something towards the fulfilment of its potential.

When I looked at the house, and the changes that seemed to have been made since it was first built in 1935, it seemed to me that the house had developed towards the fulfilment of its potential. For example, there had been verandahs on three sides to start with – it was almost more verandah than house, but two of these had been converted into bedrooms. I tried to understand the house so that I could honour its past. There was a lot to take in. The garage was full of things the farmer had left behind. So were the dairy and various other small sheds. It gave me a taste of the life that had been lived here.

We soon settled into a routine. I was travelling to school in Casino each day. A couple of days a week, the girls were going to the pre-school in town. It was a friendly place, like an extension of family, and the girls loved it. After a while we arranged for the girls to travel into town on the school bus. That was a surprise. The bus was for children who went to the primary school and the high school, but it was an important service for the valley as well. The bus driver brought the mail in the afternoons, and occasionally he brought parcels of goods that people had ordered. He was happy to take the girls.

They sat up behind his seat, and they loved the journey. In the afternoon my wife would listen for the approaching bus, and walk down to wait for it at the gate. The journey took about thirty minutes. It seemed to be a good time, living in our own place in some comfort, while having some old-world qualities. The house had an old Scottish slow-combustion stove, a Wellstood. It was not as well-known or esteemed as the Aga or Rayburn, but it was solidly, Scottishly respectable. There was a hot water system heated by the stove, and it was manageable to obtain firewood.

Young people had started to move into the valley. It wasn't yet a mecca for hippies, but older people had been moving out for years, and there were a few vacant houses. Also, properties had started to be subdivided, and people were buying bush blocks and putting up their own shelters. This was happening slowly in the valleys all around Kyogle. We were sort of in the vanguard, although it would have been hard to say what we were the vanguard of. Some people saw themselves as craftspeople; some saw themselves as alternative farmers; some thought there was scope in fruit crops; a few leaned towards traditional farming; and some, at least for now, were relying on the dole. Some, possibly, were growing small patches of marihuana and selling enough to fund their establishment.

Every valley had its own flavour. In our valley there were numerous craftspeople. One was a metalworker, one made high-class, period-reproduction furniture, one was a potter, one made musical instruments. There were numerous artists. Many expressed their creativity in how they built their houses. So, it seemed a good time to be arriving. It seemed that a community would grow in our valley, based on alternative thinking. And, a community would develop around the district. Already there was an alternative food place in town. You could eat there, they sold fresh vegetables from local farms, and they sold wholefoods. I occasionally sold vegetables there when I had too much from our home garden.

Friendships began, among the new settlers, and with the old settlers. Of course, there was suspicion too, that was on both sides, but the prickliness did not predominate. There was sufficient exchange of real goods for a level of trust to be established. Most of the old settlers in the valley worked at the timber mill in town. They had used to be dairy farmers, but there was only one man who still had a dairy herd now. The mill owner had been in business for over thirty years. He had a regular contract supplying wooden boxes for banana growers. In between, there were orders for house frames and other small buildings. It wasn't the only mill in town, but it employed most of the men in our valley.

The families also had some cattle, and on weekends, cattle were moved around. Some of the older settlers told me stories about my house. One woman had milked cows at my place when she was a girl. She remembered one time when someone was sick, and she and another girl had helped to milk the cows at my place and one other place before they rode their horses to school. In those days there was still a primary school in the valley: Upper Horseshoe Creek, which had about twelve pupils. Today there is still a pine tree standing near where the building had been.

Then, in that first year, my wife became pregnant. We thought it would be fine; the girls were more independent, and we could manage three children in the house, and we were settled in our new home. So, the months passed and she became big, bigger than before, but that, we thought, was a good thing. Both the girls had been small.

The in-laws were informed and were predictably happy. Both grandmothers were competent knitters. The birth would be in December. We were thinking it would be nice to have a boy. When my wife went into labour, I took her into the Kyogle hospital. We had organised someone to look after the girls. After a suitable period of time, the baby was born. It was a boy. Joy! And then there was a kind of flurry, unexpected, and the doctor said, "Oh, I think there's another one there!"

"Oh," I replied, in the awkward heaviness of that moment, "I suppose it had better come out, then." Lame words. And my wife was caught up in the sudden revision of the whole experience, and having to face another birthing episode. Twenty minutes later there was another boy born.

In retrospect, people say all manner of things. "Didn't the doctor know there were two babies?" "Didn't your wife realise there were two babies?" I am just telling the story the way I remember it. Maybe there were moments when the doctor had said, feeling the belly, "There seem to be a lot of limbs there." Maybe my wife had felt that there seemed to be a lot of movement. But in the settled memory of the pregnancy, the word that there were twins on the way did not eventuate until after the first boy was born.

Suddenly, all our plans for accommodating one extra child had to be thrown out, and we had to think about how two more children could be managed. There had been strains in some of our household goods. For example, our fridge was on its last legs, so I went and bought a new one, rather larger than I had intended. The car was likewise close to the end of its life, and I arranged to buy a newer, larger, station-wagon. We had to organise for more furniture. I think we were all in shock, including the grandparents and the two girls.

We had the space in the house, and everyone helped us, in-laws and neighbours. The local ladies thought it was a great blessing, and talked among themselves about how they could help. Both the old generation and the new settlers were on board. Food, washing, looking after the babies and the girls, it was all offered.

But for my wife, nothing seemed to be enough. She was sullen, cranky and disconsolate. I did as much as I could, day by day, week by week, but nothing seemed to be enough. Now and then, someone would come to visit, and for a while, things would seem to thaw out, but it was only an occasional respite. The ongoing pattern was unhappiness and moroseness. I said, "This is the hardest time. There is a lot to do. It will get better. It will get easier as they get older."

Nothing I said made any difference. Nothing I did was enough, nor anything that others did. It has to be said that this was in 1978. In those days, not so long ago, there was no language for post-natal depression, or recognition of this experience. In the face of the inexplicable reality, we were surrounded by generous help.

From this point in time, it occurs to me that my father's mother had suffered from post-natal depression. She had not been able to recover her equilibrium after the birth of her last child, and she ended up in Callan Park Mental Asylum. That was in 1920. Her husband had done what he could to maintain the family and the household. I think he kept the older children at home, while the younger ones were farmed out to various aunts and uncles. It was up to the extended family to manage the best way people could. In Kyogle, the community in the valley likewise did its best.

19 Betrayed

One week, a friend came to visit – male. He was coming to help out around the house. I was teaching full-time, so this was appreciated. And then one day, I came home from school and there was no one there. I found a note on the table. It just said, "I have gone. I have the children." On that day, the boys had been up at a neighbour's place for a few hours. They were about ten months old and took to the neighbours well. Shaking, I got into the car and went up to their place.

They told me that my wife and the friend had come up to pick up the boys and left, a few hours ago. They said there was something about it that they thought was a bit strange. When they realised that something untoward must have happened, they were struck with guilt, but of course, there was nothing they could have known, and nothing they could have done.

Where were they? I had no clues. I still had no idea what was going on. I went home, and saw that some clothes for the children had been packed. I did not think it would be helpful at this point to contact either my parents or my wife's parents. The realisation was still forming that my wife had left and taken the children. My wife had a female friend who had visited us recently, and she lived only a couple of hours away. They had worked together as mental retardation nurses at Stockton, near Newcastle. I had a phone number for her. I rang her.

It took a couple of days, but the friend got back to me and said she had an address, down at South West Rocks, a beach holiday town. She said that my wife was there, with the friend and the children. She suggested that I go and see her. I got in the car immediately and left.

I arrived. When I got out of the car, my wife came out of the house. My children were not to be seen. She approached me aggressively and just said these words: "What are you doing here?" with the emphasis on "you". I was taken aback. What did that mean? We had been married for seven years. We had four children together; surely there was something to talk about? There was a madness about it, as if she had some illusion in her head, in which I was prevented from appearing before her. What kind of a question was that? But all the time I had been driving there, I was thinking, there has to be some talking to be done. There has to be some discussion between us about the situation. But now I thought, "This is irrevocable. You have done something you can't take back." My thoughts then went to my children. I was their father, and that was irrevocable. I would always be their father.

Over the next twelve months, my thoughts reverberated between these poles, over and over. My wife filed for divorce and for the lion's share of the assets, all of which had come from the settlement of the claim over my motorcycle accident. I filed for custody of the children, as an act of sanity, a comment on the period of time since the twins had been born.

What I didn't know until forty years later was that this episode was not a spontaneous fling between my wife and our friend. I had always been led to believe that the affair had just happened during the week. But it's funny how people can reveal bits of stories a long time afterwards, because it doesn't have the same charge anymore. A friend told me my wife had written to the friend beforehand, with a plea that she needed to be rescued from me. She appealed to him as a white knight in a dire situation. He was foolish enough to take the bait.

I was told by another person, recently, that I had been impossible to live with, that I never talked and couldn't communicate. This story had come from my wife. But I don't believe that was at all true. I was constantly trying to cheer her up, and take the burden off her. I suppose that people need to have a story about events that makes them feel better. In the face of stories like that, for all the pain, I have to be glad that the marriage ended. I kept my faith with my children. Regardless of the mess, I am their father.

The difficulty is in having to tell the truth about painful events, even if it means exposing other people's stories. It leaves the question of whether those stories are malicious or delusional. I will tell the story once. After that, it is up to people to make up their own minds. I made one vow in the wake of the dissolution of my marriage: there is much of life left to be lived; I will not live my life in bitterness.

I have found that there is often a single statement in an event that encapsulates the truth of it. In this case it was the statement my wife made when I turned up where she was holed up with her new boyfriend: "What are you doing here?" If it had been a bullet through the heart, the effect would have been no different. After that day, I had to become a new person.

I read the *Book of Ecclesiastes* sometime after this and found that some of the statements were accurately, profoundly appropriate. "It is an unhappy business that God has given to the sons of man to be busy with." "To accept his lot and find enjoyment in his toil – this is the gift of God. For he will not much remember the days of his life because God keeps him occupied with joy in his heart."

20 Dream

Sometimes I have dreams, and if the dream seems significant, I write it down. In the emotionally turbulent months after my wife left, as she tried to position herself for a favourable divorce that would keep the children from me as much as possible, I tried to recentre, to become separate from her, to attain a new understanding of myself and the people around me, so that I could live again. I did not drink alcohol at all in this period; I felt that I needed to keep a steady hand with myself to prevent myself from subsiding into self-pity.

This dream was very detailed and coherent, and I remembered it after I woke up. It was about a girl who had a shotgun, who was not quite angry enough to shoot to kill, but who was angry enough to want to have the whole world at gunpoint. A man came, solid and towering, outwardly impeccable and inwardly calm, an exalted representation of the world at gunpoint. It seemed that this was his job.

He faced the girl in the heat of her anger, taking it upon himself without protest, with just a sadness that was not for himself at all. The girl was disarmed, not only her but also her anger. So, I learned from this man that no job is ever just a job.

Afterwards, I returned with the man to his home. His comment was not about the girl, or about his job, but about me: "You seem to have been tortured a lot for a young man." My first reaction was that I could not see my life that way, but the seed-thought that grew was, "If this is so, then to what purpose is my life bent? Is there something in which I am at fault, that attracts such sorrowfulness?"

That dream simmered for some time. It was provocative.

21 Divorce

During the divorce process, my ex-wife told me that if I wanted to see the children, I could go and live in the Blue Mountains, where she had gone. It was a message delivered with derision. It did not matter. I had thought about this and I knew where my home was. I would ask the court to order that the children come to visit me in my home in the valley at Kyogle. That wish was granted. I believe that my ex-wife (and her boy-friend) were angry about that for many years. It showed in the constant sabotage to travel plans for access visits. It did not matter.

    I asked myself if I was just being obstinate. I was certainly being obstinate, but it was important that my children experience their father as a strongly anchored person, not someone who had been broken by the whim of a woman who was not of sound mind, at least at the time.

    I even asked myself the hypothetical question: if the circumstances arose where my ex-wife could be accepted back, would I accept her? Long after they became adults, my two girls confessed that they had hoped for many years that their two parents would get back together. Children do. They would whisper about it in their private night-time conversations in the bedroom together. Even though it was impossible, the desire possessed both of them, impervious to logic.

    But my ex-wife had left irrevocably. There was no meeting of souls between us. Would I get back together because of the children? It was merely a hypothetical question, but it would have been only a matter of material welfare, an empty kindness. My vow was to start again, with or without the children. My ex-wife was obliged to be committed to her new choice now. It was her challenge. I was not part of her life anymore.

    I kept a place for my children in my house. They would know they would always be welcome, and I was their father. Yes, some people counselled me to give up on the children. They said it would be easier for both them and me. But, after reading the *Book of Ecclesiastes,* you don't miserably beg for the path to be easy. You ask to have the strength to stand up straight, to do the proper thing, to be loving. I believe that I did, over the years.

22 Father

How does one adhere to such a path? Is it a matter of dogged discipline? Must one be dour? I think there are moments that anchor you, and the memory of such moments. About six weeks after my ex-wife had left, I was at home, putting a load of washing on the clothesline. I was living day to day, going to work and subsisting, keeping my hopes up. I did not know where they all were, or what was going to happen next. One thought was that I might never see my children again. I just had my conviction, that I was the father of my children, and nothing could change that, not anything that anyone tried to do.

A station-wagon pulled up in the yard – this is seventeen kilometres out of town, with the creek rippling nearby and the breeze lifting the leaves briskly. No one around. A door of the car opened and two girls ran out – my daughters, aged three and four. They ran straight towards me and grabbed onto my legs, shouting and excited. That was the moment I knew that I was the father of my children, and I would always be their father.

My ex-wife and her boy-friend had come to get some more things for the next phase of their life. Nothing good happened on that visit; well, I don't even know if they noticed the one good thing that did happen. My ex-wife probably did. She would have registered this as a nuisance for the future.

23 Restabilising

I was still teaching at St Mary's, all the way through the destruction of my marriage. I didn't disclose the event to my fellow teachers or my pupils. It did not concern them, and I did not expect them to play the role of support group. I remained present, and I did my job wholeheartedly. In fact, in large measure, it was my sanity. I did let Sister Anne know after a while, but I was not collapsing. I wondered how nuns see the breakdown of marriages. Did they see it from a spiritual height, as if marriage breakdowns were part of the unsatisfactory nature of the lives that normal people lead? Did their minds leap to accusations and blame, of one party or the other, or both? I never knew, but I felt that Sister Anne was compassionate. Perhaps she was even wise.

Nevertheless, there were days when I felt empty. As a high school teacher, one does playground duty, and I would do my rounds of the playground when I was on duty, making sure that the peace was being kept. What I noticed was that some students, both girls and boys, would come up to me and say hello, and then they would hang around for a few minutes. Sometimes there was conversation, and sometimes there wasn't. They didn't seem to be uncomfortable about the silence, and after a while they would drift off again. I often wondered if they were intuiting that I was in need of strength, and they were hanging around until they had given it to me. It certainly felt that way, and I was awed and grateful.

I stayed at St Mary's until midway through 1983. I spent about three years taking stock of my life. I lived alone at Horseshoe Creek. I established a large garden and refined my gardening skills. I had raised garden beds, heavy mulch, and a system of micro-jet sprinklers. I had a spring high up in a gully, and the farmer before me had laid a set of pipes all the way down to the house. There was a header tank of forty-four gallons up at the spring. The water filled up slowly and there was a ball-cock on top. Later I built a 1,000-gallon storage tank on the hillside.

The micro-sprinklers were in sets that went down each row of the garden, and there were eight rows altogether. I usually ran three rows a night, and they lasted all night until the tank ran dry. I figured out it was equivalent to giving a garden bed one inch of rain. The prime ingredient for a lush garden is water! Of course, I had far too much food, but I either gave it away to neighbours or sold it to the alternative shop in town.

I gradually got to know my neighbours, many of whom were new. As it happened, among the new settlers, my house was one of the few established houses. Most people were living in temporary sheds and tents. Mine was also one of the few places that had electricity. The situation reminded me of how things had been when I grew up. Then, most people had lived in temporary dwellings too. It took them a few years before they managed to build a house. The difference then was that most people had electricity and running water.

Kyogle was a high-rainfall area, and it was not uncommon to have floods. They weren't on the news the way they are now. They tended to be quick floods: it would rain heavily for three or four days; it would build to a crescendo and then it would die away. The next day would be bright sunshine, and you could dry things out and fix any damage. I know other places are slower, because they are further downstream, and the water gathers together and sits stagnantly. With us, it was a matter of the road being cut off for one or two days, and then seeing if the road surface was still trafficable. We always kept a week's food in the house, not taking the road for granted.

I remember swimming in the creek the day after a flood peaked – not really advisable, but as long as you watch for a while to see if any logs are rushing down, it's fine. It was one or two metres higher than normal. The bed of the creek was clear; all the loose rocks and plant debris had been swept away. The water was light green. I had to be careful I didn't get swept downstream, because the boulders were big and you can't expect a raging creek to be kind.

It was the most refreshing swim I've ever had. It was as if the whole creek was sparkling with life.

On such days, people would turn up to my house, wanting to use the washing machine to wash their dirty clothes and sheets. They were busy days, with load after load, and yet we sat on the deck and watched the creek, drank tea and talked as well. People were keen to repay my generosity, and gave me all manner of gifts. I wondered if my house had performed a similar function in the old days. It was strategically placed, next to the road, not too far upstream, and just before a bridge. I think it had.

In fact, there were two bridges, one twenty metres from my house, and another two hundred metres further upstream. I was told this story by old-timers, because it concerned my house. They seemed to think it was important that I knew the story, and perhaps also they realised that I appreciated knowing the stories. In any case, I was told this story more than once. The house was built in 1935. In those days, ticks had emerged as a problem for the cattle, and the treatment was to dip the cattle in poison that killed the ticks. This was preferable to the cattle dying. So, it became a collaborative endeavour between the local owners and the Department of Agriculture to determine where the cattle dips should be situated.

At the time, the road was primitive, and there were multiple creek crossings – fords. These were a problem every time there was a flood, because they got washed out, and it often required a lot of work to make them trafficable again. This was a problem for the local people, the Council, and the cream carriers who transported the cream from the local dairy farmers to the cheese factory in town. The locals met and discussed it, and they came up with the idea of fixing both problems. Instead of building two dips in that section of the creek, they could build one dip and two bridges. That way, the cattle could be driven over the bridges to the dip, and the problem of two creek crossings would be solved.

The Council decided to cooperate, and in 1938 the two bridges and the one cattle dip were opened. Someone gave me a photo of the occasion, a celebration with everyone in their best attire, dignitaries officiating, and my house seen in the background. It was lovely how the history of the valley was being passed on. The sharing of the history overrode all the differences that the old and young people may have had between them.

24 Kyogle stories

Another story I was told was about a pile of rocks. An old farmer said to me, "You know how when you go to town, just as you come out onto Fawcetts Plain, on the left, under an old fig tree, you notice a pile of rocks?" In fact, I did. I had noticed it. I thought, as you would, that a farmer had made that pile of rocks in the process of clearing a paddock.

The old farmer asked me why the pile of rocks was there. I told him. It seemed obvious, and I wondered if he was taking me for a fool. "Well," he said, "that's where you're wrong."

I didn't see how I could be wrong about a thing like that. Then he told me the story.

In the early days of Horseshoe Creek, back before there were enough cream producers for there to be a cream carrier, around 1905, two Hindu men had a dairy farm up near the end of the creek. They generally had enough cream every two or three days to bring full cream cans down to the beginning of Fawcetts Plain. The cream carrier used to pick the cream cans up from there and take them into town.

Because they brought the cream cans down by horse, and the loaded cream cans were heavy, it was important that the load was balanced. Sometimes the amount of cream didn't work out, and they only had enough cream for one can. So, what they did was they would fill the second cream can up with stones, to balance the load. Then they would drop the stones at the rendezvous point at Fawcetts Plain. There was no need to take them back; there were plenty more stones back up at the end of the creek. Over time, the stones piled up, and there was no need to move them, so there they still are.

Well, that was the story, and it could have been true. My logical mind says that the better solution would have been to half-fill each cream can with the cream, but I felt it was the kind of situation where that comment would have been a spoiler. But I think the horse would have been on my side.

So, it seemed that I was gathering stories about Horseshoe Creek and Kyogle, and people were sharing them with me. This happened informally for years. Kyogle was the main town in a very large shire. Kyogle was towards the eastern side, with dozens of creeks flowing into the Richmond River as it flowed south towards Casino, and then east to Ballina. This made Kyogle separate to Lismore, because the river that ran through Lismore was called the northern arm of the Richmond River. It flowed south to Woodburn, which was where it joined up with the Kyogle arm. In recent years, the river through Lismore had its name changed to the Wilson River.

West of Kyogle, and part of the shire, was the northern arm of the Clarence River, which ran right down to Grafton. There were a couple of small towns out that way: Urbenville and Bonalbo. To get to them, you had to drive north of Kyogle almost up to Woodenbong, then down the Clarence Way until, after Bonalbo, you got to Sandilands and headed east to Casino. A big circle.

Deciding that I would stay at Horseshoe Creek was the beginning of my recovery, the recovery of my self. I also realised how much I had suppressed myself for the sake of the relationship. I was used to an atmosphere of cold judgement. Now I was free to explore what I wanted to do and be. I started reading, and writing. I wrote short stories, just to see what they might be like. And I still wrote poems, attracted to that form of expression.

I read novels, particularly the novels of Tom Robbins. Why was he important? He had a zany sense of humour, and I liked how he made that an aspect of life. Having a serious, sober appraisal of life in our society did not have to mean having an approach to life that was overly serious. I think I had often committed the sin of seriousness.

Things I know

One can be too serious, but it can take a while to learn how to lighten up. "Absolute seriousness is never without a dash of humour." – Dietrich Bonhoeffer.

25 Adult education

I must have been getting known around town, because a man called Richard contacted me. He was an odd fellow, and yes, he was serious. He was working for a funded organisation working with unemployed youth. He was young, but not really long-haired, but nor was he "straight". I suppose what set him apart was that he did not seem to be a part of any group. He was a loner. He had done some unusual activities with the youth, things that some people in the town didn't approve of, but which I thought were innovative.

Richard organised day trips to Brisbane by bus for groups of youth. He took them to the Commonwealth Employment Service (CES) centre and arranged meetings with potential employers. This was frowned upon by some employers in Kyogle (the loud ones) because they wanted youth to get jobs in town so they didn't leave. The reality was that this wasn't happening and it wasn't possible, so Richard was giving the youth the best chance possible. Some people could see the value in what he was doing, and he didn't seem to mind that he wasn't everyone's favourite youth worker.

Richard wanted to talk to me because one of the other initiatives he had instigated was a program of adult education courses in Kyogle. He confided that he was thinking of leaving town and he was looking for someone to take over the adult education courses and build them up. It wasn't really a job; the pay would amount to about half a day a week. But, it was feasible for me, because I was still working as a teacher. It wasn't as if I had a family to attend to. I could use my time well.

Accordingly, I took over as the coordinator of Community Education Kyogle in early 1982. It was the perfect context for me to get to know people around the district, looking for potential tutors of courses, and the program would offer the same opportunity to local people, both new settlers and traditional folk. Our program offered a wide range of subjects – ceramics, aerobics, yoga, meditation, patchwork quilting, massage, floral art, wood-carving, plant propagation, creative writing. There was more: woodwork, leatherwork, stained glass, floral art and macrame. We were enthusiastic. It was the early days of computers, so we offered word-processing. We offered microwave cooking – it was early days for that, too.

It was exciting, and people were keen to be part of it, both as tutors and as students. We were well-supported by townspeople and organisations, so advertising was easy, and venues were available. I felt that we crossed the lines and helped to bring people together. It was surprising who enrolled in the various courses – young, old, traditional, alternative, male, female – there was a healthy exchange happening. I did this for three years, and the program built up, and the numbers. People were making suggestions about what to do next and how it could work. You could see an evolution and development happening.

Adult education tapped me into a different stream of people: beyond Kyogle, people around the far north coast region who were interested in adult education. For them, it was an expression of a belief in the capacity of adults for development. They fostered adult education programs in their own towns, and were working at developing a regional group to support adult education and encourage state government funding. So, adult education for me meant not just involvement in the town that I had decided to settle in, it meant being tapped into a burgeoning group around the region, and its enthusiasm.

One of the pioneers of this group, Bill Sippo, wrote a paper on the philosophy of community adult education. He wrote, "Its essence is that it is based on the needs and wishes of a local community rather than of the State or even of a local provider. It accepts that all people can learn and progress. They can become better informed, more thoughtful, more understanding, better aware of problems and more confident in tackling them. A better sense of community can be developed. Only those who try can hope to reach the unreachable. If this is the philosophy of community-based adult education, it has something for which it can proudly fight."

I still have a copy of the paper, typed on a typewriter and printed on a Gestetner machine. I was stirred by such sentiments. It looked like the birth of a worthwhile movement. The people involved were committed. They were not necessarily credentialled but they were clear, deep and passionate thinkers. I did not have a great deal of residual respect for the credentialled, and this looked like a new field of activity that could set its own rules. Bright minds, free thinkers. They were already compiling materials to teach tutors and adult educators, some of them drawing on their own education in teaching and psychology. You could see they had the intelligence and the resources to devise a tertiary education course, but their emphasis was always practical – how to support adult education programs.

The idea of going back to university had not altogether left me. The other technics teacher and I had devised the course for pupils from Year Seven through to Year Ten, and the other teacher had discussed with me the possibility of my going back to university to get a teaching degree specialising in technics. He was thinking it would bolster both my career and the credibility of our small department. Although I was tickled by the idea, I wasn't profoundly moved in that direction, and I let it pass.

I was more pleased by the fact that we had put together the course for technics in book form. I was prepared to say that this was my first book! It was 1982, and processes were still manual, not digital. We typed material, inserted drawings, and physically assembled the book and bound it. The front cover was printed by hand, technical-drawing-style.

The only reason I gave up adult education was that it had a natural limit in a small town, and I was eventually looking for a full-time job. I was ready to end teaching. Teaching had not been the plan in the beginning, and it was time to intervene in my own life. I was prepared to admit that I had learned important life skills in teaching, and that those skills would follow me into whatever else I would do. I could not see, at this point, a pathway into writing. At most, I had taught an adult education course in creative writing: "Satisfy that urge to write. The course aims to develop your discipline and imagination in expressing yourself and organising your thoughts. (six weeks)" I imagine that I was a good teacher of creative writing.

I handed in my resignation at St Mary's. Some of the pupils were shocked. I had been there for five years, and the current students assumed I would be staying. They were hurt. But I also found it difficult, really difficult. These people, the pupils and the teachers, had helped to keep me sane over the last few years. A group of pupils flocked around me the day after the announcement, and one pupil said, "Why are you leaving?" It was like that child-statement that implies "Is there something wrong with me?"

And that was so far from the truth. In moments like that, the truth sneaks out. I said, unplanned: "You can't stay at school all your life." So then I had to explain what I meant by that. I said, "I have to get out. I have loved it here, but I have to try and find out what I'm supposed to be doing with my life. If I don't do it now, I never will."

And it was true. I was in my mid-thirties. And I was so comfortable there that I could have stayed for the rest of my working life. But then I would never have done any of the things I was supposed to do with my life. I had to take the next step. (Indeed, at least three of the teachers who were there at that time were still there at retirement age, about thirty years later. That's wonderful, but I had not started out with the intention of being a teacher.)

On my last day at school, at lunchtime, a crowd of pupils came up to me in the quadrangle and surrounded me. There were designated leaders, and they had prepared speeches. It was quite emotional. I felt a lot of love in that place. They had collected money and bought me a set of six beautiful crystal glasses as a farewell gift, which I still treasure. But it was still necessary to go.

26 Youth worker

I ended up in the place where Richard had worked, working with unemployed youth. It was a Federal Government funded program. I saw my immediate future as being in some form of community development. It was not a long-range plan; it was simply the next step. Some people (like my mother) saw it as a step down from teaching and were disappointed. But for me it was a step like a step from one boulder to another when you are crossing a stream. Boulders go up and down; the point is to focus on getting across the stream (even if you can't see it).

For me, the general direction was towards community development. I had given up on writing, except in private. The idea of community development had been inspired by my involvement in adult education. I had attained the position of treasurer of a new state body for community adult education. The money we were handling was insignificant; the important thing was to be part of the conversation, part of the movement. Although, I admit to having reservations about being involved in political endeavours.

In my reading, I had come across William Irwin Thompson, *At the Edge of History* (1971), and he had categorised all the functions in society into four groups. This resonated with me. He started with two groups: scientists and technicians in one group, and managers and critics in the other. Strange groupings, I thought. Does that account for all the functions in our society? But then he starts to fill it out to make four groups, and it begins to make more sense.

The Science group includes education and religion. Okay, so this is about forms of knowledge, and passing knowledge on. The Technicians include industry and the military; this is about the functional, practical aspects of society. Then there is the Managers group, and this includes government, politics and the instruments of the state. And lastly, the Critics include the media and the arts. When I sit with this for a while, I believe that it does cover, adequately, all the things that happen in a society.

The big question, of course, is, where do I fit in? Am I a part of education, or industry, or the arts, or the machinery of politics and state? As a teacher, I was clearly in Education. As the owner of a bush property, with a big garden, was I in Industry? Or was I something outside all of it? And moving into the service for unemployed youth, was I in Government, Industry or Education? And what did it matter? Where did I want to be, in terms of these different functions?

I won't say I have ever answered this question, but the question does engage me. I think it means something. I think there are times when I feel I should be part of Education, or Government, or the Critics, or the Arts. I think you can describe your passage between these functions over the course of a lifetime. There is a dynamic at play.

In fact, there is a prior layer to Thompson's four-groups model. Before society, there is the tribe. He asserts that the same four functions exist in the tribe. They are: Headman, Shaman, Hunter and Clown. These are the primal versions.

The headman takes the lead and organises, and is allowed to do so by the others; it makes for comfort, peace, and simplicity. The shaman has special knowledge, and also the responsibility to handle the unknown and the daunting. The hunter is a worker and a provider with his own special skills. Which leaves the clown. Why is there a clown? The clown has two roles: to be a communicator and interpreter, and then, to offer an alternative perspective, or psychic relief.

The four primal roles transmigrate into complex society, but the roles remain: they are an essential aspect of human nature. Perhaps my challenge is to see how any particular role could combine elements of many of these different functions. So, as a youth support worker you could be an educator, an artist and a politician; and a manager!

I didn't spend a long time in that service. It was turbulent. I got the sack once, I was given my job back, then I resigned, then I was offered the job back again. The organisation was governed by a community-based committee. I had had some little experience of this in the community adult education group, although there were no high stakes there, and the committee was largely a non-event. The committee for this group, the Community Youth Support Scheme (CYSS), was political, with members drawn from across the town's businesses.

The President was one of the local publicans. He had numerous casual staff at his hotel, so his ideas about managing staff came from there. There were other shop-type businesses represented, and one of the local solicitors. There were two of us youth workers. Prior to us, there had been a project officer who had thought that the role of the service was to be friendly to the youth, and provide a place for them to hang out. This had led to the influx of elements who wanted to trade in drugs. It had been explosive, and had involved the police.

My orientation was as an educator and with a focus on community development. I thought that we could offer training programs that would help young people to find jobs. The committee thought this was a healthy response to the situation. However, some of the young people who had established the place as a hangout were not prepared to be shifted. It was a delicate situation for a while, involving persuasion, rewards and conditions. We made headway and we established worthwhile training programs that were well-attended. We also cleaned the place up and painted it, and got some money for more appropriate furniture and facilities.

The trigger for trouble was not any of this situation. We were managing it quite well, and anyone would have been pleased with what we were doing. We had enthusiastic support from some youth, grudging support from some who had been enemies at the start, and new youth who were appearing each week. We were building up confidence and attempting more as each week went by. The trigger was the President, who informed us that he was sacking us. This was somewhat of a shock.

He then informed us that this action was regular; that they (that is, he) sacked staff at the end of each funding period because they did not know whether they would get funding for the next period. He cheerfully informed us that we were welcome to re-apply for our jobs. However, I had come out of an environment that was more civilly regulated, and I thought that the civil rules should apply here also, not the one-man rules of a man used to the jungle.

In an instant response, I informed him that I did not accept the sacking, and that he had no right to do that. We were employed on a permanent basis and that was that. I also informed him that the correct procedure would have been to sack us in the event that they did not receive funding for the next period. He insisted that the sacking stood, and we could re-apply for our jobs. I said that I would be taking action, and I went home.

I did not usually get involved in confrontations, but I felt that what had been done was wrong, and it had to stop. I didn't even feel personal resentment towards the publican, but he was taking his personal attitudes into a public arena. I was partly influenced by the fact that there was a solicitor on the committee. The solicitor also had to know that this behaviour was unacceptable. He should have already known, so better that the lesson should come from the outside.

What the publican didn't know was that I had joined the union for social workers. In the employment atmosphere of the youth service, I had felt that I needed its protection, and I also kept this knowledge to myself. But now, I rang the union in Sydney and explained the circumstances. I said I thought it was an open-and-shut case. I had a contract, and there were no grounds for my dismissal. The person undertook to take the case to the industrial relations commission and to let the committee know.

27 Lady 2

While this was happening, my domestic situation had changed. A lady had come to stay. She needed somewhere to stay, and a friend in the valley, a midwife, referred her to me. Perhaps the friend thought it was time I gave up my retreat. It had been three years since my wife had left. And, rocky as the arrangements for access visits often were, I had persevered with having my children visit in school holidays. The children seemed to appreciate it as a home that in some way was theirs. That was even true of the twin boys, despite the fact that they had been taken away before they were twelve months old.

The lady settled in, and helped keep house. She obviously needed somewhere quiet, stable and peaceful. There had been trouble before. She had come up from Sydney with a boyfriend and they had stayed at a hippie shack further up the valley. But there was turbulence between them that was not fixable. Soon after the lady came to my place, the man went back to Sydney, and that was that. Before long, the lady and I ended up in the same bed, and that seemed good. Life seemed stable and pleasant.

If I have cause to refer to my ex-wife from this point on, she shall be Lady 1. My current visitor became Lady 2.

So, when the dismissal crisis occurred, I was open to new responses. Lady 2 and I went on holidays for a week, down to Yamba. I very seldom went on holidays, but in this situation, I was unusually calm. I felt that it would all come out right.

And it was so. We had an enjoyable week at Yamba, enjoying swimming at the beach and nightly seafood. At the end of the week, I received a telephone call from the person at the union, informing me that the committee's action had been overturned by the industrial relations commission, and I had my job back, with a week's holiday money. I went back to work.

I expected some grief from the publican, but strangely enough, I seemed to have won some respect from him. He was more polite to me after that. Interesting.

I worked with a new partner, who had a different background to me, not teaching, but we worked well together. The energy level of the workplace was high. However, suddenly we found ourselves in the middle of a war. The former project officer had come back into the picture, getting himself appointed onto the committee, and a small group of youth seemed to be making a last-ditch effort to wrest back control of the centre as their hang-out.

There were incidents that involved mysterious night-time damage to the centre and threats of violence. I thought this was bizarre as well as childish. It came to a head when the two of us were threatened in the centre, and were backed up by the ex-project officer who had got onto the committee. We quit on the spot and walked out. What followed was a town feud. It was absurd, because there was no chance that the murky ex-project officer could win control of the centre and the organisation.

Well, we supposed that there was, if they were allowed to get away with it. I suppose that in Thompson's schema of all the functions in a society, there are corresponding anti-functions, and we were looking at an example here in this little country town. We decided that we would see this through. We went to see all the former committee members, including the publican and the solicitor. The difficulty with all of these people was that they all had jobs and were busy. They were happy to be on the committee as long as there was no trouble.

We communicated with the federal officers, given that this was a federally funded government project. They could see there was a groundswell of support for cleaning up this mess, so they were willing to become involved. After a few weeks – with the centre being closed over this period – a public meeting was called, with the federal officers chairing the meeting. A new committee was elected, and the ground rules for the functioning of the organisation were clarified. It was a sound victory for the town.

The two of us were offered our jobs back. Neither of us accepted. We left it for others to become involved. I felt that I had had my experience. It had been valuable, and I had learned a lot – educator, trainer, administrator, planner, politician, manager, communicator. I went home. The garden needed tending. (I wrote about the episode of my involvement with this organisation in a book, *Sustenance*, published in 2011.)

I had had a period before when I didn't have a job. I had found legitimacy in sitting and thinking. And doing practical things at home. How did I justify this? I felt that I had spent most of my young adulthood thinking abstractly. The issues that consumed me were climate change, capitalism, education, spirituality. What I had neglected was the practical side of life. Did I know how to use a saw or a screwdriver? Did I know how to fix household items that were broken? Did I know how to grow plants and cook meals? Could I paint a house? My father had been a painter; could I paint a house?

I felt the urge to be independent in my surroundings, not silly and helpless while in possession of fine abstract ideas. I could see it in the older generation of people in the valley and around Kyogle. All the farmers could fix their own fences, and any other job you cared to name. It wasn't exceptional, it was just expected. I had already embarked on my own learning. Before I started work at St Mary's, there was very little I could do of a practical nature. But if I wanted to keep my job, I had to learn basic woodwork and metalwork. I thought, the school only goes up to Year Ten and I am an intelligent adult: I have to be able to learn that much, surely. And I did. I even went to the Casino Technical College and learned welding, and how to use a metal lathe and a milling machine.

There was satisfaction in knowing these skills. It gave me a feeling of power in my home environment, that I wasn't helpless. As Bill Sippo said, adult learners "can become better informed, more thoughtful, more understanding, better aware of problems and more confident in tackling them." I was realising that this was a holistic vision. The revolution was fading away, and I could see that many of the revolutionaries were impractical. Perhaps that was just another symptom of the ailments of our society.

It didn't hurt to spend a few months at home. Money was meagre but generally sufficient. I had not divested myself of the adult education coordination position yet. It had bubbled along in the background while I had been working at the unemployed youth centre. The program of courses was always broad and interesting, catering to a wide range of tastes. We didn't have a defined groove. Later on, many adult education programs became de facto vocational centres, with job skills and business management skills in the foreground.

None of the adult education people I knew wanted to go down that road. There were already technical colleges. The brief of adult education was adult development in its broadest sense. We did cater to practical interests, but then, personal development begins with personal mastery. Wasn't I doing that in my own life? We offered automotive maintenance and aerobics. But we also offered a course in alternative medicine, and one in astrology. We offered soft-toy making, photography and bonsai. We offered family days too – candle-making and silk-screening. I found that it was an interesting exercise to think about balance in all this. It was like holding William Irwin Thompson's paradigm in mind.

One time, a young man came to us and wanted to offer a discussion group called "Facing the Threat of Nuclear War". I think that he was a son of one of the town families, a solicitor, and that he didn't live in town all the time. I suspect that he was the older brother of a girl I had taught at St Mary's in Casino. He was very dignified. He had been educated in the city. I realised that we were tapping into very diverse streams, and stirring up seeds of change. We offered that course, although there were not enough takers for it to run.

I wondered who else in town knew that young man, and what they might think of us for putting up that course. But mostly, one did not know, so one simply had to use one's judgement. He was an unusual but welcome addition to our fare. I think that our program of courses in Kyogle was aimed at personal fulfilment rather than revolution. It was an expression of the adult development creed, to become the fullness of one's self, liberated rather than oppressed. That way, a healthy social milieu was most likely to ensue. It was good enough for me.

28 Skills

One of the skills that I developed during this period was the ability to put together a program, and also to compile it into a suitable form for printing. This was the era just before the personal computer appeared. Most people didn't even have a typewriter, so they had no way of presenting textual material or layout. Life belonged to the secretary, and there was a huge gulf between the low end (handwritten) and the high end (printing machines).

The first program I put together for adult education was handwritten by me and printed the same way that I printed material for students at school: on a Fordigraph machine, a spirit duplicator. While I was at St Mary's, they bought a small offset printing press and I learned how to use it. That was satisfying. It wasn't such a great leap when personal computers arrived, because I was used to using a portable typewriter and preparing materials for duplication; I was involved!

Over time, our programs for adult education became more professional-looking, and it was a concern that needed to take centre-stage. It wasn't taken for granted as it is now. I think the difference it made to be in the lead in these areas was that we had a commitment to being professional, as good as the technology allowed us to be, and we became known for that. It became a global impression of everything we did; it had a halo effect.

Things I know
Everything occurs as the next step, not as part of a grand plan.

29 William Irwin Thompson

I was still digesting material from books I had read about social change, counter culture and alternative lifestyles (although I hated the word "lifestyles"). The William Irwin Thompson book, *The Edge of History*, reverberated in my head for years. Consider this: "For all my expensively acquired knowledge, I had no knowledge that was of any use in this world…. I had been travelling sideways to many interesting places, but I had not moved one inch up…. It was all disembodied knowledge that didn't yet belong to me" (p. 35). I was seeking to live out the antidote to that indictment by leaning towards the practical.

Even more pointed was this comment: "It became obvious that if a man could not survive the subtraction of his job from his identity, then there wasn't really much to him in the first place" (p. 27). I spent most of a year at home, apart from the time I spent on adult education business. There was a lot of Thompson to digest, on multiple aspects of self and society. He had a humorous depiction of the current social unrest. I know he was talking about America, but it still held resonance for Australia:

"We were all caught in a shoddily built house in which all the lights had gone out. The hippies wanted the penny jammed behind the fuse, the radicals wanted to burn the house down and make for the exits by the light of the flames, and the moderates wanted to call in the 'experts' who had built the house in the first place." (p. 36)

He thinks of the hippies as drug consumers, whereas we need to break that down into drug consumers and followers of alternative lifestyles (which included religious persuasions, both Christian and Eastern, and non-religious grassroots folk). But the sentiment is salient; sitting in a valley outside of Kyogle, I could reflect on all of these social forces.

Thompson distilled some grand ideas in that book, and even tiny fragments were significant: "There are times when a man of learning must withdraw from political and social involvement, from all action, and wait patiently for the appropriate historical moment" (p. 73). I felt that I had withdrawn and was waiting, although I did not know for what. And the statement kept any sense of guilt at bay – "A man should be working; he should be doing something useful for society in the workforce". Otherwise you are lazy, and unfairly depending on others to support you. My feeling was, I just need to hold things at bay for a while. Keep it at bay – it sounded as if society was like a snarling wolf.

One of the grand ideas in Thompson was that society would let things become so bad that we would find ourselves in the tragic situation that whatever any side decided to do, it would be wrong.

Some people wanted a political revolution. That would not be enough. Some people wanted to focus on technology ("Technology will save us"). Some people thought the answer was in religion – of one sort or another, and they would be extremes. In the midst of all this were managers who were primarily interested in power, and they had learned that the best way to preserve power was to give the illusion of reform and constant innovation (p. 67).

I was happy being retired, albeit temporarily, from the fray. I had renovated my house, my garden was fertile and productive, and Lady 2 and I were enjoying life.

In time, Lady 2 became pregnant. We were both happy about this. She liked the prospect of being a mother. I liked the prospect of having another child. She had met my other children and, amid all the tentativeness that one might expect on both sides, it was a happy interaction. The child was born in winter. It was a boy. The birth happened in Lismore Base Hospital. It was slow, but it eventuated without mishap. Lady 2 was disturbed by being in a hospital atmosphere, and she begged me to take us home, back to Horseshoe Creek.

I was hesitant, but the friend from further up the valley who was a midwife assured us that she would help, and so we went home that same afternoon. And indeed, the situation was fine. The baby was calm and happy to be alive. And so, things went on for a while yet. This was a good time. Perhaps it was partly because I was older and I had more idea of what to expect. I knew that it would be manageable.

30 Council

About three months later, I received a phone call from the CES saying that there was a job available in Casino. One always dreaded what they would offer. It was often something wildly inappropriate that could only have been offered out of malice, and had no regard for your knowledge or skills. Nevertheless, I would go for an interview.

I had an interview with an officer from the CES. He explained what the job was. It was a twelve-month contract with the Casino Municipal Council as a Community Profile Officer. I had never heard of such a thing. However, as he described the job to me, I realised that I was probably one of the very few people in the district who had any chance of mastering what it seemed to require. I had been at home long enough; I wanted something to sink my teeth into, to use the wolf metaphor.

In terms of the ideas that William Irwin Thompson had fed me, I felt that I could start re-involving myself in society in a small way. I would not be seeking to accuse the world, change it or fix it, but I could work on one small part and see what was possible. And I was being given an opportunity; I was not brandishing weapons, or trying to force the world to listen.

I had an interview with some people from the Council. I had already been subject to interview panels, so I was prepared for the wildly disparate directions that questions could come from. One has to be both firm and cautious. Years later I went to a job interview with a panel, and I took an instant dislike to the man heading the panel. I decided quite early on that I did not want the job for that reason, so I answered questions in ways that I thought would niggle him. My strategy was successful: I could see that he was niggled, and I did not get the job.

The Council interview included the Town Clerk, another staff member, and two Aldermen (this was a municipal council with a concern only for the town, not for a shire dominated by farmers). The Town Clerk was cemented in his position and had been so for over twenty years. He wore a highly starched white shirt, dark tie and charcoal grey suit. The staff person was responsible for health and building and was not the least bit interested in this Community Profile Officer thing, whatever it was.

The alderman was obviously one of the agitators who had stirred up interest in getting federal government funding for the position. He was a semi-long-haired, middle-aged "radical" (as he was seen in this town). In terms of William Irwin Thompson's four primal roles, he was the clown. I had never really met someone like this before, and I wondered how he survived in a town like this. He was a school-teacher; I guess that explained why he was in the town.

I think that my background appealed to them, given that they were committed to taking on a person for this job with the preposterous title. Who knew whether I could deliver the goods? But some of them didn't know what the goods were, and some of them didn't care. Those who were advocates also didn't have a great idea what it was, but they were interested to see what would eventuate.

The brief of a Community Profile Officer was to undertake research to produce a community profile of the municipality. This would describe the various aspects of the community and then explore what services were needed in the town. How did one do a thing like that, and what would it lead to? It was clear to me from the interview that most people on the council thought that the council had enough to do with roads, water supply and sewerage, and keeping a check on building works. It had no business getting involved in social services; that was for the other levels of government.

To take the job on, which was strongly preferred, given that it would get me off the list of unemployed people in the district, meant that I would have to take a stance towards society. I had had the luxury of ignoring this for the last few months. I had got the idea from Thompson that the appeal to "work within the system" was wielded by systems managers who know that "the mass of the liberal humanists is nothing against the inertial mass of the system itself." Perhaps it is cool to recite that dictum these days, but it was a novel thought then.

I figured that this position would give me wide scope to define it myself. I might be "working within the system", but I could irritate it if I wished, and I could give it options that it might find uncomfortable, which it could consider as it wished. But what was the accepted understanding of the role? Apparently, the role had been created a decade or so earlier, among local governments that had a more sophisticated range of services, mostly in cities. There, it was not so easy for councils to ignore social needs. Apparently, too, this idea had been explored for a long time in other countries, and there were frameworks for describing the various sorts of social needs.

I managed to obtain some information about community profiles that had been produced in other local government areas. It wasn't a great deal, and it wasn't easily obtained, because this was the old world of libraries and librarians, ordinary mail and telephones, not the unleashed space that the internet has sprouted. However, I felt that I could apply myself well and produce something that was intellectually respectable, and perhaps even practically useful.

The model I used was called UWASIS: The United Way of America Services Identification System, although it is possible that another candidate would not have even adopted a framework. The model asserts that there is a set of social goals that are of interest to people and organisations who have the task of managing social welfare. There are the basic needs to maintain life (food, clothing, shelter, health and safety), participation in society (work, benefits and involvement in decision-making), equity (fairness in sharing resources and assets), and development of each individual's talents and capabilities.

The framework then looks at eight specific areas: basic needs, health, education, income and employment, protection, social functioning, community development, and environment. So, I gathered information in all of these areas, using the Census and other data sources, and looked at what bodies were involved in providing for or fostering each, and who was considered to have responsibility. This constituted my report. However, I thought that unless I had a host of practical recommendations for action, the report would disappear from Council's attention within a week. I had to look for possible initiatives that would be beneficial to the community and would reflect well on the council.

Accordingly, as well as the report, I produced a Community Services Directory which set out all the existing organisations in town, looked at in terms of the UWASIS framework. The benefit of this was, as I suspected, that most aldermen were surprised about the range of organisations that existed. I also produced a Housing Report, which resulted in Council's participation in constructing housing for low-income families. I facilitated community activities for senior citizens and for International Youth Year, and I instigated a movement to establish a SkillShare service in Casino (the successor to the youth unemployment service I had been involved with in Kyogle).

All in all, it was a busy year, and I thought it was time well spent, both for me and for the town. It also meant that I was known to many people in the town, and in Kyogle too, given that there was a newspaper that covered both towns, and I made sure that the initiatives of my job were reported.

The attitudes of the various constituencies of Council did not change much. The Town Clerk met me once or twice during the year. He was not miserly in the help that he offered me. For example, he made sure I had access to a typist when I needed it, but he still felt that my role was irrelevant to Council's real purpose. One day he invited me into his office. It was a large room, evoking the time of Charles Dickens, and he sat at a large desk, all in dark wood, sombre. Behind him were all the volumes of the Local Government Act, ready for if he ever needed to consult them.

He explained to me that he had worked in all three types of government. I wondered how he could have been involved in Federal or State Government, but I waited to hear what he had to say. He said he had worked for Shire Councils, Municipal Councils, and County Councils. I nodded. I had learned something. I understood that he had reached the pinnacle of his working life, and that his conception of his role was to sit there until someone required his knowledge of the hundreds of provisions of the Local

Government Act, and then he would give them the benefit of that knowledge.

There were very few staff meetings at the Council, but I remember the longest one. Modern life was occurring, despite all the efforts of people in Council to prevent it. A symptom of this was that many of the Council employees now came from out of town, so they, like me, might have to travel forty-five minutes or more to work. Currently, lunchtime was a set time of one hour. The local employees needed this time because they went home for lunch. Their wives actually cooked them lunch. (This is, of course, to ignore about thirty percent of the employees who were young women in clerical roles.) They came back to work slow and contented.

The out-of-town employees were not interested in one hour for lunch because they brought a cut lunch and they wanted to go home as soon as possible so they could do all the things that work kept them away from. One employee, an engineer, was starting an avocado farm. This was the longest staff meeting, because the pros and cons needed to be debated, and it was emotional. Some people wanted to interfere with other people's rights! The obvious solution of having a flexible lunchtime rather than a fixed time period was not even mentioned. I had this in my mind, but I thought: I am only temporary, I am just an observer, and I just want to see if it will be brought up. It was not, and nothing was resolved, so nothing was changed.

Thompson would have said: "Human society becomes a many-body situation in which values can only be achieved in conflict with opposites. This structural situation makes conflict itself a necessary function of organic differentiation" (p. 80). I hadn't thought of conflict as being a necessary condition of the stability of social groupings, but perhaps it was.

I finished the project, and everyone seemed pleased with what had been achieved. There were initiatives that came to life in various sections of the community. It seemed to have been a good thing for the town. I was unemployed again, but Christmas was coming up, my four children were coming up from the Blue Mountains, and I could spend time at home with them and Lady 2 and the new baby. It was a good place to be in summer. There was a track from the house down to the swimming hole in the creek, and we all spent lots of time there. Occasionally we went to the beach, maybe down to Evans Head, or over to Ballina where my mother lived.

31 Challenge

My leisure time did not last long. In February 1986, I saw an advertisement for the job of General Manager of the Casino Branch of the Challenge Foundation of NSW. It was a service for people with intellectual disabilities. I knew about it because it had been one of the services I had listed in the Casino Community Services Directory. It seemed that this job was a new position. The local organisation managed a children's residence, an adult training centre and a respite care service. It was nominally part of a state organisation (there was an office in Sydney which was called the Head Office), but to all intents and purposes, the branch managed itself. It decided what services it should offer, what staff to employ, and it managed its own funds, which came directly from the Federal and State governments.

I had not managed an organisation before, but it was the next step from what I had been doing. And it was clear to me that the next thing I needed to learn was how to manage an organisation – money, staff, funding, services, even strategy (a word I had not used before). Could I do it? Well, my experience to date had been that yes, I could, and also, there were probably few other people around the district who could. When I saw the advertisement in the local paper, I thought immediately, "This is my job."

Again, the interview involved a panel, that included committee members, the manager of the local branch of a building society (he was the President of the committee), someone from the state government's Department of Family Services, and someone from the local Neighbourhood Centre. The questions covered a broad range of topics. I realised that most people asked questions about issues they themselves were wary of or nervous about, but I was ready for this, and I was modestly confident.

I was given the job quickly, and I started work the next week. The organisation was in a rudimentary state. There was no office, just a two-drawer filing cabinet in a room that served the staff of the adult training centre. When I looked through its contents, I found a file about the recruitment process for my job. I wasn't shy about looking at things that fell into my lap. The file noted that only two candidates had been interviewed for the job. The other candidate had been the project officer at the youth unemployment scheme in Kyogle, the bully who had taken over the committee for a short time until he was routed. I was clearly the best qualified candidate for the position I currently occupied!

I attempted to come to grips with the dimensions of the role. I spent days meeting staff and other interested parties from the three services. It seemed a very strange configuration of energies. I guessed I was being initiated into the culture of disability services – the people with disabilities, their families, the staff who came to work here, and the people who played other support roles, including fund-raising. There was definitely a dynamic of various forces.

The big new thing for me was to get to grips with handling money. The services received funding from state and federal departments, so there had to be accountability measures. Apart from this, I had to learn bookkeeping, and this was all being done manually. We were still in the days before computers. At this point, big business organisations had computer-based accounting, and some larger organisations in the welfare sector also had systems, but it was rare for small organisations to have a computer.

The word was that Apple had devised a "personal computer" which would be accessible to everyone who wanted one, and this would revolutionise what computers would be able to do, but we were in a country town, and that news was a long way away. The more immediate issue was that the books of the association were not available. They had been with the auditors for three weeks, and had not been received back yet. Moreover, the auditors were not being forthcoming about their report.

Despite the absence of the books, the President was happy to meet me and talk about the nature of the organisation, and talk enthusiastically about its future. He bought me lunch at a hotel. I asked him about the books, and he said, "There's no hurry. Just familiarise yourself with the services themselves, and the staff." But after a few more days, I had done what I could credibly do.

I received a phone call one night at home. This was unusual. And it was one of those doomsday phone calls. It was a member of the committee, and he informed me, sombrely, that the President had been arrested for embezzlement. The President was in police custody, and tomorrow morning when I came to work, could we meet at the auditors?

What did this mean for the organisation? What had the President embezzled? Was there anything left? Would the services be able to survive? Was there even a job left for me? I was merely one week into the job. I didn't even know how to do the job yet, although I was quite confident of learning how to, but could I manage a crisis in these circumstances?

In retrospect (that is, now), I realise that I could have left at that point. I could have just said, as people do nowadays, "This is not working out." But even now, I think that would have been a second-best option, even a cowardly one, and I don't think I would have driven off and left them to it. If everything begins, as Thompson said, with the tribal roles of Headman, Shaman, Hunter and Clown, then at that moment I was the whole tribe, and I would play all the roles I needed to until I could differentiate them and parcel them out to the people around me. What was the situation?

The President, being also the manager of the local branch of a building society, had used his position to fiddle the organisation's books. He had done it with great appetite. The organisation's money was banked in his bank. Then he had convinced them to operate on an overdraft. The cleverness of this was that he had not only stolen all the money they had, he had stolen up to the limit of the overdraft. The auditing firm, to their shame, had not detected the obvious conflict of interest the year before, and the eager young President had "gone for broke" in the current year.

It was madness, of course. There was an obvious end to it. There was no way out; he was going to get caught soon. In retrospect, people realised where he had spent the money. He had spent it prolifically, in public, and people thought he was being generous. He would buy pizzas and beer for everyone in the room at an organisational event. He chartered a plane to fly to the next town – to pick up a cheque for money raised in a television fund-raising event. And then spent that money too.

I eventually wrote this story in a book. It was twenty-five years later, well after it was all over. It was the first novel-type book that I wrote. It was called *The Ten Thousand Things*. I am telling a different story now; my centre of focus is its part in the progression of my life. The irony is that I was thinking about how the world was falling (or throwing itself) into the hands of managers, yet it was the skills of management that I needed to develop, and quickly.

It is also true that I needed some elements of all the tribal functions. I learned how to lobby politicians in the first month, and I obtained enough money from the Federal Government to keep the organisation going and rebuild. I felt it was quite an achievement to convince the government to give us money when our predecessor has just stolen everything. But I put the new money to good use. I also had to weather the public eye, to convince the local media that I was capable of cleaning up the mess. And I had to establish myself with the staff – they didn't know me and I didn't know them.

The week after the arrest, the Chief Executive Officer (CEO) from the Challenge Foundation office in Sydney turned up. I thought this was interesting. He hadn't turned up when I was recruited or when I arrived to start work. Why now? What was he after? You see? I had learned already that a manager has to be suspicious. And I was right to be wary of him, because he told me I should sack some of the staff. He said they were just burnt-out mental retardation nurses.

What he didn't know was that my first wife had been a mental retardation nurse, so I knew that this was an irrelevant judgement. I decided I would make up my own mind. Also, I thought he would probably have forgotten this conversation by the time he got back to Sydney. He would have been happy just to have expressed a confident opinion and intimated presumed, superior knowledge.

32 Lessons

It was a momentous time for me, and a time of great achievement. But also, it was a tumultuous time, six years of it. I grew things five-fold in that time: five times the budget, five times the staff, along with additional services. We were widely known; we had visitors from around the region and from inter-state, from other services and even from government officers. The Governor of New South Wales, Sir David Martin, paid us a visit with his wife.

We were considered to be successful pioneers of new models of service. However, the job caused me grief, because success leads to power struggles, and I was beaten. At the end of this time, I was sacked and driven out.

Part of our success was that we became early adopters of computers. Not the conventional PC computers, but Apple. Not even Apple Macintosh but, at least to start with, the Apple IIC. And our first bookkeeping program was not even off-the-shelf, but a bespoke program written by the Treasurer of the committee, who, in his daytime job, was a medical practitioner. I became the de facto consultant to the Treasurer in the design of the program, because he was an enthusiastic coder, not an accountant, and he needed guidance.

It was all a little bit beyond belief, but it worked. So, the story of our growth was partly the story of how we mastered the administration of processes and money. I was working on developing systems to simplify every aspect of our functioning. We used Apple's first programs for word-processing, spreadsheets and databases. Eventually I had to persuade the Treasurer that we had to purchase an accounting program because we had to switch to double-entry bookkeeping so that we could track assets as well as cash. For him, that was heart-breaking.

That was probably an element of enemies accumulating. Neither of the two of us was untoward, but we were still swayed by emotional responses. Other people in the picture were not so innocent or forbearing. Everybody wants to be in control, but I was turning out to be the one that others wanted to control.

The worst of being beaten is that you become subject to the stories people tell about you. In the local paper, the one that served both Kyogle and Casino, after I got the sack there was a front-page story that insidiously implied that I was either incompetent, dishonest, or both. I knew where the story had come from, but I was powerless to do anything about it. And what do you say? "The accusations are false!" "Well, that's exactly what you would say, isn't it?"

And in the wake of it, someone came up with the expression "just a burnt-out school teacher". One wonders who came up with that, but then, one must be careful not to drown in the morass.

I could have run away in the beginning. I could have said: "It's just not working out."

Did I build anything lasting? I felt not. I felt that most of the services I built up were smashed down. Sure, there were remnants. The plant nursery remained as a viable commercial business and an adult employment service. It earned money, both for the clients, as wages, and the organisation. That was a laudable achievement from the starting point of a few plants potted up by a few clients at the adult training service. That had been an initiative of two of the "burnt-out mental retardation nurses" that I was supposed to sack.

I can say that I learned a lot, about a lot of things. I could ask, would I do it differently now? But the answer is, of course I would! I know things now that I didn't have an inkling of then. In effect it is a nonsense question, futile philosophising. The main difference would be this: when the last days were upon me, and the pressures started to mount, I was keenly aware of my enemies, and how dishonest and scheming they were. This was a new revelation. Prior to this, despite my introduction to the organisation and the President's arrest for embezzlement, I had been naïve. I didn't realise how political, devious and self-serving people could be.

While I was in this turbulent state of mind, struggling with the idea that people could be so deliberately dishonest, and lie to your face without batting an eyelid, I had a dream one night. There was a snake, just a vivid impression of a snake. The image stayed with me, although I had no meaning to attach to it. It happened that the next day the family and I went down to the coast, to Byron Bay. We wanted to get out of our normal routines and the heaviness that our home environment was becoming as a result.

We went to the beach and it was enjoyable: no weight, no encumbrance of fraught business affairs, just the sun, the sky, the sand and the beautiful view. We went into the town to get some food, and there was a bookshop nearby, so I went in. I had no purpose or plan; I was browsing aimlessly, pulling a book out here and there. I pulled another book out, and the image on the front cover was a snake. The snake, my dream – was this the meaning? The book was *The People of the Lie* by M. Scott Peck. It was about people who exhibited the kind of behaviour that I was having trouble accepting the reality of, or dealing with. I read that book very quickly, and it was a breakthrough: it gave me a sense that I was not crazy, and not alone.

In the face of the reality that I could now at least accept the possibility of, my determination was to be brave. I had always suspected that I was a coward at heart, and I wanted to show, in these circumstances, and with so much at stake, that I could be brave. And I believe that I was. However, for this very reason, I was probably occasionally unwise. In the dark days, it was probably unwise to tell the CEO of the Challenge Foundation in Sydney to mind her own business. Not that my retort was unjustified, but it probably did not help the course of events.

In that respect, and probably others, my actions today would be strategically different to what they were then. I use the word "strategically" with appropriate humour.

This period of time was significant in my working life. It was a critical time of coming into competence, coming into power, and refining a direction in my working life. Yet, it ended up in a shambles. What could be said now: anything of value? Well, I learned a lot about the role of manager – all that it entailed, and the different ways you can approach the role. I learned what my inherent strengths and weaknesses were, and how to work on the aspects you are weak at, or how to compensate for those weaknesses.

However, I always thought that I would not be a manager for life; I was doing it in order to learn how to do it. Why? Perhaps I was going to teach others how to be managers. Or, would I write about it? I didn't know. In any case, a lot had been happening at home in the meantime.

33 A breakdown

Lady 2, with whom I now had a child, had come unstuck. Her previous problem had been heroin. Since she came to my place she had been "clean", and for a year or so after the child was born, things were fine. But then it became shaky. She said, "You're boring", and threw things around. And yet the boy was lovely, easy to be with. It made no sense. There were friends and neighbours who came to visit. It didn't help. It was all empty to her.

She craved drugs. If I was not there, she would drive to Nimbin and score heroin. Money went missing. If I asked questions, I would be told lies. I wasn't used to that, at least, in my home; I didn't know what to do. I would come home and she would be unconscious in bed, and the boy would be wandering around by himself, or keeping an eye on her, as a three-year-old trying to be the adult.

I organised a flat for her in town, and we shared custody of the boy, but it wasn't a solution. She went to Sydney, and took the boy with her. She went to her parents' place, then to a flat she shared with her twin brother. I thought there was a peculiar kind of madness in their dynamic, plastered over with a veneer of cultural superiority, underpinned with the venom of snakes. As I had become familiar with the family, I saw that what the lady and I had had in Horseshoe Creek was a time of peace, but it had been fragile, and it had taken so little to break it.

I think I was angry with myself, as well, for not being able to help to change anything. It was a train wreck going to happen. After going to Sydney, she had taken up with a man, and they were living in a house that was owned by another man. There was an incident of high drama. The man who owned the house rang me one night at midnight. He said he had found my phone number. He said there was trouble in the house, and he thought that my boy was unsafe, and I should come and get him.

There had been fights between the two men, including a physical fight. The lady and her new man had been taking heroin. The owner wanted them out of the house. The situation was obviously urgent. I said I would come. By the next morning, I had driven to the Gold Coast and got a plane to Sydney. I had also rung a male friend in Sydney, and asked him to come with me. We turned up at the house that morning. I didn't want them to spirit my son away. She was there, and looking wasted and crazed, and she tried to put me off, saying they had to go out. But I was not about to be put off. I said that I was going to take the boy back with me. She didn't keep up the argument; she didn't have the stamina.

I packed up the boys' few things and we drove off. It wasn't pretty, but it was cleanly done, and with no violence.

The friend and I drove to Chinatown and we went to a Chinese café. The boy wanted a bowl of noodles, and he ate as if he had been starving, finishing the entire bowl. It was ten o'clock in the morning. He and I flew back up north, and we were back at Horseshoe Creek the same day.

This was not the end of things, because I did not want the boy not to see his mother again. The difficulty was to devise the circumstances in which he was not under the control of her or her parents.

This is the point at which the report of the events hits a wall. The rest of the story – there is more to tell – is worse, and I don't want to tell it. The boy emerges into my custody; that is the positive side. The circumstances of the transition were unpleasant.

One reason not to tell the story is that it is damning of certain people, and to tell that story properly, I would have to dig up pages from an archive. I would probably find critical facts missing, like dates, so anyone affected could claim that I was being unfair. Or I would have to spend more time digging into the darkness. And then we come to the question of principle: should some stories be allowed to die? Does it serve anyone's interests to tell the story?

Today, there seems to be mostly a relentless insistence on telling any story that a person wants to tell, brushing aside all objections. From a family history perspective, the argument for telling a story is that in a subsequent generation, it will be seen that there is a thread that came through from the past, so it is important. I have many instances from my rather large family history.

One instance: one of my sets of great great grandparents had eight children. The last child was called Thomas. I knew where all the names of the other children had come from – the father's side, the mother's side, but not this one. And then I found out. She came out to Australia as an unmarried single female immigrant, on an assisted passage. She left from Glasgow; she was nineteen. But one month before she left, she was in a boarding house in Glasgow with a one-year-old son, called Thomas. I discovered there was an orphanage in Glasgow at that time (1841), and my surmise is that she left the boy there so she could leave the country as a single unmarried female.

So, I would say, she had to leave home because she was pregnant, and she couldn't go back home, and she couldn't keep the child. But she never forgot the boy she had to leave behind. And I didn't have to tell that story, but I have, and it gives deep meaning to the name of her youngest child.

Similarly, you could argue that I should tell all of the story of Lady 2. But I don't want to. In years to come, it might not hurt so much. I suspect that my great great grandmother left a clue to her story in the name she gave to her youngest child. I think she wouldn't mind that I have discovered the facts and I've told the story now. Time heals wounds, and that is the path I choose to take. Someone can dig up the bones of Lady 2 in years to come.

34 Lady 3

There was more to my domestic life than this. Things had settled down after the turbulence of Lady 2. Another lady turned up after this. I might not have noticed, but she was someone I had known when I was about twenty. I had met her and her husband (she had married young) at a Christian group, and we had become friends. I remember that we had all laughed a lot, that kind of hilarious, unstoppable laughter. Afterwards, you think, that was extreme. What was I reacting to in the rest of my life, and what was it they were reacting to in the rest of their lives? But it was fun. And then, as young people do, we drifted apart.

This lady turned up again. Let's call her Lady 3. She was working in Lismore. Time had moved on, and she had divorced some years ago. She also had a boy, but no current partner. Her boy was about the same age as my boy. When we realised our connection, we connected up again. I was still at the Challenge Foundation, and it was not long before the last days. Things were hotting up; the enemies were gathering. I know it sounds ridiculous, and seen in retrospect it was indeed ridiculous, but it was the way it was. No one seemed to see that it was ridiculous.

Eventually, Lady 3 and her boy moved in with me at Horseshoe Creek, and my boy arrived as well, after the drama in Sydney. The two boys went to school in Kyogle, and Lady 3 and I participated in the war in Casino. It involved lobbying, preparation of reports to counteract lies that were being told, and a public meeting, which filled out the room at the Community Health Centre with over eighty people. The President and the CEO came up from Sydney, thinking that they would hose the situation down with a few slippery but authoritative-sounding words.

The truth was that the game was nasty, and the intention of the people from the office in Sydney was to close everything in Casino down, strip the assets, and take the money back to Sydney. They had their own political game they were playing with the federal government funding body, and they needed a war chest. After the public meeting closed down abruptly in a noisy furore, the President from Sydney walked past me, close, and he whispered, "No hard feelings, but business is business."

In that moment, I understood that for some people, life is not life, it is just business. Perhaps at some distance there are human goals, such as looking after people with disabilities, but that has all faded from view, and in the fore ground there are only strategies. It can be bloodthirsty, because they have come to believe that that is necessary. They will say, when questioned, that is the way the world is: occasionally, you have to draw blood. Business is war. I suppose they will rock up to the gates of heaven expecting a red carpet, because they fought the good fight.

I went home (again). In any case, I had a full house. Everyone was getting used to a new situation, so it was positive. Everyone was settling down after tumult, so there was some laughter and joy.

35 An intimidator

I had a small job that continued after I was dismissed from the Challenge Foundation. I was carrying out the administration of the respite care service. During my last twelve months with the Challenge Foundation, I could see that trouble was brewing, and so did the lady who was the coordinator of Respite Care. She asked me if there was some way of saving that service from the looming troubles. And there was. It was becoming trendy for services to be incorporated separately. The rationale was that this avoided conflicts where one organisation had control over all aspects of a client's life.

The rationale was valid in theory. However, in small country towns, it was generally a moot point, because it was most likely that the same people who would end up on the management committees of all the different organisations. But the popularity of the rationale made it easy for us to put up the idea of Respire Care being an organisation separate from the Challenge Foundation.

One of the people on this new committee was problematic. The coordinator of the service knew this – he was the parent of a client of respite care. I was told that he had spent time in far north Queensland, and he taken lots of magic mushrooms. That may have affected his brain functioning. I met him. He was a big man, and one of those big people who like to use their height and weight to dominate others. In one conversation I had with him, he told me that someone had given him a whole library of Scientology books. He swore that he had never been a member of the Scientology group, but he had read these books. He also told me that he and a friend had invented a car that ran on water, but it was difficult to get funding for development. I couldn't see that he was doing much work.

One day he arranged a meeting with me in the respite care office. He was going to audit all the administrative procedures. He was authorised by the committee to do so. The office was a shopfront in the South Casino shopping block. I was somewhat wary of his intentions. We sat down in the office, and once again he was trying to use his physical size to dominate me. But for that to really work, the other person has to feel intimidated. I was stone-cold calm.

He began asking questions, and it was obvious that he was working from a script that he had got from an accountant friend, and he knew far less about accounting or management procedures than I did. So, I fed him the answers in authoritative fashion, slow and steady. I could see that he felt he was losing the game, whatever it was he thought was going to happen. Was I supposed to collapse or panic? Then, as a finale, it seemed, he asked me about insurance, whether we had insurance.

"What if," he said dramatically, "a vehicle was to smash through the window into this room and kill everyone?" He emphasised his words, and gestured as if to simulate this wild, frightening event, obviously hoping to intimidate me. At this point I have to say that when I dressed for this meeting, I put on a long-sleeved shirt that was deep blue. It was a really bold colour, and I didn't wear it very often. It seemed to have an effect on some people, as if it were an aura.

All the time we had been talking, the man had been reciting his lines, following the script that was meant to dominate and intimidate, but his delivery was flat, as if the energy had gone out of him. Normally, you might say this is fanciful, but this was not a normal situation. This was not an ordinary man, and I was not dealing with him in an ordinary manner. My use of voice was deliberate, as if I was re-tuning him. When it came to the finale with the loaded question about the insurance, I said very calmly and firmly, "I don't think that is very likely to happen, but yes, we do have all appropriate insurances. Will that be all?"

I didn't see much of him after that. I continued to do the administrative work, but during this year I realised that I had to make a move. I had to change course and move in a new direction.

36 Teaching again

After a while, I started casual teaching at Kyogle High School. I decided that if you only teach at one school, you get to know the students and the teachers, and then no one keeps testing you out. You just become an accepted member of the family. And that's how it was. After a while, everyone also accepted that I could teach a range of different subjects credibly. I was a mathematics teacher, but I had also taught technics (woodwork, metalwork etc). And I taught English and history. One desperate day they asked me to take a sewing class, but there was a girl in the class who was accustomed to taking charge, and she masterfully orchestrated the lesson. She was applauded at the end.

Of course, I knew that I had earlier walked away from teaching, and I did not want to be back, sealed in that fate for the next thirty years. After the awful mess of the Challenge Foundation, it would also have been an expression of failure. I was a competent, experienced manager, despite the occurrence of bad press. However, the other side of the truth was that I was having trouble getting another job around the region. I applied for quite a few, jobs for which I was eminently qualified, but I did not even get to the interview stage. The far north coast is, in employment terms, a small pond, and I was a hot potato, to mix metaphors. Many employers would have thought, "He may be innocent, and he may be competent, but why take the risk? There are plenty of job applicants around."

37 University again

During this time, I went back to the niggle in the back of my mind, the one that had been there for twenty-five years: I should go to university and obtain a Bachelor degree. When I started discussing this with people, they leapt to the conclusion that I should do a Master of Business Administration. I was mature-aged, and I had six years' experience as the General Manager of a complex organisation. That was enough to get you into admission.

However, I had the idea that I had not completed two Bachelor degrees, and I should start by completing one. I did not want to be the hare that leapt to the finishing line; I wanted to be the tortoise that could tell you every rock and flower along the track. I thought it would be satisfying to complete the whole course, and also, if I did so, no one could accuse me of having deficiencies in my background. (I was sensitive to criticism.) Accordingly, I enrolled at the growing university in Lismore. It had previously been a Teachers' College. Of course, I would not do Psychology if I could help it.

So, when I walked on campus for the first time and heard The Doors, it felt like I had made the right decision. I was right about the feeling of satisfaction: in every unit I studied, I read the textbooks and could describe immediately the relevant work situations I had encountered and dealt with. Looking at my fellow students, I could see they were just reading the words. They had not yet experienced any corresponding reality. I highly recommend doing your first degree after you have had twenty-five years of experience! (Perhaps not if you are a doctor.)

I was encountering concepts that made sense of so many of the situations I had experienced. So often I felt, "So this is what I was doing, or this was why I was feeling the tension I was experiencing!" Also, I was writing. I was writing essays. I had acquired experience in writing while I was a manager, because there are reports to write, submissions for funding, business cases for proposed ventures, newsletters, reports to committee, media releases and correspondence. I had been observing how much writing is (or can be) part of the manager's job. Once I became accustomed to the academic medium, I was rewarded with good marks. I got Distinctions and High Distinctions all the way through.

It was occasionally hard to juggle my studies with casual teaching. There is a point of good balance between the two, but casual teaching was a random event, and it usually came in the morning with no advance warning. For two terms, it was more intensive than that. I received a phone call from the Deputy Principal on the first day of term, just as I was getting ready to go off to Lismore to lectures. He asked me to come in and talk to him. That sounded serious. When I visited him, he told me that a mathematics teacher had gone off sick.

The teacher had been losing confidence, and in the morning of the first day of term, he had sat at his staffroom desk at bell time, shaking, and said, "I can't do this anymore." He went on sick leave for stress. The Deputy Principal asked me if I could take over, and it could be for up to two terms. That meant a full-time engagement. I had to consider, would I be able to keep up with my studies, which were also full-time, at least notionally? The money would certainly be useful. I decided I would do it. I was a mature-aged student; I had to be able to do it. Young people worked too, as well as studying at university.

The first week in that teacher's job was torrid. He had obviously not been actively teaching for some time, and the students were used to being out of control. They tried to run over me, as if it were a game. However, I was no longer young. I had not been assertive when I started teaching, because I wanted it to be a soft and gentle experience. I did not like the authoritarian teachers, who were mostly sadistic and mean. But now I realised the truth of what a lecturer at Teachers' College had told us: "The first part of being a schoolteacher is being a pirate captain. If you don't assert your control over the group, you will never even get to start your job as a teacher."

This was a radically new perspective for me. I hadn't needed it at St Mary's. It had been a tame environment where I hadn't needed to step outside of myself. Here it was a matter of surviving. If I didn't step up, I would be dragged out of there in tears after a fortnight, just as the former teacher was dragged out. So I stepped up. I raised my voice. I ran my classrooms from the front of the room. I demanded attention. I was fierce.

When some of the students complained that they didn't want to learn maths, and didn't need to, I gave them my standard lecture on the subject: "You learn mathematics so that you can look after yourself, otherwise people will take you for a fool. I don't want you to go out into the world helpless, so you are going to work and learn. That's what you're here for."

I kept this up for a fortnight. I went home with a sore throat every day and a smile on my face. After a fortnight, I toned my voice right down. I did it on the spur of the moment in the middle of a lesson. The students looked me strangely, wondering what was going on. I told them: "You don't want me to be shouting at you all the time. But we are here to work. Let's do it." And we did. The students felt safe now, and they didn't test me out anymore. And some of the other teachers thought I had done an awesome thing. And I had, but it was real; I wasn't just playing a game.

I kept things strict. If a student kept pestering, either me or other students, I would throw them out. When I got a break from teaching the lesson, I would go out to them and give them a stern lecture. I think some of them were afraid I would send them to the Deputy or the Principal, but I never did. It was my classroom, and I would run it myself. I didn't need anyone else to lean on.

Here is a paradox. The first week I was there, one of the students said, "You look like Ned Flanders!" (Homer Simpson's neighbour from the cartoon.) And I suppose I did. The beard had gone by now, and I just had a moustache, and my hair was moderately short, and it wasn't yet grey. So, the name began to stick, despite my shouting all the time. And I suppose it meant that they knew that the shouting person wasn't the real me. I didn't get angry about the name, and I didn't try to stop it, unless it was part of them being rowdy and disrespectful.

Mostly they used the name quite courteously, just as part of the teaching lesson. "Could you show me how to do this, Mister Flanders?" We both accepted it. It was the one licence I gave them, and I suspect it meant a lot. Several weeks later, I got a measure of just how much the name was accepted. I took a Year Eleven class that wasn't usually mine, because their teacher was off sick. They were working quietly, as there is plenty to do in Year Eleven, and most of it is self-directed work.

A girl asked me for help: "Can you show me how to do this, please, Mister Flanders?" And a couple of the other girls tittered, and the girl looked puzzled. They said to her, "That's not his real name. His real name is Mister Martin." And she went red, acutely embarrassed. So, then I had to defuse the idea that she had done something wrong. I had not reacted adversely to being called Mister Flanders, and she was confused. I had to explain that I didn't mind; I considered it an acceptable way to be addressed, even affectionate, as long as the student wasn't being disrespectful about it. I explained about my struggle to rein in the unruly classroom spirits in the younger groups, and how the name Mister Flanders had been the ground on which we had met.

It took her a while to get over her embarrassment, but we all had a good discussion about it after that, and laughed. One is always dancing between devils in the classroom. I was present when I was there, but I always kept in mind that my purpose was to keep energy free for the other things I was doing, at home and at university.

38 Beardless

There are three stories about my shift from full beard to moustache only. The first is about the time I shaved my beard off. It was a birthday party at home for one of the boys. It was an excuse to invite a bunch of people over, so there were about twenty people in and around the house for the afternoon. I suppose I must have had the idea in my head about shaving the beard off. I had had the beard for almost twenty years, so all the people I knew around Kyogle and the north coast had only ever seen me with a beard.

It was a relaxed afternoon, and people were sitting on the verandahs talking, or playing in the yard with the numerous children. I went into the bathroom, looked into the mirror, then shaved my beard off. I left the moustache on. There wasn't a lot of thinking involved, or agonising over a decision and what people might think about it. I just decided that the beard had been there long enough and that I was always going to shave it off one day, and lo and behold: today was the day.

I walked back out into the throng. People noticed; some people noticed instantly. Some were aghast, as if to say, "How could you do that?!" To which my answer was, "Hi. My name is Glenn. Pleased to meet you."

Some people seemed to think my action was ill-considered. Others were busy making the adjustment, but their reaction was positive. They seemed to accept that I would be the same Glenn they had known, and we could still be friends. Some accepted the change, but seemed to be wedded to my former appearance, and were disturbed by the change. Or, perhaps they were disturbed that they were disturbed by the change.

I think this next incident may have been at the same time, but I can't quite work out the dates. I shaved my beard off on the weekend, and I went to school on Monday; this was at St Mary's. I walked into the classroom and the students looked at me strangely.

One of them called out, concerned, "Where's Mister Martin? Who are you?" It was a serious question.

I thought that was interesting. It suggested that school students tend to see the outside of you; in fact, they depend on that to recognise you. Which suggests they see you primarily as your role in relation to them, the teacher, not as a human being first. This is okay, of course. This is what you would expect, but you don't see the evidence of it very often.

It was the school holidays soon afterwards, and I drove up to the Blue Mountains to pick up my children for the holidays. When I got out of the car, my children came out to meet me. Then one of the girls stopped and looked at me carefully. She said, "I know there's something different about you, but I can't figure out what it is."

I stroked my chin, and then she saw it. She thought it was funny – that I had shaved my beard off, and that she hadn't seen it straight away. I have always compared her reaction with that of the school students. There was a fundamental difference. My children saw "me" first, and my physical appearance came second to that. Isn't that extraordinary? I wouldn't have thought there was a difference, but how else do you make sense of her initial reaction?

39 Career

I wasn't sure what I would be doing after I finished the degree, but I was now in my forties, and I felt that I had to pursue something like a career, and in a direction where I was likely to earn decent money. I had no intention of growing old poor. One of the ideas that was forming was the idea that I may have to leave Kyogle. I was beginning to think that a career in human resource management was feasible, and it might pay well. When I considered all the things I had done as a manager, much of it had been about "managing human resources".

I was aware of how ludicrous the language was, but I also knew that people are dialecticians. If you wanted to be heard and heeded in a particular field, you had to speak that language, seamlessly and without embarrassment. It was the dialect of that field. Speaking it suggested that you knew what you were talking about, whereas not speaking it proved (as far as they were concerned) that you did not know what you were talking about.

I was once given a dramatic example of this syndrome (from real life), not with language, but with attire. A lawyer walks into court as the case begins. He is late, he is flustered, and he is not wearing his suit coat. The judge looks at him and says in his deep voice, "Mister Mason, I cannot see you." What does it mean? It means that the judge will not recognise his presence in the courtroom until he is wearing a suit coat. Mister Mason rushes out of the courtroom and finds a colleague in the corridor and begs him to borrow his suit coat. He rushes back into the courtroom and things go back to normal.

Mister Mason's learning, qualifications and knowledge of the case prove to be meaningless until he is wearing a suit coat.

Things I know

You have to speak the language of the world, or it will treat you as if you are ignorant, and then you will be poor.

Another thing I know: The people who made up the language mostly know what they are talking about. This is not so much true of the people who use it every day.

40 BBus(Hons)

I was getting Distinctions and High Distinctions. Of the lecturers, the ones who were my age and older were mostly respectful, and modest about their own knowledge and status. They accepted me as an equal among themselves. This was not so much true of the younger ones. I had one incident when I had to ask for an extension on an assignment (remembering I was also working full-time as a teacher at this time). I went to his office to see him. He had a visitor present, a lady. When I asked him for the extension, he launched into a lecture about taking university work seriously, and was I managing my time properly?

The lecture was longer than that; this is just the essence of it. I heard him out, and just said, "Sure. Thanks," and left. I wondered whether the lady told him, after I had left, that I had worked with her on devising the constitution for a new Rudolf Steiner school in the area. Just to let him know that I probably could manage my time well enough. From my silence, she may have deduced that I saw the lecturer's performance as mere vanity, and mostly for her benefit.

I made it through three years of the Bachelor of Business degree successfully. My first degree! I won the Suncorp prize for being the top student ("Outstanding") in Human Resource Management (HRM). I think it was worth $100. I was still doing casual teaching, and money was not desperate. I decided I would stay at university, and undertake the Honours year. All this time, I had been thinking about ethics, and in particular, the issue of why people act unethically. I thought I could address this question in the context of HRM as the subject of an Honours thesis.

I had joined the Australian Human Resources Institute as a student, and I thought I might be able to make use of this connection to run a survey among its members. I got their permission to do this. Somehow, I got printed copies of the survey to its annual conference and they were handed out to delegates. (I had a computer now and I had learned to do layout of documents.) The institute returned a bundle of the surveys to me. This was still prior to the internet.

My thesis was called "Ethics and the Role of the Human Resource Manager". I obtained a hundred and sixty completed surveys. It was sufficient to give me data to analyse. My main idea was that HR managers knew about the relevance and importance of ethics to their role, but they had not thought about it a lot. The result was that they often gave contradictory answers to ethical questions. My data seemed to bear that out.

My aim had been to do something that was modest but credible. I think I achieved that. I had done a lot of reading and thinking, so I felt that I had painted a respectable canvas in which to locate my question. I had done all my own work, from analysing data – and I used Excel for this, not a statistics program – to doing the layout of my thesis in Word. At the end, I had reservations about my fitness as an academic, but I had many of the useful competencies of an academic. For example, my reading was wide and my referencing was solid.

A marker of one of my assignments remarked, "This is more of an essay than a paper", but I think this was tantamount to saying I was more of a writer than an academic. I found it hard to take this as an insult. It was more a word of caution about going down the academic pathway. At the age of forty-seven, I had an Honours degree, First Class Honours, and I was awarded the University Medal. I was pleased about that.

The awards ceremony was held in Lismore in March 1997. It was a sunny day, and there were many people, friends and family, who were happy to celebrate it with me. It felt like the sun coming out after a season of darkness. My photo was in the Lismore newspaper. I felt that this was for all the people in the region who had harboured doubts about me. I had seen many of the dubious people I had had conflicts with slink away and disappear. I was proud and standing, with undeniable merit.

I had no illusions that my achievement at university would lead to glory. There is an annual churn of students through universities. Most of them get swallowed up by ordinariness, for all the flurry of honours that are handed out, the certificates and the medals. During the year I applied for many jobs. I had widened my scope to far beyond Kyogle. I was resigned to the idea that I would have to move. I applied for jobs around the north coast of New South Wales, the surrounding regions, and Brisbane and Sydney.

I had one offer of a job at a university. It was a sweet offer: to be an Associate Lecturer in human resources, and at the same time to carry out work for a Doctorate of Philosophy (PhD). It was at Toowoomba. The catch was that the work for the PhD had to be as a colleague in a major, funded project, for a professor who was doing research into downsizing, which had been a major phenomenon in the 1980s and had ongoing effects. At this point I became obstinate. If I was going to do a PhD, it would be on my topic, not as an adjunct to someone else's topic.

Sanity says that I should have swallowed my pride and accepted it. I would have had a PhD within two years, and I would have had a job lecturing at a university as a fait accompli. However, I did not waver from my conviction, and I turned down the role. In the meantime, I had a part-time role at a university in Brisbane as a tutor in Business Ethics. This was more within my envisaged range of possibilities.

I did that tutoring job for all of that year. It was interesting. The "tutoring" classes were a complement to the lectures, but there were approximately eighty students in each class – hardly the realm of tutoring. It looked like a good business proposition for the university, but it was not a forum for teaching. To make it more interesting, most of the students were from overseas, here for the duration of their course, and their first language was not English. The languages included Chinese, Thai, Vietnamese, Cambodian, Spanish (from South America), German, and Arabic.

What the students wanted from me was not tutoring. They wanted me to explain what had been in the lectures. Tutoring was like third base, and they were back on first base. I thought this would be a worthwhile service, and I was able to perform it, so most of what I did was in lecturing mode. The students had to perform one exercise where, in groups of three, they took a business ethics question and presented their perspective to the whole group. I was fearful that this would be a disaster, mostly because of the language issue, but I gave them what preparation I could about the presentation process, and how I wanted them to approach a specific business ethics issue.

For the most part, the students did remarkably well. Their presentations were salient, coherent and logical, and spoke to the ethics issues that needed to be discussed. Most of them managed their work as a group quite well, sharing the responsibilities. I wanted them to be able to talk about ethics issues in ordinary English, not just relay the moral philosophy terminology they had been fed in the lectures. They made some progress towards this end.

The experience helped me to appreciate how unsatisfactory the business ethics curriculum was. The course had been written by lecturers from the philosophy department, and they were interested in imparting the truths of Moral Philosophy, not in addressing the real, harder-edged world of business. It seemed that the students could at least grasp what the ethical issues of the business world were, and appreciate the difficulties one might face in resolving them, especially if one was involved, and was young and powerless, and one needed to survive in the business world. The students appreciated that if one held a position in an organisation or company, issues were not merely philosophical; they concerned power and money.

I wrestled with this, trying to think of how you could address this in training courses within organisations. Later I did a Master of Education where I took up this issue.

41 Driving

The part of the job at the university in Brisbane that I liked the most was driving to Brisbane. It took me three hours. I parked at South Bank and got a ferry across the Brisbane River. I had never caught a ferry to work before. It is nice to cross the water; there is something mythical about it. However, the best part of the trip was the first part. From Kyogle, one drives north, past Wiangaree and then onto Gradys Creek Road and through The Risk. It was crazy to think I was doing this to get to a job, but the job might lead to something better….

The Risk is called that because in the early days, which was about the 1880s, small settlers were arriving in the Kyogle district to start up dairy farming. Most of the land was in the hands of big squatters from the 1840s. In the 1880s, it was legal to take up a parcel of land (say, 100 acres) along the creek, but the squatters would do their best to bully you and drive you out. That was why it was called the "The Risk". The name stuck. Many years later, the New South Wales Geographical Names Board tried to get the local people to change the name. They said it was inappropriate to call a place something like that. But there was a lot of passion for the name; it represented an important part of their history. In the end, the Board relented.

It is a beautiful drive up that valley. Then it goes onto the Lions Road, which also requires an explanation. In the 1950s, the Lions Club of Kyogle thought a new road could be built through that valley to link up with the existing road to Brisbane on the Queensland side. They thought this would be good for tourism, because it would shorten the distance between Brisbane and Kyogle.

There were some enterprising and influential fellows in the Lions Club, and they knew people in the Australian Army. The result was a joint project between the club and the army, and a road of about twenty kilometres long was built. It was a bit steeper than the road authorities liked – long, sweeping hauls through several valleys – but it was approved, and it is a lovely road to drive on, despite being all gravel, joining up to the highway on the Queensland side near Beaudesert.

Just before you cross into Queensland there is a little gully where the bellbirds sing. You could guarantee it. When you got close, you wound the window down and listened for them. So, it was a long but special trip to get from Horseshoe Creek to the Queensland University of Technology a couple of times a week.

42 100+ job applications

I applied for over a hundred jobs during the year, so many that I decided to teach myself how to use a database program on the computer, and track my experiences. I had fields for employers, arranged by type (private, public, not-for-profit) and industry, and for recruitment agencies. I tracked the time to get an initial response, an interview, and notification of final outcome. The longest it took for an organisation to notify me of the outcome of a job application was five months. There were also some who did not reply at all. I did comparisons on various characteristics between public sector, private sector and not-for-profit.

In the end I saw that I had sufficient data to write it up as an article, which I did. I submitted it to the Australian Human Resources Institute's magazine, *HR Monthly*, and that was the first article I had published in a professional magazine.

In October 1997, there was a large advertisement in the *Sydney Morning Herald* looking for an Editor/Writer on human resources. Previously I had been applying for jobs in human resources. This was a little delicate, because I couldn't apply for a high-level job – I had just got my degree – but at the same time I was not an entry-level candidate – I had lots of pertinent experience.

As soon as I saw the advertisement, I thought to myself, "I don't want a job in HR; I want a job writing about HR!" I had heard of CCH Australia. Most people have seen their volumes in the offices of accountants and lawyers, lining the shelves behind the professionals' desks. The niche that CCH Australia fills is writing practical material for professionals. It is not academic, but it mediates academic and legal materials for professionals in their everyday lives. I had what was needed for such a task in the human resources area – practical experience bolstered by an understanding of legal and academic concepts.

I had found that living in Horseshoe Creek had been a drawback in applying jobs in the major cities. I think that as soon as they saw my address, they would think either that the logistics of interviews etc would be too difficult, or they would think I was not a serious candidate. However, the people at CCH Australia seemed to have a more highly tuned sense of equity, and they took me seriously. I did a written exercise for them, and then they invited me to Sydney for an interview. I thought the interview went well, and they rang me within a couple of days and offered me the job.

This led me to the next hurdle. I was contemplating leaving my home after nineteen years. I would have to rent out the house. Later, perhaps I would have to sell it. I needed to prepare the ground for all of these possibilities. I decided I needed a few weeks to clean up, get rid of "stuff", and fix things so that I wouldn't have any trouble with tenants (we had our own septic tank, and our own water system – one part tank water, and another part spring water; all this had to be faultless). A house in the country is like a machine: you have to know how to run it and maintain it.

The upshot was that, having accepted the job, I said I couldn't start for six weeks. I waited to see what their reply would be. Amazingly, they said that it would be okay. I explained by saying I was leaving my house after a long time, and I needed to leave it in a fit state. I said I was excited and grateful to get the job, and I was committed to moving to Sydney.

When I did arrive, they told me I was replacing two pregnant women who were going off on maternity leave, and that they had a bit of flexibility with dates. It's nice to know you are replacing two people, or perhaps not, if that were to mean you were going to have to do the work of two people.

The main job I had to do in the six weeks I gave myself, apart from cleaning out what I finally had to accept was rubbish, was to restump the house. It was one of those long-standing jobs. The house was bearable as it was, but it was obviously going to be much harder to deal with any issues from Sydney. I thought I could manage the job well enough, and I had the tools to do it. I took it on as a hybrid job, because many of the existing stumps were fine; some were dubious, and I would replace them. I would also try to level the house up. This would be the first rebalancing effort since 1935. The highest stumps were just over a metre, and the lowest were only about thirty centimetres. It was tight working underneath that part of the house. However, it all got done, and the house was good for another sixty years.

We rented a house in Sydney while we were still in Horseshoe Creek. How? Lady 3's brother worked in Sydney, and he found a house not far from where the job was located. He went to the house and walked through it while he talked to us on his mobile phone. He described the layout of the house and its features, and all the rooms. We decided, on the basis of this "inspection" that the house would be fine. And it was. The only significant feature that had not been described was the high-tension electricity stanchion next door to the house.

That was a judicious omission; although, we were only renting. Presumably we would work out what we were going to do before too long. We were unlikely to be staying in the house for the long term. So, a humorous tick of approval for the inspector. The real estate agent that we dealt with in Beecroft was called Clay Burton, a distinctive name.

After we moved to Sydney, I was faced with the need to rent out the Horseshoe Creek property. Before I left, I went to a real estate agent in Kyogle and discussed it. I had taught two of his younger brothers at St Mary's in Casino. He seemed decent. I had enjoyed teaching his brothers: they had good technical minds and an honest work ethic. After we were in Sydney, he rang me to say he had some potential tenants, but he wanted to check with me first.

It wasn't an ordinary family, that is, mother, father and children. Instead, it was two sisters, who had both been married but were now separated, and they each had a child. What did I think? Their names were Burton and Clay. Really? Sometimes, one feels that the universe is nudging you in a particular direction. I said I was sure it would be okay. So, the ladies moved in, and proved to be good tenants.

43 Sydney

When I thought about coming back to Sydney, I finally decided that it would be okay as long as I didn't go back to the area where I grew up. I didn't have a great deal of love for the area. It had started out as ravaged bushland with roads made of clay when I was small, and ended up as claustrophobic suburbia by the time I was in my teens. The Parramatta River was my boundary; as long as I was on the north side of the Parramatta River, it would be okay. So, CCH was at North Ryde, and our rented home was at Beecroft, and it didn't feel like I was caught in an old trap. We were close to the bush, and that was important too. I had to be able to walk out of the streets and houses and into the bush. That was also true of the house we bought at Cherrybrook.

It was interesting, I thought, to have such an adamant belief about something that would have meant nothing to most people. But it was a belief that sat deeply within me. It didn't feel like it was trivial, or superstitious. It was not dismissable! It was important to my sense of well-being.

In recent years, since I took up investigating my family history, I found a remarkable parallel. One of my great great grandfathers, William Archer, was a lively personality. There are many stories I have written about him in my family history books. He was a convict, transported to Sydney in 1838 for theft. He was twenty-five at the time, single. My reading of the theft is that he was one of those men who hang around pubs who often have something for sale. "Psst, psst. I've got some shoes for sale. Lovely stuff. They've just come in. I'll give you a good price. Have to get rid of them quickly."

The theft for which he was transported was for twenty-eight pairs of "high shoes" and the cart in which they were being carried. He ended up serving his time in the Hunter valley, found a wife (in fact, the lady who came out here as an unmarried female after having had a son and leaving him behind in Glasgow). They had all those children, and then William got the idea that he wanted to go back to England. They packed up and left in about 1870, with most of the children (some were already married).

So, here's the thing. They stayed in England for several years and he had an orchard. (Ultimately, they came back to Australia.) But where was the orchard? Was it in Hertfordshire, where he was born and lived, and where he committed his crime? Hertfordshire is to the northwest of London, north of the River Thames. No, it was at Rickmansworth in Kent, south of the Thames. So, I wonder whether William had the same kind of feeling that I did – it would be okay to go back to the land where he was born, but there had to be some kind of barrier between him and the past. If he did have that feeling, I can relate to it.

44 Separation

I had not seen Sydney for several years, and I had not lived in Sydney for twenty-three years. I wondered how I would find it. I had been thinking seriously about the possibility of coming back to Sydney for three or four years. I did not want to live in a city, any city, but it seemed to be necessary, otherwise I would be stuck in some low-paid, meaningless job around Kyogle until I was too old to work, and then I would be poor.

At the same time, the idea of coming back to live in the city in my late forties was ludicrous. How could I exchange a property in the country for a house in the city? I was also aware that one of the reasons I was coming back to Sydney was that Lady 3's family was in Sydney, and she had been complaining for years about her distance from them, and her isolation in the country. Coming back to Sydney was a last-ditch effort to stop the complaining, to put it crudely.

It was also an opportunity for the two boys. There were limited options for them in Kyogle. It would be good for them to be in Sydney. It meant that their future study and work options were unlimited. We sent the boys to two different schools. It prevented any competitiveness between them.

I had a battle to get my son into a school near to where we were living. The Department of Education told me that the appropriate school was Peter Board High School in North Ryde – we were in Beecroft. I found out that this would involve three bus rides for him each way. I also found out that the school in question was scheduled to be closed down in twelve months' time. The department had not told me that. The closest school was one mile away (okay, 1.6 kilometres) and he was willing to walk. Part of the walk would be through the bush to Pennant Hills Station, and he was looking forward to that.

I spoke to Pennant Hills High School, but they wanted to stick to the department's guidelines. I thought, "I am not coming to Sydney and starting out with a defeat in the face of mindless stupidity." So, I talked to the local State Member of Parliament. I figured that their primary function is to assist their citizens in just such ridiculous situations. To his credit, he took the time, he understood the problem, and he intervened. Suddenly the school was willing, although the lady in the school office wanted to be peeved. I didn't care. My son was at the school he wanted to be at, that he was entitled to be at, and he was happy there.

Otherwise, things were not going well with Lady 3, and I had emotionally withdrawn from her. She was good at fighting, but her philosophy was that the angriest person in the room always wins. The dynamic with her child was unhealthy. She was indulgent with him, and it caused problems with my son. He repeatedly went into my son's room and stole things and broke things. When confronted about it, he would deny it, however obvious the truth was. His mother refused to allow the problem to be addressed. Finally, I resorted to installing a lock on my son's bedroom door.

Lady 3's response was, "You can't put a lock on a door inside our own home." And my response was, "The boy has a right to feel safe in his own home."

Soon after this, I was at a conference in Melbourne, for work, and I spoke to her brother, who had moved there, about the issue with Lady 3's son. I suppose I was distraught. He and some friends shared a big house, and they said, "Send him down. We can help him to get straightened out." On reflection, I thought it was actually feasible.

When I came home, I explained the offer. To my surprise, the boy accepted, and packed his bag within a couple of days and went. I think that he knew he had run out of slack at home. He had descended into a directionless mess, not going to school and living in filth. Any moves I had tried to make to correct the situation, seeking collaboration with Lady 3, were sabotaged. The remarkable aftermath was that very soon after, Lady 3 went to Melbourne for a visit, and when she came back, she announced that she was moving to Melbourne. I was greatly relieved.

After that, I told her I wanted a divorce, and that was that. She commented, "I suppose it was inevitable." I simply said, "Yes." Financially, it cost me, but I had to consider what I wanted the rest of my life to be like. About the experience of my marriage to Lady 3, not everything needs to be said.

When you go to the Woodford Folk Festival in Queensland – six days at the end of December – on the last night they have a huge effigy, which represents all the things that happened that year, and they burn it. Maybe 20,000 people watch this fire, the stick-and-paper figures, several stories high, gradually collapsing into the flames. And then they talk and sing about the qualities it would be desirable to bring into the new year. Let there be a fire for the marriage to Lady 3; let it all tumble into ash.

45 Apprenticeship

When I started work at CCH, people were curious about me. Here I was, a man in his late forties, starting work as a writer and editor. Most of them had been at CCH since their early twenties, so for them I was starting out twenty years late. Then they asked me where I had been up until now, and I told them I had lived in a house in the country up north, seventeen kilometres out of town in a valley, in the bush.

They looked at me aghast. "And you came back here, to the city? A lot of us dream about doing what you've been doing for the last twenty years. What are you doing here?"

It was a tough question, but as can often be the case, I had an answer before I started thinking about it: "I'm living my life backwards."

Afterwards I wondered whether that was just a trite, silly statement. I suppose one perspective is that I was unhinged when I was in my early twenties. The death of my father could have been part of that, the motorcycle accident could have been another. And you could add whatever else you like into that mix. So, in those terms, I was just getting back to some sense of things, say, some sense of a career. But, I also think that's all nonsense.

However, there is no harm in launching on a new career path when you are in your late forties. In fact (yes, I remember, I have written this elsewhere), it is the best time to change your career path. If you have children, they are probably nearly grown up. You still have some energy to invest in a new endeavour and new learning, and you probably have a good body of knowledge and experience that you can apply to a new field, and the wit to generalise that across silo barriers.

I have known numerous people who have made such a transition in their late forties. (I'm not going to continue this thought. I just got the whiff of a colonel with a curling moustache, warming up to regale his readers (he is always regaling) with the wealth of his knowledge about an obscure niche of inquiry.)

Starting work at CCH was my real apprenticeship in writing, and my introduction to the concept of producing a body of knowledge that was always up-to-date. I was given responsibility for a reporting service called *Managing Training and Development*, and I contributed to other services too, on human resources management and employment law. I was grateful there had been a solid load of legal units in my Bachelor of Business degree. I wrote and updated commentary on training and development, producing four reports a year. As well, there were newsletters which I produced, so I researched for them and wrote articles on current topics.

I had to produce work every week, and it was submitted to a team of sub-editors who corrected it – for grammar, punctuation etc (not for content). I was in my element. I realised that this work environment leant heavily towards the law. Many of CCH's information services were about tax, accountancy and corporate law. I was in the Human Resources section. Likewise, most of our services were based directly on the law: employment law, industrial relations law, equal opportunity law, work health and safety law. However, another stream of writing had crept in, related to good practice in these areas. Accordingly, the commentary had an undercurrent that was concerned with values, intelligence and insight.

Many of the writers were a little uncomfortable in these areas, because they saw themselves primarily as interpreters of changes in the law. They even saw commentary on professional practice, separate from a legal framework, as being illegitimate and frothy. But there was a demand for it from the audience – professionals of various kinds – and if CCH was to report on changes in law, it also had to report on the conversations that professionals were having – context makes sense of text. Accordingly, we attended conferences and reported on what was being said there. We had a fast turnaround on these jobs, often releasing articles in the same week as the conference. At conferences, we often wrote at night and sent articles back to the office.

Well, if I had avoided becoming a journalist when I was twenty, I was having the experience now. I heard and met many national and international "thought leaders". I was able to join several professional bodies, in training and development as well as human resources. This tapped me into a wide field of literature. I also branched out into academic literature. Often, the people who spoke at conferences were academics who were addressing themselves to the wider professional audience, not just other academics.

That gave birth to the idea that part of my role was to pick up academic papers and provide an interpretation of them for a professional audience. Sometimes I spent several weeks focused on "an idea that was trending" in order to produce commentary that might serve innovations in professional practice. An example was "knowledge management". This endeavour meant that I was sifting through a wide range of articles from Australia and around the world, and sorting out the hype from the helpful.

Occasionally I had an idea of my own! Given that I had been a manager for several years, I wondered about the question of how a person makes the successful transition from worker to manager. Moving from being an ordinary worker to being an expert is still continuous; you are just doing more complex versions of the same thing. But becoming a manager is a radical change in the nature of your work. Many new managers don't realise this, and think it is just an extension of what they were doing before. But this means they try to micro-manage their workers, and take over their work. So, I started researching this topic, and writing articles about it. By now, I was getting work published in other professional magazines as well as CCH publications.

As a result of my articles on the new manager, I was invited to speak at a conference. It went well, but I didn't know how to manage myself into a career in that direction. It didn't happen. This modern world seems to depend on a lot of marketing; that wasn't my forté.

At the back of this writing was the concept of what we were doing at CCH, the concept of having available to a professional field a body of work that was comprehensive, useful, easy to navigate and use, and always up to date. You can see the application of this in a legal field such as employment law. It breaks down into some specific topics, all of which can be tracked back to specific legislation. If that legislation changes, you have been tracking it, and you report on those changes. You do it in two ways: you change the commentary on that topic, and you issue a newsletter which informs the reader what has been changed.

CCH had strong systems for carrying out this work, across a great number of fields. Those systems were strong enough to survive the transition to the digital world. I happened to be at CCH just at the time this was happening. There were months and years when all the data in a reporting service was sent to a company in India to be converted. There were fears about this – would it be a disaster? But, for the major part it seemed to go well, or well enough.

The people who started CCH (I don't tell their story, but I think it is a worthy story to tell) were conservative. They used a program called XY Write instead of Word to begin with. Their fear was that if they used Word, Microsoft might at some point claim copyright over any material written in Word. I don't think their belief was outlandish. For example, I use a computer program for family history, and if I print out a family tree chart, along the bottom of the page it says that the copyright of that chart belongs to the company. But it is *my* family history information, all of it, not theirs, none of it! The software is a tool only.

It's a bit like the manufacturer of a hammer saying that it owns the house you built using that hammer. There are many things I love about the modern world, but there are also many things I hate. I know, people like to argue the point, but we live in a world where many businesses have been built on the basis of shifting the paradigm from ownership to renting. For the most part, this is sleight of hand. And in the case of my family history chart, the company's claim to ownership of the copyright is a fraud. I may be "renting" the software, but it is a tool I am renting; it does not follow that they own the results of my mental effort and labour.

I was interested in the concepts that underpinned the commentary, because in the human resource management field, many of the topics are about professional practice, and the law is only a minor part of it. For example, recruitment is a necessary function, and organisations need to have systems to manage their recruitment processes. Some of this is about the law, for example, complying with discrimination law, but the system requires much more thought than just legal compliance. And, the elements of the system need to have some perspective on ethics and intelligence.

When I was conducting recruitment at the Challenge Foundation, I often had to involve a panel in the interviews. This was fraught with peril. I would try to coach the people on the panel about what was appropriate and helpful to ask, but they were usually busy people, so they didn't listen beforehand, and they just expected to turn up and unleash whatever was in their head that day. I devised policies for recruitment and I tried to instil procedures in likely panellists, but it wasn't always enough.

One time, we were recruiting a lady for a job working with children at a residence we managed. It became known that she had a child of her own, and I had one person on the panel trying to grill her on how she was going to get to work, and who was going to look after her child. It was unfair and inappropriate. I figured she would have addressed that question before she ever decided to come to the interview. These days, asking that question breaches anti-discrimination law.

So, I had a clear ethical perspective in the commentary I wrote, and I am not apologetic about that. I see it as necessary and honest. If an organisation wishes to act immorally, I think it is best that they are clear that that is what they are doing. I never had any objections to my commentary on recruitment (or any other topic). In fact, I was often asked to adapt existing commentary for other publications, and I think that was because the values I was expressing are in fact societal norms, clearly expressed.

I always thought that the genesis of CCH was noble – the concept of offering a helpful service to the business world: information that was always current. It was insightful and intelligent. As it branched out more into the human resources world, somehow a conceptual framework permeated through the publications. I never saw it written down, which I thought was remarkable, for a company whose business was writing knowledge down. Writers, who were mostly internal, but sometimes external "experts", would produce commentary on a particular subject, and the various blocks of commentary would be broadly commensurate with each other – in organisation, scope, volume and treatment. And mostly, in tone as well.

One week, I drew a diagram (a mind map) of what I thought the template was. "If someone is to write a body of commentary on a particular topic, it will consist of…." There were about a dozen items in my template: definitions and key concepts, description of the context or environment, relevant history, purposes and objectives, policies and guidelines, values/beliefs and assumptions, structures and procedures, stakeholders, implementation of policies and systems, skills needed, obstacles and challenges, review and evaluation, case studies and examples, and resources for further exploration.

When I showed it to people, they assented readily, as if to say, "Oh, so this is what we've been doing!" My explanation for that is what they say about fish. You can talk with fish (theoretically) about specific things in their environment (rocks, seaweed, other objects, other fish etc), but you can't talk to them about water, because it is everywhere!

The bigger question was, can you keep track of a field of knowledge, or was it a pretension? (Or was it just a successful business proposition – a mirage?) From that I got into questions such as: what is an expert? What is competence? How does a person move from being a novice to an expert? At a certain point I realised that some people were just interested in business for profit, while others were interested in the field itself. It was an intrinsic/extrinsic distinction. How important was that distinction? Could you influence it?

46 Poetry collections

However, I realised there were some things I wanted to clear up first. Some things had been sitting around, metaphorically, for a while, and some had been sitting around for a long time. After Lady 3 left, I was starting to get my life back (my son was still with me), starting to get a sense of expressing things that were important to me, and starting to develop my own expertise.

During 1989, in Horseshoe Creek, I had had a year after Lady 2 had gone, and I had delved into the poetry I had written over the previous twenty years. Now that computers had arrived, and I had bought one, the possibility of self-publishing was closer. The project of writing the history of the Kyogle Shire (in 1988) had given me enough money to buy a computer. Today, that sounds ludicrous; the price of a computer would be a fraction of what you would get paid for such a project. But that was the state of things then. I had bought a top-of-the-range dot matrix printer as well. I was contented. Life is a one-step-at-a-time journey.

I sat on the floor of the living room, and over many nights compiled two small volumes of poetry, sorting through a mass of notebooks and pieces of paper, and making selections. I had in mind two themes: flames in the open, and love and armour. I liked the idea of a small fire, where the weather is mild enough for it to be in the open in a small clearing. It could have been a metaphor for my life. So too was the title of the second volume: *Love and Armour*. I liked this because "armour" evoked the word "amore", French for love. But I saw love as being in constant competition with conflict and war. Hence the need for armour.

Anyway, I finished the two volumes, and I was pleased with them, but there wasn't any easy way to get them into print. I managed to print out a specimen copy of each on the dot matrix printer, and that was that. It was a private project; I wasn't in search of a publisher. So, the two books went back into storage for many years.

It was 2007, and I had the time and space to bring the two volumes out of storage and reconsider them. I was on computer number 4, I think, and I had current software with which I could tackle a book project. To quote one of the poems: "After days and days, the sky was clear and the sun that shone did not remember pasts. Purposes that had lain silently awoke, and knew how soon to seize their ends and means. Spirit touched the fuel of hearts and came burning through, the day moved with true aim from the mystery of source to new heights." ("After days") I think that is a fair description of my 2007 project.

I still liked the poems, which was nice, because often poems do not survive the shift to a different time of your life. I didn't change either of the collections, but I thought it would be nice to add some autobiographical notes. To me, the poems and the stories belonged together; they made sense of each other. I know that some people frown on this: "The poems should be able to stand alone." Do I care? My statement stands: the poems and the stories belong together; they make sense of each other.

My last statement in *Flames in the Open* (2007 version) was this: "This sequence of poems started in want of a dream. All I really had to work with was a pugnacious refusal to accept the small vision that was given me – get a job, fill your allotted place in society, be content. I like the sequence because of what it tells me about how a dream emerged out of that.

"During that period of time it surfaced, was pushed down, resurfaced, took shape and filled its wings with hope. It lives and dies and transmutes itself from lead into gold. It finds its feet, weathers storms, refuses to wear a tie, and Mr Wright [my high school principal] would not recognise it. He would wonder, though, whether there is land on the other side of the great water, and if it is true that hearts can be light."

I was in the next phase of publishing history: I could do the layout and design the cover so that the books could be printed professionally. My 1989 version had been amateurly printed on my dot matrix printer and is not nice to look at these days. Now, there were printing houses who could do short runs, and I had both the collections printed this way: one hundred copies of each. I had no plan of what to do then, but I didn't (and don't) believe there is much of a market for volumes of poetry.

In fact, there was something else going on. Among the aspects of my life that needed awakening was my thoughts on the debacle in Casino with the Challenge Foundation. I was writing professionally now (that is, it was my job), and I wanted to write a book that looked at the ethical questions that surfaced in the Challenge Foundation struggle. In my researching for articles and commentary on human resource management and training, I had come across books and articles that opened up new lines of thought for me on ethics.

I realised that ethics issues are not adequately dealt with solely from the perspective of moral philosophy. You need to look at psychology and sociology as well. So, I came across the idea of human development of values. People in business and public life disagreed about ethics, or acted differently, because they were at a different stage of development in their values. If no one recognised this, it would inevitably result in arguments and acrimony. I explored that idea deeply enough to arrive at my own understanding of it.

There was one other aspect: a model of what a person is. Freud had the model of the Id, the Ego and the Superego. Other psychologists and thinkers in various religions had their models of the human being. Slowly, over years, I derived a model of the human being, consisting of five dimensions, which made sense of ethics and the different stages of development humans passed through. This became my first book after the two histories of Kyogle. I thought of it as my substitute for doing a PhD.

I tried to find a publisher for this book, but the only questions the publishers seemed to be interested in were, "Are you a lecturer at a university? How many students have you got that you can sell it to?" I wasn't a lecturer and I had no students, and none of the publishers was interested in what I had to say. But after I gave up on this path, I had no intention of leaving the book to sit in the cupboard, so I used the same printing house who printed the poetry books to print the ethics book. It was called *Human Values and Ethics in the Workplace*.

Occasionally, someone was interested in hearing about the book. I gave a few talks for professional organisations, but it never built momentum. For a few years I had stacks of boxes in my garage of ethics books I had no way of selling. Eventually, sadly, I threw them all out. In the meantime, I created a website. It gave me the satisfaction of knowing that my books were "out there", and occasionally I sold some books, but I was thankful I had a job.

47 Bliss

I went back to my poetry books to ask myself, "What is it that I am trying to do when I write poetry?" I thought it was a fair question, because some people are telling stories, and I wasn't trying to do that. I couldn't go along to a Poetry Slam Evening and bellow out a ballad. I wasn't Henry Lawson or Banjo Patterson. I couldn't entertain with a jolly jingle where everything was threaded together with rhythm and rhyme. I wasn't T.S. Eliot; I wasn't a representative for global angst, although perhaps I had some of his style, having studied him at an impressionable age.

When I trawled through the poems again, some themes seemed to stand out: join no crowds; keep your hands free for waving; my eyes see me pressing ahead, grappling with the complex living.

And these fragments:

"Beginning in the dark we taste what the light would do, hope, and occasionally stand defenceless, tempting the fire-bright.

"At night you may find him, spinning out the tracks of the stars.

"How is it that the poor man advances? By listening and seeing with his heart.

"All rivers enter into the sea; with that as his end, the stranger listens to the pitter-patter of rain and sees a sailing twig caught momentarily on a creek bend.

"Do you hear him singing in the morning? He calls upon the mountain to move.

"In fatigue or confusion he remembers his resolve and finds again the union of soul and purpose. Wake to the moment, move higher, abandon false dreams, false desire. Flashes illumine the one course, clear to the heart of the one source.

"The roof sighed but kept the rain out another year, we shouldered another morning, packed away questions of the heart, climbed the hill again, until we dissolve, either we or the hill, until the river answers, until..."

I think I am trying to express bliss. And perhaps this is unexpected and therefore hard to relate to. I think a lot of poetry is observational, about the ordinary events of life, or non-ordinary events. It seeks to express an unusual or lyrical perspective on the event, or express humour, anger or misery. So, I think I understand this now. Since I published the two volumes in 2007, I have published three more volumes. One of them dug deeply into my early poems, starting from my first recorded poems when I was eleven.

There was a book launch for the two poetry books and the ethics book. I was a member of the NSW Writers Centre, and they had an event where authors could showcase their newly published works. You got fifteen minutes on stage where you could launch your book(s). I did two sessions: one for the poetry books and one for the ethics book. I invited friends, and I asked some people to speak about the books. It was a pleasant day, and I sold a few books. One has to accept it as a nice day and not expect any flow-on outcomes. That's how it was.

I sit with that thought: amid all the dramas and difficulties of my life, I write poems about bliss.

Things I know

Bliss exists in parallel with the vicissitudes of your life, and one day, perhaps, you may integrate the two. So, plunge ahead. Take the risk.

48 Writing a story

I had not integrated bliss and ordinary life. Nevertheless, I say, nevertheless. One continues on. After realising I was not going to attract an audience for the ethics book, I started thinking about the original impetus for the book: the situation at the Challenge Foundation in Casino. After I had been dismissed from there, several people had said to me that I should write the story of it. It had high drama, and I had kept to a brave and honest path in the midst of it. But I had always resisted. The story was too complicated, too emotional, and would I end up having to deal with people wanting to sue me for libel?

Accordingly, I didn't do anything about it. I was working on a follow-up book to the ethics book, because there is always something else that needs to be said. I had worked on a few chapters, but the truth was, I was bored with it. And if I was bored, how could I expect readers to be interested? One day I was discussing this with my son (he was about twenty). He was talking about writing as well. He had muddled his way through school, with rather ordinary results at his Higher School Certificate. He had even gone to university for a while, to study computer programming, but he didn't have a high opinion of the syllabus or the teachers. He thought it was all backward.

However, he found himself a job at a telecommunications company, and suddenly he was in his element. He was working with big systems as a technical person. Their training seemed to be ad hoc, but he seemed to find his way, and before long he was respected among his co-workers. I used to ask him questions about how he learned. I was interested in whether he could verbalise that. My experience was that people who were highly competent were often not so good at describing how they learned. But my son impressed me. He seemed to know what he was doing, and could verbalise his processes of learning quite well.

As is often the case, once he blossomed in his area of work, he blossomed more broadly. He had started reading science fiction books, many of which were de facto philosophy, psychology and sociology texts. He was building his own library. (I was pleased with that!) And the thought had germinated that he could write a book, or story, himself. Hence our conversation in the kitchen over a cup of tea. He excitedly told me about a website called "National Novel Writing Month", or "NanoWrimo".

The idea is that you try to write a book in a month: November (30 days), the only rule being that it has to be 50,000 words or more. There is no real prize, and there is no assessment of your manuscript. You upload the contents of the file and their tool merely counts the words. They give you a digital certificate with your name on it that says you are a winner. You also attain the right to buy a tee-shirt (your money!). I liked the whimsy of it. There are options for interaction. In some places, people set up groups so they can meet.

I resisted. I told my son that my book was non-fiction, not fiction, so Nanowrimo was irrelevant to me. He persisted. In the end, he used the magic words: "Write it *as* a story!" I don't know why these words were magical, but they were: they clicked. I immediately went to my computer and opened an account on the Nanowrimo website. On the first of November I sat down to start. I stared at the blank screen. I had no plan at all. I started by describing myself, sitting in my library. I kept going. After a few hours, it hit me. I was going to write the story of my experiences at the Challenge Foundation in Casino.

Because it was a story, not history, I didn't have to use people's real names, and I didn't have to agonise over the exact dates and places, minor details that would have made the account ponderous and dry. And because I was writing the story in thirty days, I had to stick to the main story, and not get dragged down all the side tracks. It was remarkable how that sense stayed with me every moment of the way: is this part of the main story, or is it a side-track?

On the last day of November, I got up at six o'clock in the morning and I wrote until just before midnight. I was pulling all the threads of the story together, and I did. I did it! The next day, I printed it all out, sat down and read it all through. I felt that I had achieved the task; it was coherent and it had the essence of a good story. It also gave me a tremendous feeling of release: the story was out there now.

One of my twin sons had studied graphic design recently, so I asked him to do the layout and design for the book. The book was called *The Ten Thousand Things*. That was based on a quote from the *Tao Te Ching*: "The Tao that can be told is not the eternal Tao. The name that can be named is not the eternal name. The nameless is the beginning of heaven and earth. The named is the mother of the ten thousand things." My "ten thousand things" was the mess I was embedded in at Casino, after my period in retreat at a secluded distance in Horseshoe Creek, peaceful but not really doing the work I needed to do in my life.

Once again, I went for a print run with a printery that did short runs. I got one thousand printed, and I held a book launch at a popular bookshop near the city: Gleebooks. I put some effort into asking people to come, and I asked two people to speak about the book for me. About eighty people attended, in the upstairs room above the bookshop. There was afternoon tea, and my books were for sale.

I was pleased; I thought the day was a success. There was also a family celebration for the book, a picnic at Fagan Park, Galston, where I stood up and said a few words about the book, in the presence of my children and their families.

Later on, I gave a presentation at a conference about my experience at the Challenge Foundation, as a morality tale about leadership. If I had thought that this might lead to wider coverage for the book, I was wrong. However, this time I did have a few people whom I asked to read the book and give me a testimony, and when I reprinted the book, I included some of their comments. The comment I liked most was from the man who read it on the plane trip from Sydney to San Francisco. After he arrived, he sent me a text message that said, "When I had finished the book, I sat and savoured it, and I carried that feeling with me for days."

Another person said, "It was a delightful and insightful journey of personal exploration and reflection. A compelling journey into one's quest for inner peace and mastery in life. Glenn has inspired me." Another comment was: "The book is unusual in that it highlights the important ethical dimensions of the leadership role and the inevitable pressures and conflict potential that come with it."

And one more: "Probably because it is based on a true story, the book is both a moving account of the events and a bit confronting to the reader when the extent of the nasty politics is revealed."

49 I Ching

There is a bit more to be said about the book, in the interests of full disclosure. Its subtitle was: "A story of the lived experience of the I Ching". I have used the I Ching since I was in my mid-twenties. It is called an oracle, and is widely treated as a means of divining the future. Many things have a superficial nature and a deep nature. At a shallow level, one can ask questions of the I Ching and it will give you an answer, which you can interpret. "Should I start a relationship with this woman?" "If I apply for that job, will I get it?" Et cetera. The Tarot operates likewise.

At a deeper level, it is more about what it would be good to do in order to act steadfastly and uprightly. Alfred Huang, who has a commentary on the I Ching, says, "The I Ching offers guidance for favourable actions and to avoid misconduct that invites misfortune".

While I was the manager at the Challenge Foundation in Casino, I often put my dilemmas before the I Ching to see what it had to say. When it came to writing the book, I didn't have those notes anymore, but I thought, "I wonder what would happen if I threw the I Ching (throwing the three coins six times to get a hexagram) as I went along? So that's what I did, as I was writing, and I discussed the readings in the book.

This was novel (so to speak), and it annoyed some people deeply, but others accepted it as a way of looking at things that might be helpful, and as a quest to look for spiritual meaning in the troubles that come to pass. Sometimes the experience was unexpected and confronting for me. When I was about to write about the scene where I was dismissed (it had been a few days before Christmas, as it so often is), the hexagram I got was 58, Lake/Joy. I thought this was a bit unsympathetic of the universe! However, it did force me to see another side to the situation.

In writing the story, I had become immersed in it, and I was emotionally embroiled. As I had done when it was happening, I was determined, and I just kept digging deeper. The I Ching was telling me, "This is not all there is in life. There is life after this, and it is time you were taken out of that dark hole".

One of the testimonies for the book mentioned the I Ching: "I very much liked the story that Martin told. It is compelling, and his search for inner guidance and wisdom through the I Ching, illuminating."

I had written the book in November 2009, and it was published in 2010. I had been ambivalent about overtly referring to the I Ching, but I decided it was worth doing it. I didn't have anything to lose. But the I Ching has little exposure in society, especially in Australia. Occasionally it pops up in movies. In *You've Got Mail*, Tom Hanks refers to it as an oracle of wisdom when he is contemplating offering advice to Meg Ryan. It is something we all know about, but at the same time, we know nothing about it. It sits there for him as a cultural icon next to the movie *The Godfather*.

William Irwin Thompson refers to the I Ching in *At the Edge of History*, but not much. It comes up first as something that hippies know about. The only comment he makes about the system itself is when he says, "like coins tossed for the I Ching, we created a geometry larger than ourselves." I liked that comment, given that the I Ching is based on the yin-yang binary, and there are sixty-four hexagrams. But you don't hear about people meeting in I Ching groups or organising I Ching readings. Perhaps it is because there are sixty-four hexagrams, and it sounds complicated.

Things have to be simple. For a while, I studied an approach to leadership called the Leadership Architect, created by Lominger. I even qualified in the methodology. I was impressed; it was the most comprehensive approach I had seen, and I thought it was valid. It was consistent with the model of a human being I had created in my ethics book. The system had six clusters of factors (strategic skills, operating skills, courage, energy and drive, organisational positioning skills, and personal and interpersonal skills). In all it consisted of sixty-seven skills, plus some more that dealt with how to deal with troubles.

Most people veered away from the model. Sixty-seven skills were far too many. It was enough to talk about four factors, like DiSC (Dominance, Influence, Steadiness, Conscientiousness) or use the MBTI (the Myers-Briggs Type Indicator), which was developed from Jung's personality model (extravert/introvert, intuitive/sensing, thinking/feeling, perceiving/judging). The latter model gives sixteen personality types. However, these systems were just about personality, not leadership. Are the discussions actually a proxy for talking about leadership?

There are plenty of websites that talk about these two models, and it intrigues people to try and map their own preferences. Lominger was more focused on performance in a job, and looked at the intellectual, emotional and moral strengths one needs to cultivate in order to be a good leader. I thought that it was much more useful, and relevant to leadership, than the other approaches, but fear of complexity is widespread.

In the same way, the perceived complexity of the I Ching discourages people from looking into it. But for me, it was the place where I belonged. Also, it is better to look into one thing deeply than to look into a lot of things in a shallow way. The I Ching's allegory for this is setting out to dig a well, and starting a new hole when you have only gone down a metre or so. The water is deep down, and you have to dig deeply to find it. A dozen shallow holes will not yield what you need.

Despite my allegiance to the I Ching, I was more wary about referring to it overtly after *The Ten Thousand Things*. Some of the meanings are evident, but much of it assumes deeper knowledge of the whole matrix of hexagrams. If I talked about 29, it can be called the Pit, the Abyss, or the Ghost River. It consists of the trigram Water, doubled. The image is of water rushing down a ravine. The only thing to do is to keep going, straight ahead. If you are sincere, you will have success.

But then, it helps to know that 29 is paired with 30, which is Radiance, Fire, Bright Omens. In the beginning there is Heaven and Earth (hexagrams 1 and 2), and then the ten thousand things are created. They are formed from the tension between Fire and Water. And people go through cycles of growth and development, facing struggles and obstacles, and thereby come into their fulness.

In the end, cycles are completed (63 After Completion) and new cycles start (64 Before Completion). In 63, Water is above Fire, while in 64, Fire is above Water. Just think, after completion, one is boiling water on a fire to make a cup of tea. When fire is above water, things are not yet in their proper position. It is a way of thinking.

Gradually, one imbibes the thinking and becomes part of it. The answers to specific questions do not matter so much, because there are always a lot of things going on (which can be called complexity), but you get clues, which are about how to balance the yin and yang within yourself, and in your relationships with other people.

Occasionally, life is unimpeded. In 14, Great Abundance, it is supreme everywhere, a great harvest. But one must always be steadfast and upright. Noble souls use their abundance to benefit others. And they always seek to curb evil and foster good.

Moreover, they understand that abundance does not just refer to material wealth. There are four aspects: wealth, power, health and spirituality. And finally, Great Abundance is, like everything in our world, subject to change. After all, the I Ching means Book of Changes.

50 Leadership (1)

I find myself talking about leadership because in the commentary we wrote at CCH, the topic took centre-stage quite often. In the whole management field, and training, and human resource management, everyone talked about leadership. It seemed humorous to me, because (a) much of management is procedural, not heroic, and (b) most people don't want to be leaders. To put it another way, much of the work of people in management positions is about management, not leadership.

I wondered whether the talk about leadership was a proxy for something else, say, the need to feel significant. It's certainly easier to talk (in suitably vague terms) about leadership than to talk about the necessary components of an appropriate recruitment system, or the procedural requirements to ensure fairness and justice, or the systems required to ensure goals are achieved. While I was the General Manager at the Challenge Foundation (today, would I be called the Chief Executive Officer, as I was responsible for five separate services?), I was asked what my "management style" was. The person asking me would have had no idea what he was talking about, but I knew he wanted me to say something tough, like "Make decisions!" and "Get stuff done, no matter who or what is in the way!"

Instead, I said something like, my goal was to get things done effectively and harmoniously. I could see him cringe. He was a head-kicker. Later, I found out that this was literally true. He had beaten up an old man who got curious about what was going on in his business.

My attitude towards the concept of leadership was coloured before I ever got to Sydney, with its self-confident, brash corporate world. I discovered W. Edwards Deming, the originator of Total Quality Management (TQM) in the 1950s. He was American, but he went to Japan, and is given a lot of credit for the rebuilding of Japanese industry after World War II.

Deming's concept was that, to be successful, a company had to work out how to foster quality in its products. He was an engineer, not an economist. He believed that quality was established as a system. In other words, one must understand how everything is connected, and that everything can affect everything else. The system must be based on continuous improvement, and employees must be involved; employee relations must be co-operative, education and training must be ongoing. At the heart of it, for managers, was the idea that one must have a "profound understanding" of the context – the environment, the elements of the environment, and the dynamics at play.

I thought this was all obvious, and right. What is the alternative? Cut the costs, maximise the profits (we are thinking here in the short-term, of course; Deming's view was the long-term). By the time I came to Sydney, TQM was on the wane, and it was being treated as a fad. Of course, there were new fads. Everyone tut-tutted knowingly about fads, but they kept coming, in waves, and everyone nodded wisely about the new insights.

What did Deming have to say about leadership? Only that the important thing was one's overall philosophy, and as long as one had the TQM perspective, leadership would take care of itself. The important thing was to have a deep understanding of the industry one was in. I was working in a singular type of publishing company. That was different to being a retailer of white goods, or a merchant bank. On the contrary, when I arrived, CCH was employing a bunch (a phalanx?) of young people (mostly male) who had MBAs and zero knowledge of CCH's business.

Zero knowledge of the business wasn't seen as a problem. All the principles of business were seen as the same: they were taught in the MBA courses! A smart young manager could adapt them to any context. Mostly, one needed good marketing collateral and a flashy marketing campaign, followed with a hard-sell team of salespeople. In some of these marketing campaigns, companies were sent goods they had not requested, together with an invoice. The sales were booked as soon as the goods were sent, to get them into the current revenue period. Bonuses obviously depended on it.

Some of those forced customers didn't understand that they had the right to return those goods, at no cost to themselves. But it was just business. Now, when I hear someone say, "It's just business", I think: "When someone says that, it means their business is dirty business."

51 Dirty business

I had my own experience of dirty business. We (I was married at the time) came to Sydney and bought a house after two years renting. It was hard, because I had not yet sold the Horseshoe Creek property, and we certainly had no spare cash. There were many loan brokers around, and I thought it would be sensible to talk to one about our options. "No problem!" said the broker. "The solution is to buy a third property! Then you rent it out, and use that money to cover the mortgages, and soon enough, you'll be ahead."

The numbers made it look possible, and we were short of options. We were given a contract for a loan to cover the purchase of the two properties, and the Horseshoe Creek property was to be collateral. There was a fee of $10,000 to be paid to the broker upon fulfilment. Part of the enticement was that the loan specified a very particular interest rate (let's say, 5.72%; I forget what it was), so I understood this to mean that the loan was secured. But, as the weeks passed, nothing was happening.

We were stuck, because the purchase of the property at Cherrybrook was riding on this, and there was no way to hasten the sale of the Horseshoe Creek property. Finally, the broker demanded his $10,000 fee, but we didn't have the loan. He threatened me. At that point, I went to a solicitor. I was new in Sydney, so finding a solicitor was guesswork. I briefed the solicitor, and he wrote a procedural letter (half a page) to the broker, merely to request copies of all the paperwork. A couple of weeks went by, and the law firm told me the solicitor had moved to another job, and could I come and brief another solicitor? This happened once more, so I had briefed three solicitors in the same firm on the same matter. They sent me a bill for $5,000.

It was a big law firm; they had consolidated three times in the last couple of years. Obviously, greater revenue was a primary issue. I was tired. I couldn't fight them as well. I paid the bill and asked them to give me all the paperwork, which they did. I decided I would do it myself.

It took me about forty hours of work to trawl through the pile of papers, which was about five centimetres high. I decided to take it to the Consumer Claims Tribunal (the name might be different now). I decided that an ordinary, intelligent person should be able to get to the bottom of this problem. And I did. The truth was, the broker did not have a loan; the 5.72% was pure fiction. And the decisive fact buried in the five centimetres of papers was that several banks had refused to offer a loan because they wouldn't accept the Horseshoe Creek property as collateral. The general rule seemed to be that, maybe they would accept a house in a regional town, but they would not accept a property seventeen kilometres out of town, in the bush.

So, the loan was dead, and the broker knew it, so he was putting pressure on me to pay him, without telling me the truth about the loan, that is, that it did not exist.

I compiled the relevant information, referencing it to the pages in the five centimetres of papers I had, and packaged it up for the tribunal. I went in for the hearing with some trepidation. I had no experience in making a presentation to a tribunal (with one exception, but I will come to that later), and as a young man I had consciously refused to go into a career that would require me to stand up and argue in public. But I told myself that I had the weight of evidence on my side, and the broker just had bravado.

And in fact, the hearing went my way. After the tribunal member had heard from both of us, he asked us to go to a conference room and see if we could settle it ourselves. We did that. I even did the classic thing: I got my cheque book out and put it on the table, and said, "You're a liar. Nothing you've said is the truth, but I'll give you $2,000 now to just go away." Greed is a wonderful thing: he refused! That fired my determination! I thought, "I will get you now."

We went back into the courtroom and informed the Tribunal Member the outcome of our discussion. He decided in my favour, which is to say, the broker lost, and we were free of him. And then the Tribunal Member said a profound thing. He said, to both of us, "You don't have to let this rest here, Mister Martin. You can take this further if you wish."

I understood that he was telling me I had a provable case of deception and fraud against the broker, that I had the evidence to make it stick. I appreciated that immensely, but I was tired. All this had been on the top of work and the rest of life. I let it go.

Subsequently, I sold the Horseshoe Creek property, and life was a bit easier. Selling it was a big wrench for me. I had spent nineteen years of my life there. For comparison, when I was growing up, I lived at Greenacre for nineteen years as well. I haven't lived in too many places in my life. I know some people have lived in dozens, and some people move around a lot. But not me. That's how it is. So, now I was really back in the city.

52 Tribunal

And yes, there was one other time when I appeared before a tribunal. It is topical to mention it, because as I write, there is a Royal Commission going on into the previous government's Robodebt scheme, and my story is a parallel to that. My story goes back to 1997, when I had finished my university degree (the Bachelor degree and the Honours year). During my studies, I had received Austudy sometimes, if I was not doing casual teaching. (I am no longer sure if that was the name of it, but I don't feel obliged to keep the names of government support schemes in my head.)

I received a letter from the Department of Social Security (DSS) that charged me with wrongly taking money from the scheme, and doing this with the intent of defrauding the government. Yet, I had been so careful to be honest, not only because that is my personal value, but also, I was studying ethics. To be convicted of stealing money would not be a good look! I had reported all my earnings, and I had done so in a timely manner. I certainly didn't think that I had received more money than I was entitled to.

I was also upset because this accusation attacked my entire course of study. Going to university was my path out of the malaise I was in after I had been given the sack. I could not get a job anywhere, at anything. My only option was to reinvent myself, and that's what going to university was all about.

I examined all the information I had been given by DSS, and I compared it with my bank records. I was given a date for a hearing at the tribunal. I had to go to Sydney for that, to a building in the city. I appeared before three people. I presented my case, and I explained the effect of the department's claim on me. I didn't want to make the case about my emotions, but I did want them to know the effect of their wrongful accusation on me. The department's approach towards me was as if they were a bunch of back-alley thugs – and this was the government!

I had the evidence in my bank statements and my correspondence, and it was quite clear that I had no case to answer. The tribunal members dismissed the charges, and apologised for the department's actions, and told me they were satisfied that I had done the right thing at all times. I wouldn't have told this story, I'd forgotten it, except that the current Royal Commission, and hearing some of the affected people's stories, brought the memories back. It was unfair and unjustified then, and so it seems now. In any case, to call something "Robodebt" gives you some idea of the mentality of the people behind it. It is disgusting, and it is depraved, both as a name, and as a methodology.

53 Leadership (2)

Leadership again: I am still intrigued by how much leadership books and training programs emphasise the self. "What kind of a leader are you?" A big part of good leadership is understanding the context. You may need to be a different kind of leader in different situations. What about my own performance as a teacher in a classroom of schoolchildren who have been essentially unsupervised and unrestrained for weeks? Was I the same kind of teacher as I liked to be in more normal circumstances? Hardly. So, context is important, not my personal style, and any decent training program should make this clear.

Later, I was working as an instructional designer for online learning, and I was trying to guide teachers in the preparation of materials for online courses. I coined the phrase "Text without context is a con." It was a dramatic way of emphasising the importance of context in creating meaning.

Another aspect of leadership is making the best use of the people in the group. A more mature model of leadership could be called synergistic. It makes the best use of all the talents in the group. A good example is the response of various governments to COVID. Suddenly, medical personnel were upfront at media conferences, and political leaders were deferring to their advice. And it was accepted by the public, because the public could see the good sense of this approach.

In most situations that involve groups that have leaders, the good leaders defer to the persons who are experts in particular fields, when the time is appropriate. And, they do not do this as a way of shifting blame. Further, when ideas are needed, good leaders elicit them from anyone and everyone in the group. They encourage it. A healthily functioning group is synergistic. People work together harmoniously, not competitively. The opposite of this is when the leader seeks to take control over everything. An unfortunate effect of this kind of leader is that people respond by shutting up. If they have a good idea, they don't speak up. Even if it takes a lot of effort, they keep silent!

Another symptom of poor leaders is their attempt to reduce everything to routines. Following Deming, I think good leadership combines a profound understanding of the field, and imagination. What is the opposite of this? I have seen an example of it. The publishing company brought out a young executive from Holland to carry out a group exercise whose goal was to generate new products. The group consisted of some workers (non-executive writers and editors), and a lot of managers and senior managers – more than a dozen.

The exercise took two or three full days. It involved many A3 sheets of paper with tables drawn on them, one for each of maybe fifty products from the various areas (tax, accounting, corporate law, employment law etc). The idea was to fill in certain characteristics for each product according to where it fitted in the market. But, to trigger people's imagination, the exercise started with a free-wheeling effort to describe "the typical customer".

What does the typical customer look like? Well, is it a man or a woman? What kind of clothes does he/she wear? What kind of car does he/she drive? What does he/she do on a weekend? And on and on. After a while, people began to get into the spirit of it. (What other choice did they have?) Laughingly, the group decided that the car was a Volvo. And of course, they decided that the wine was a chardonnay.

Where do they live? Well, that question was a bit sensitive for me. I had grown up in Greenacre, and when I came back to Sydney, I decided to stay north of the Parramatta River – for my own personal reasons, not through any sense of social superiority. I thought that most people who worked at the company lived within a radius of a few kilometres of North Ryde. But the customers? Many of them would live in the richer suburbs, obviously. But how was this supposed to help us think of new products, or imagine what those products should look like? And how did it help to tap into my personal history of places I have lived and prefer to live?

At one point in the proceedings, when I was mentally fatigued with the exercise, I calculated what the cost was of all these workers and managers for two or three days, plus the cost of bringing the person out from Holland. I forget the figure, but it was a lot. It was silly. The value of the exercise was not zero; it was negative, because it killed the possibility of any ideas arising. Why did it happen? It happened because it produced a lot of spreadsheets, which induced the idea of action and certainty. Managers (and executives) like certainty. Not knowing what the future will bring is a scary thought. We try to eliminate it.

Needless to say, the entire exercise produced not a single piece of fruit. And subsequently, I have thought about what would have been a better exercise. It doesn't help at all to try to describe "a typical customer". It doesn't matter whether or not they drive a Volvo. However, what is worse about the exercise, is that it ignores all the drivers who have BMWs or Audis, or anything else. What might be actually helpful? To forget about that, and think of the processes that a person in the relevant role (human resource manager, for example) undertakes, and the situations they encounter. Think about the life cycle of the manager.

Note that this brings context to the forefront. Once you have done this exercise, then you can think about the products in relation to that context, and you can think about gaps in the existing products. I went back to my desk, three days behind in my work.

I suppose the "typical customer" exercise is a bit like using DISC or the MBTI as a proxy for exploring leadership. At the end of it you have a set of descriptors, most of which you can relate to emotionally, so you feel you have been "seen". But beyond this, there is little of practical value to enable you to develop any positive leadership qualities.

54 Contracting

I worked at CCH as an employee for several years, but eventually I was dissatisfied and I wanted to leave. At one point I applied for a management position, but I didn't get it. My theory is that I was too valuable as a writer and editor. The person who was appointed to the position was far less qualified than me in all respects, not least of which was management skills and experiencee.

I had a number of different managers. The last one was the most difficult to work for. This was when I started thinking seriously about how to leave. I had also watched these gung-ho young managers systematically dismiss all the senior staff who had been with the organisation for more than twenty years. Seldom a week went by when you did not hear someone say, "Did you hear about so-and-so? He (or she) has been made redundant." And it would be someone whom you knew about, at least by reputation, someone who carried a wealth of knowledge in their head. The young bloods were systematically gutting the organisation of its most important asset, its employees' knowledge.

I liked the work I was doing, but I didn't like the work situation. At this time, the company was starting to use more external contractors as writers and editors. The idea I formed was that I would leave, but I would "take some products with me", that is, I would leave and become an external contractor, but I would work on the same publications. That would mean I could work on the things I enjoyed, but I would not be subject to the same managerial supervision and intrusion.

The condition was that the company was willing to allow the products to be worked on externally. Now that the company had shifted to working digitally, this should not have been a problem. I could set up a VPN connection from home and work directly on the products. I thought about this for twelve months, and gradually fed the idea into conversation. I also stopped arguing with my manager. No matter what I thought about her decisions and actions, I did not argue. I stayed silent and did my work.

At the end of the year, I broached the subject of becoming an external contractor and writing for the same products that I was working on then. She agreed, to my relief. She also remarked on "how much our relationship has improved over the last twelve months". Indeed it had, but only I knew why.

For a time there, most of the team felt disenchanted with the atmosphere. There were no overt fights. This manager had sacked two people, for gratuitous reasons, in her first month in the role. It was her signature approach. But, mid-morning, we would all walk out and go downstairs for coffee. At first, we spent fifteen minutes having coffee and talking. As the atmosphere continued to decline, the time spent drinking coffee became gradually longer, until it was up to an hour. It was an interesting building, because it had an open atrium, so you could see downstairs to where we were drinking coffee from the open office space upstairs.

The manager never confronted the team, or any one individual, about the coffee-time ritual. I think this behaviour would be called passive-aggressive. These days, passive-aggressive behaviour is viewed negatively, but there are times when it is appropriate.

One time, I went to the Human Resources Department (HR) to complain about the manager. I argued that her behaviour was wrong. She had been bullying a young writer relentlessly. I don't think there was any particular reason, except that she liked having a victim. It was serial behaviour: when she stopped with one person, she would start with another. Perhaps she felt that she was systematically improving the team. The young writer had come to talk to me to ask me what she should do.

The person in HR that I spoke to was not sympathetic. I explained the effect of the manager on the whole team, and about the bullying of young staff. The conversation wasn't going anywhere productive, but then the person started talking about my feelings. She said that I seemed to be upset, and that perhaps I should consider how to reduce my stress levels.

It was in that moment that I had a revelation. I said, very firmly, "I did not come here to talk about my feelings! I came here to present a serious management issue to you, and I want that addressed!"

It was the first time I had been aware of how the "emotions agenda" can be abused. This was a brazen attempt to divert me from the issue I had come to discuss. It was also a dishonest attempt to subvert me. I left in disgust. That episode was one of the incidents that prompted me to think seriously about leaving.

I advised the young writer that her most productive course of action would be to leave, and not waste any time doing so. I was serious. And she took my advice. Within four weeks she had another job, and when our paths crossed a couple of months later, she told me she was happy there, and she thanked me for my advice.

You could say it was ironic that I was having these altercations with the HR department when HR had been the specialty of my degree. But, you could also say it was ironic that the HR department could be so, shall we say, less than ideal in a company that published commentary for HR departments. However, it had been my view from the beginning that in most cases, HR is far less than what it should be or could be.

My Honours thesis explored the hypothesis that there is no consensus among HR managers on ethical issues, but they display a high level of congruence with the values of the organisations for which they work. To state this in the worst light, HR managers are the organisation's henchmen. They do not constitute an independent force that fosters the organisation's ethical behaviour. Rather, their primary goal is to protect the CEO.

55 Drinking

The period of time before I converted to contractor status was not my finest. At the company's Christmas party I drank too much. I was usually quite moderate, but I was feeling poorly about my situation. The company supplied the alcohol liberally at Christmas, and I did not exercise sufficient restraint on this occasion. Afterwards, realising that I was drunk, instead of driving home I went to a Harry Potter movie. I knew it was three hours long.

I slept through most of the movie. I thought I would be okay to drive home. However, about halfway home there was a police check and I showed up as over the limit. I faced the ignominy of having to leave my car there and get into a police car to go to the police station, where I was breathalysed again. I was charged with drink driving and had to go to court. This was my first driving offence in over thirty years driving. The person before me in court had been charged with speeding and he wanted to argue with the magistrate. I had no argument. I was in the wrong and that was that. The magistrate let me off: no fine, no disqualification, no bond. I haven't been back to court since.

I realised that I had let my despondency about work lead me to drink excessively. After that, I was more disciplined about focusing on my goal of becoming a contractor, and more content. Another incident that occurred before this was also confronting, but not in a galling way. One of my twin sons was living at home at the time. When I came home after work, we would often discuss things that had happened during the day. And I would tell him some of the awful things that were happening at work.

One day, I had told him about another incident, and how much I didn't like my workplace, when he retorted, "Dad, if you don't like it, leave. Don't keep whining about it." And I thought, laughingly, "Well, there is wisdom in that!" I had to stop complaining about it. Or, as one of the commentators of the I Ching puts it: "Do not lament your troubles." It was very good advice.

56 Visiting Greenacre

After the time it took me to make the transition to being a contractor, I settled in happily. At home I had a double garage – two separate spaces. The owner before me had been a stained-glass craftsman, and the space that was not the garage was his workshop. At first, I fixed it up as a living space, and it was used as sleeping quarters for whichever of my children was staying with me/us. Each of the twins spent some time there. After that, slowly it became an office and library. So, when I began life as a contractor, it was my office. It had the pleasant characteristic of being very large. I had the luxury of space!

The study/office/library is the same size as the temporary dwelling that our whole family lived in for five years after we first moved to Greenacre (mother, father and three children). That was a single large room with a kitchen at one end. On the side was an unlined bathroom and laundry. The toilet was down the end of a pathway (the pathway had the luxury of being concrete!).

When I moved to Sydney, I thought that I should visit Greenacre one day. It took me several years before I did so. I drove down the street, slowly realising that I did not recognise anything, not a single house. In the intervening years, the modest suburb had been built upon and built upon. The 1950s houses had been reclad and had a second storey added, or they had been demolished entirely and replaced with a two-storey modern edifice. I suppose it is an architectural style with a name: "Modern Sydney" perhaps.

The next time I rang my mother, who was now living in Ballina, I said I had visited our old home, and it was all different. Our house was gone. She laughed. She said the family that bought it had demolished the temporary dwelling, then moved our house back onto that space, and built a new house in front of it.

What was interesting about my visit was that, when I looked at the space where our house had been, and it was gone, I felt okay. It wasn't really relief, that wasn't the right word. It wasn't as if I had been mistreated there, and I wouldn't want to imply that, but I felt quite okay that it was now all gone. That part of my life was over, finished. I had moved on to new things, and none of that life needed to be repeated or perpetuated.

I hadn't expected that feeling. It was a surprise. So, then I had to think about that too! I think it is about a distinction between things that are worth preserving, and things that just served their purpose for a time and can now be let go. It is the central question in preserving history. Some people want to preserve everything; some people want to preserve nothing. I haven't articulated the rules for this, but I know what my preferences are. There was that house I looked at before we bought Horseshoe Creek that I just wanted to bulldoze, but the Horseshoe Creek house, built 1935, I loved. Likewise, the house I currently live in was built, I think, in about 1920, and I love it, imperfect as it is.

57 Maturity

The other important thing about my office was that it was separate from the house. I think it is so important for your workspace to be separate from your home. You have to be able to leave work! I loved walking to my office each morning, through the garden. I never set up tea-making facilities there, because when I wanted a cup of tea, I walked home, all twenty steps of it.

Another benefit of being a contractor was that I could take on other work. It also meant that I was more disciplined about the time I spent on my CCH publications. But also, I was quite experienced and knowledgeable by now, and I was interested in seeing how that manifested. My systems and routines were more refined. Also, being in my library meant I was always close to reference material. Since I had come to Sydney, I had started building my library. I built lots of shelving, and I made all the shelves the same height – 330 mm tall, so that all my books could be categorised by topic rather than being messed up by some books not being able to fit on the right shelf.

I think my experience manifested in being able to work faster. I knew the employment law material and its context very well, and I was up to date. If I was revising a given piece of commentary, I was quick to see what was needed, and I knew how to write what was appropriate. I think it also helped that I had been part of a very experienced team of writers for several years. In many ways we were seamless. We were the ones who had decided that this was where we wanted to be, and we grew into that. I think we were an example of what Daniel Goleman was trying to describe in his book, *Social Intelligence*. I think it was why we were able to write commentary that was so cohesive despite the fact that there was no template written down about what it should contain or how it should be expressed.

In my first year of being a contractor, I did a huge amount of work. As well as writing regular reports (that is, updating commentary) for five CCH services, I wrote commentary for several other HR services, and wrote training courses for several online courses on compliance topics (equal opportunity, sexual harassment, work health and safety). I also wrote material for several other companies, including one in Hong Kong. And I edited two books for other authors and attended several conferences.

It sounds like this must have been exhausting but, to point to the I Ching again, the situation that is really exhausting is when you are trapped in a confining environment. For the hexagram Exhaustion (47), it uses the image of the bonsai tree, trapped in a confining container and unable to expand into its fullness. (True, there are other, aesthetic perceptions of bonsai, but this one is intuitively salient.) I felt that I had been released, and I was spreading my wings.

I could say that hexagram 63 applies at this point. It is After Completion. But then too, the end of every cycle sees the beginning of another. Sixty-three leads to sixty-four: Before Completion. The order is deliberate.

Glenn, aged two, Punchbowl (and cat)

Home: "Temporary dwelling", Greenacre, 1954

Glenn, about June 1973, at home from hospital, in plaster

Identity photo as psychiatric nurse, Parramatta Psychiatric Centre, 1974

Glenn in Mackay, 1975 – shelling peas, with first daughter

Garden at Wyndham Creek, 1977

One of Glenn's five prizes for vegetables at Kyogle Agricultural Show, 1977

Glenn enjoying Horseshoe Creek swimming hole, 1979

Glenn with other students from bonsai class, Community Education Kyogle, 1982

Glenn with students in technics class, St Mary's High School, Casino, 1983

Visit of Governor of New South Wales, Sir David Martin (no relation) to Casino Branch of Challenge Foundation, November 1989. Pictured with client, Mary Tolle, Governor's wife, and Glenn Martin, General Manager.

Glenn receiving his BBus(Hons) degree from Chancellor of Southern Cross University, 1997, and wearing University Medal

Glenn at Horseshoe Creek, beardless

Glenn in Hong Kong, 2006

Glenn and CCH sub-editors at statue of Hanuman, Kuala Lumpur

Glenn speaking at Woodford Folk Festival, December 2006

Fire ceremony at Woodford Folk Festival, 1 January 2006

Echidna at Gumnut Place, Cherrybrook, October 2008

Glenn speaking at family celebration for *The Ten Thousand Things*, Fagan Park, Galston, 2011. Grandson sharing stage.

Book launch for *The Ten Thousand Things*, Gleebooks, Glebe, 2011

Tane Mahuta, "lord of the forest", kauri tree, Waipoua Forest, New Zealand, 2011

Glenn and friends at book launch for *The Search for Edward Lewis*, 1 February 2019

A view of Glenn's library

58 Concerts

One of the bonuses of coming back to Sydney was being able to go to concerts. I had not thought of that. While I was living in Horseshoe Creek I went to a few concerts, but not many. If a big artist was coming to Australia, sometimes a bus ran from Casino and Kyogle up to Brisbane, and they sold packaged tickets: bus plus concert. That way I saw Dire Straits with Mark Knopfler. It was at the QEII Stadium, standing in the middle of the ground. It was both the loudest and the clearest music I had ever heard. The set included "Telegraph Road", all fifteen minutes of it (I wrote about "Telegraph Road" in my book, *Future*), and "Private Investigations", where the middle is almost silent and then there is the tremendous thump of the bass.

Some people don't like Mark Knopfler, because he is not demonstrative, like, say, Mick Jagger. He just stands up there at the microphone and performs the songs. But I just want him to perform the songs, and I think he is present in every note he plays on the guitar. So that was a good night. And then the bus brings you back, and you end up getting home to bed about four a.m. in the morning.

The other act I remember seeing in Brisbane was Genesis. This was in the days when Phil Collins was becoming famous as a separate act, but this tour belonged to the band, Genesis. It was in a concert hall, but I don't know the names of concert halls in Brisbane. I remember that the music was wonderful, but also, I remember that this was the first concert I saw where the light show was something in itself. I had never seen anything like that. I was dazzled.

On another trip to Brisbane, I remember something else I saw. We were going past a theatre, and on the side of the building, in huge letters, was the name "Sarah McLaughlin". I had never heard of this person, but I thought, "The letters of her name are so big! I wonder who she is." And there was no reason to remember the name of someone I had never heard of. Yet I did. It was years later, after I came to Sydney, that I came across her music, and liked it. And it was years later again that she came to Sydney and I went to see her in concert, and it was quite special.

The first concert I went to see in Sydney was Sebastian Hardie. I was driving to work one day when I saw a poster on some telegraph poles. It was surreal. Sebastian Hardie had been a band in Sydney in the early 1970s. They only had one album: "Four Moments". It was in four movements, like a symphony. Some people who played rock music were incredibly talented. Sebastian Hardie had this symphony that was beautiful and also really moving: "For a moment it will hold you, for a moment it will hurt you". And then they were gone, just like Tully.

So, seeing their name on a telegraph pole in 2003 was surreal. The concert was at the Metro, in George Street, Sydney. They performed the album, and a few other numbers, and I was as enchanted as I ever was with their music. However, the highlight came later. I began to pay attention to the advertisements for concerts in the *Sydney Morning Herald*. At that time, that was the primary way that concerts were advertised. It is bizarre to talk about this as history, as something that is no longer true, because all the advertising for concerts is now online and by email.

Ticketek announced that the band Yes were touring in September 2003. This was significant because, while I had seen numerous bands in Sydney when I was young, Yes came out in 1973, and that was the year I was in hospital. I did not get to see them. The closest I got was that some friends came into hospital to see me, and told me how wonderful the concert was. So, now, after all these years, I was going to get to see them.

To make it better, the combination of the touring band was the one that was the best, in my opinion. Yes was one of those extraordinary bands that kept going through multiple changes of personnel, and people left and came back. There were around twenty people in all who had played in the band for a period of time. But this concert was to be Jon Anderson, Steve Howe, Chris Squire, Alan White and Rick Wakeman, the ones who had released "Fragile", "Close to the Edge" and "Tales from Topographic Oceans".

This is where Sebastian Hardie comes back in. They were the introductory act. Wow! (I know: superlatives.) I had a seat in the second row, up close. I figured that most people would not know who they were. What did they do? They came onstage and played all of "Four Moments", the whole album. That was their entire act. And after it, the man sitting next to me exclaimed, "Wow! What the hell was that!?" As well he might. It was stunning.

No matter. The Yes concert that followed was just as amazing. It made up for missing out on seeing them all those years ago. This and one other amazing concert sparked off a period of time when I saw all of the artists and bands I had loved in my early twenties. It was as if they had all dried out from the drugs, got their lives and their health back together, and went back on the road to show just how good their music had been and still was. It was something for which I feel truly blessed.

Things I know

What is lost? Nothing is truly lost. In the blink of an eye it can be restored.

59 Santana

The "one other amazing concert" was Santana. One concert I did see in 1973 was Santana. I was out of hospital, between operations and still on crutches, and my brother took me to see him. It was exhilarating. I remember that, at the end, we all thought the show was over, and were on our feet making for the exits when he reappeared on stage and performed for another twenty minutes.

There I was, standing and hanging onto my crutches, and happy to stand there unmoving for twenty extra minutes of bliss.

This time, March 2003, thirty years later, Santana was playing out in the open, in Centennial Park. My youngest son (aged eighteen) came with me and we went by public transport – train and bus. It was a big band onstage, about ten of them, with lots of rhythm. The journalist who reviewed the concert in the *Sydney Morning Herald* described the guitar-playing as "coruscating", which is a word you save for special occasions such as this. The journalist complained that at times the rhythm section was a bit too dense and it threatened to submerge Carlos Santana in its midst.

My son and I agreed with that assessment, but I was also mindful that Santana never stood alone. He was always part of a throng and he encouraged a sense of community. That was reinforced when he brought Yothu Yindi, the Aboriginal group that was popular for the song, "Treaty", back onstage to perform a song together.

After the concert, we attempted to get a bus back to Central Station, but thousands of other people had the same idea. We decided to walk. Walking down Oxford Street in Paddington at 11:30 at night, we came across a bookshop that was still open – Berkelouws. Neither of us had seen such a thing before, so we went in. There was a café in there as well, and plenty of people. It was lively. So, that can happen too.

Perhaps I should explain why I am able to quote from a newspaper review of the Santana concert in 2003. After I had been to a couple of concerts, and I realised that this was going to be an ongoing phenomenon, I got the idea of having a scrapbook with all my concert tickets in it, and the advertisements for the concerts. It is a childish thing, I suppose, but what a delight! And yes, it was certainly an ongoing phenomenon. Within a year I had been to see Bonnie Raitt, Brian Cadd, Fleetwood Mac, Jackson Browne and Deep Purple.

In December 2004, I went to see the Finn Brothers (Neil and Tim Finn from Split Enz and Crowded House) at the State Theatre. That evening I had been to a Christmas cocktail event for the Australian Human Resources Institute, so I arrived a minute or two after the first artist had come on stage. I hadn't known who the support act was going to be, but I recognised who it was. It was Missy Higgins, who was very young and who had only just started to become known. She had been discovered on the Triple J radio station's Unearthed competition, and she had just released her first album, "The Sound of White". Walking in at that moment, into the beautiful State Theatre, I felt this was a huge bonus and a great privilege. Missy Higgins was sweet and unassuming, and I loved her songs.

Missy Higgins also made me realise that there was still good music being made. While I was living at Horseshoe Creek, I was prepared to believe that there was no decent music made after the 1970s (apart from Dire Straits and Genesis).

My scrapbook filled up over a period of a few years. I saw R.E.M., Nora Jones, The Moody Blues, Jethro Tull, Carole King, Eric Clapton. I saw John Williamson at the Dural Country Club. I saw Anoushka Shankar playing along with her father Ravi Shankar, at the Sydney Opera House in 2008. Ravi was eighty-eight, and he died in 2012. It may sound tiresome to say it was a privilege, but that was how I felt. He had played at Woodstock in 1969. He had played a leading part in bringing Indian music to the West. He had brought a new sensibility about music into our lives.

Anoushka Shankar was also impressive. Her fingers just danced across the strings, she had a bold sense of drama about her playing, and she was mixing Western sounds with Eastern. I saw her again in Sydney many years later. Several artists I saw more than once, and under different conditions. I saw Jackson Browne play in a band line-up, but another time I saw him play alone. The latter occasion was at the State Theatre. Onstage with him was one piano and seventeen guitars – I counted them.

Jackson Browne was the first major artist I had seen play without a set playlist. After he had performed the first couple of numbers, he asked the audience what they wanted to hear. He said he couldn't guarantee everything, because there were some songs he had not played for several years. So, someone would sing out a song, and he would think about it, and say, "Oh, yeah!" And then he would turn around and look down the row of guitars, to choose the appropriate one for that song.

So, the concert went that way, every bit a live experience, unprecedented and exciting. I understand groups having a playlist, because songs usually require rehearsal, and audiences expect a seamless performance. But, the extreme of this trend is that performances can sound recorded, and then you think you might as well have stayed home and played the CD.

One time I saw a band, when I was still living up north, and it was like that. It was Stan Ridgway at a Byron Bay venue. The band sounded really good: very tight. But, after the band went off stage, the venue put on the band's CD, and it sounded exactly the same. It was a strange thing to do, to put on the band's CD directly after they had played, but it also did them a disservice, because it made them sound as if their whole performance was pre-recorded.

Jackson Browne was definitely not pre-recorded.

I saw Simon and Garfunkel at a huge stadium arena at Homebush. It was called the Acer Arena, but it changes its name every few years. When I went to London in 2018, I went to see the Royal Albert Hall, which was wonderful. It has only ever had one name. It was magic seeing Simon and Garfunkel. Their music arrived when I was in my mid-teens, so it was a very impressionable time. And its magic lasted. The traffic jam afterwards, however, was unfortunate, although, it is kind of special that one concert caused its own traffic jam. It took me two hours to get home, when it would have only taken forty minutes as a clear run.

Enough of the music. I am not a music journalist. I am now up to my fourth scrapbook. Since the digital world took over, I have had to resort to reverse engineering. I copy the images from the advertisements on the computer screen, paste them into a Word file, print them out and paste them into the scrapbook. Sometimes I am able to do that with the ticket as well, but now the tickets are migrating to the mobile phone and it is not always so easy to capture them for the scrapbook.

60 Nashville

One more concert: one of my sons took me to a concert, and it was when tickets could first be sent to a phone. When he showed the tickets to the usher on his phone, her machine didn't work, and she got frustrated. In the end she said, "Just go in. It will be fine." One likes to tell stories about technology when it doesn't work.

Here's the story about that concert. It was at Star Casino in Sydney, so we had to walk past all the poker machines to get to the concert hall. I didn't know who I was going to see. I suppose I could have done some research and found out, but this was a present for my birthday, so I left it as a surprise. The artists were Emmy Lou Harris and Rodney Crowell. I hadn't heard of Rodney Crowell, but I knew that Emmy Lou Harris was a big country star. I hadn't listened to her much, but I am not averse to new experiences.

It was a great concert, but what I remember most about it was the chemistry between them. It was if they were joined at the hip. It was riveting, far above the ordinary. It was a joy to see such magic at play. But there was something else that made it much greater. The night before, I had discovered a new series on Netflix: "Nashville". It was set in Nashville, about a country singer who was past the peak of her fame (Rayna James), in competition with a young rising star who was brash and success-driven (Juliet Barnes). In the mix is Deacon Claybourne, who is Rayna's guitar player and her former lover. In the series, he comes back into her life. Onstage (there was plenty of music in the series), they lit each other up.

I was so taken by the series that I watched the first three episodes that night: most unlike me. At the Emmy Lou Harris concert, it was as if I was watching the "Nashville" series playing out in front of me. Seeing the synergy between these two stars was like seeing Rayna James and Deacon Claybourne in real life. I don't know what the relationship was between Emmy Lou Harris and Rodney Crowell, but certainly they related to each other onstage the way Rayna James and Deacon Claybourne acted in the "Nashville" series.

I won't promise that there will be no more music stories.

61 Memoir

I have said elsewhere that I resist the term "memoir". For me it conjures up images of an ex-colonel with a suitably impressive moustache, reclining in his spacious and luxurious library, and regaling the reader with tales of his heroic feats in the field of battle. It reeks of self-importance and self-absolution. He never did anything that was imperfect. To distinguish myself, I no longer wear the moustache I had when I was known as Ned Flanders. I would not like my life to be seen merely as a series of battles. I was seldom in a leadership position, and the older I get, the less inclined I am to allow myself to occupy such a position. And the closest I have got to heroism is to try to stay honest.

This book is a memoir in the sense that it does not coat events and people with a veneer of fiction. It may be somewhat coy in identifying some people, but that is merely because I have no wish to expose them to public view or vilify them. And indeed, they may not be the same people today. Most people learn from their experiences in life; one hopes so.

As a memoir, it is extremely selective. Partly this is because I have written about many events and episodes elsewhere, and I do not wish to commit the sin of repetition (well, only in a limited way). A couple of years ago, I decided that I should create a "book of books". It is a booklet that describes all the books I have written, and it says something about me as a writer. It is called *Glenn Martin: Profile of the Writer's Work*. In that booklet, you can see that I have a stream of books called "reflections on experience". The booklet is available on my website; you can download it as a pdf from https://www.glennmartin.com.au/contact

So far, there are five of the books called "reflections on experience". To quote from the booklet: "they are mostly told from a first-person point of view, and they are more or less autobiographical, but they are also a stepping stone to meditations on the meaning of events and the values by which one should live. Robert Pirsig's *Zen and the Art of Motorcycle Maintenance* would be a reasonable parallel. (Pirsig's books have been described as philosophical novels.) David Whyte is another touchstone (*Crossing the Unknown Sea*)" (p. 8).

In 2012, I tackled the question of why I had left Sydney as a young man, and why I eventually came back, around twenty-three years later. The book was called *To the Bush and Back to Business*. On the back cover, I said:

> "A young man who should have found a corporate ladder somewhere and climbed up it, turns his back instead and goes off into the bush. Years later he comes back to the city that he left. In this book he rakes over the ground: the search for a viable livelihood living close to the earth, the search for an alternative community. He asks himself, was the questing anything more than loss and failure? What do those young-man dreams look like now? And what does business look like?
>
> "This is personal archaeology, not a work of tidy history. The only records he has to call upon are a stack

of papers, folders and exercise books in a box. We have to glean the history from what comes out of the box – poems, short stories and notes on scraps of paper that ignite memories. This is archaeology that brings us face to face with ideals and desire, loss and hard circumstance, and passions that endure."

I had been back in Sydney for over a decade. Was it enough to have erased any memories of the bush? No, but it was enough time to consider whether I had gained any perspective on that part of my life. The result is not a treatise. It is more poetry than proposition. The covers of the book tell their own story.

I design my own covers. I am not a designer, but if I am going to publish my own books, then part of the enjoyment of that is to determine what the books will look like.

My house in Horseshoe Creek was in a valley, towards the end of the valley, with just the creek and a dirt road through it. It was a narrow valley, heavily treed, so that in winter, the sun did not come up until about eight a.m., and it disappeared over the hills by about four p.m.. We had lots of birds. One year I decided to track the types, and I had noted sixty-two different birds at the end of twelve months.

One of the birds was the Red-Tailed Black Cockatoo. Mostly they would come around when the weather was going to turn wet. When you could smell the rain in the air, they would turn up in the trees near the house and cry their distinctive cry. Usually, they were in packs of around six, in pairs. Their habitat was northern Australia, so I didn't see them again after I came back to Sydney. (You can look at the map in Simpson and Day's *Field Guide to the Birds of Australia*.)

However, the environment is changing, the climate is changing, and so are the habitats of birds. Just after I finished writing the book, I heard that distinctive cry, and when I went outside, a flock of six was sitting up in a tree in the yard. Fortunately, it is a deciduous tree and it was winter, so I managed to get a photo that showed them in silhouette perching there, contrary to the admonitions of Simpson and Day's authoritative guide.

I used that photo on the back cover, and then used it again in negative form on the whole cover. It seemed to be an apt comment on what I was wrestling with when I wrote the book.

That was my bravest book so far, because it crossed the boundary between prose and poetry. It wasn't a business decision; it was an inspiration! I decided to open up the writing box which contained all my scraps of writing going back to when I was about ten. Once I had started using poems in the book, I would be writing a passage and the words of a poem would come to me, something I had written, maybe twenty years ago or more. It was all still living in my head.

The other initiative of this book was to have some short stories at the end of the book. This was not unprecedented. I had read Hermann Hesse's book, *The Glass Bead Game*, and he had several short stories at the end of that. They were Joseph Knecht's posthumous writings: "The Rainmaker", "The Father Confessor" and "The Indian Life".

I thought, if he can do it, so can I! My stories were all written when I was living at Horseshoe Creek, and they represented that time for me. My stories were: "Prevailing Myths", "Rambril's Story" and "Yunwin". "Yunwin" is a favourite with me. I showed it to someone once, and she said, "I love it, but there must be more. Where is it?" But I have not (yet) written anymore of Yunwin's story.

Now that I have the thought, I might put some stories at the end of this book. Yes, there have been more stories since Horseshoe Creek.

Perhaps I should note that I have only had book launches for a few of my books. After *The Ten Thousand Things*, it was a long time, until 2019, when I had another book launch.

The year after *To the Bush and Back to Business*, I wrote another book of "reflections on experience". I would say I was continuing my train of thought. This book was called *The Big Story*

Falls Apart. I wrote a description of it when I assigned an ISBN to the book. The National Library of Australia gives you several hundreds of words as a limit, so I used them:

> The big story is the story that sits behind all our other stories. It is the story that provides the stable context for our lives. The author describes, in first-person perspective, what it means when the big story falls apart. He grew up in the 1960s, so there were plenty of socially based reasons for feeling that all the certainties were crumbling. And there were personal reasons too. An inability to even choose a career.
>
> Part 1 is The Disintegration. It finds the author leaving the city. Fleeing. But he finds a place to settle, in a valley that has walls of refuge. It is a place of retreat. It is good enough. He is telling this story as it happened, that memory returns to him after so long.
>
> He gives up books, he takes up gardening. He never stops thinking about the big story. But he ventures back in to a town, to a job, a tumultuous job that required him to learn the art of war. Books come back in, and music. Eventually there is a return to the city, wondering if it will be different.
>
> Part 2 is The Renewing. He says he is on a campaign to find the roots of the world tree. Writing about human resources and training in the day time, finding peace and joy in music. But he knows what he is finding in the stories, when his experiences turn into story. It is love, and morals. And some of the stories are in song.
>
> Part 3 is Onward. The author has to come back to the present, but he is called away again by Mu, the chanter who has been here before. Mu's desire is to dance at the music festival, and we think he intends to stay, but he comes and is gone, with just a nod to the tawny frogmouth sitting in the tree.

Part 4 is Reframing. The author is older. He is making principles. Now he knows that heaven and earth are working together. At the end, the story goes on. The energy flows in all directions.

Now I think that this book is an extraordinary stream of thought. It remains dear to me.

Things I know

You have to be content before you do anything. You have to **be** content before you **do** anything. It doesn't work the other way round. This is usually a hard lesson to learn.

62 Attempted PhD

It was 2013 when I published *The Big Story Falls Apart*. It was the fourth time I had used the NanoWrimo framework for writing. The framework meant that I wrote consistently, just about every day for a month, and then I had a draft to work with. I came back to NanoWrimo in 2016, and the topic this time was family history.

In the meantime, there had been many changes in my working arrangements. I won't attempt to describe all of them, but I could try skipping over the surface of some of them. In 2011 it was suggested to me that I should enrol to study for a PhD. I had veered away from this before, but now I had completed and released the Human Values and Ethics book, so perhaps I could build on this. I was accepted at a university in Sydney.

There were warning signs. One suggestion made by a supervisor was that I should look around at completed PhDs and choose something that I could relate to. Then I should replicate it. For example, if the subjects used to gather data wore blue shirts, I should do essentially the same study, but with subjects who wore white shirts. Or brown. This told me that the emphasis for the PhD must be on data, not ideas. Oh dear!

I gave a copy of my ethics book to another supervisor. I don't know if she ever read it, or even opened it, but she did tell me to just forget everything I had ever thought about ethics and start clean. But I don't subscribe to the "blank slate" theory. And besides, wouldn't it be better to build a vehicle for testing the ideas in my book?

So, it was not a good start. I said I did not wish to focus on quantitative methods; my approach would be qualitative. There was no blank refusal of this, but I could feel the frown. Qualitative methods were obviously alien. The months went by. I wrote some preparatory papers to draft out my direction. A response to one of these evaded mentioning the content and merely said, "You've got a lot of references." I could tell by the tone that it was a criticism.

What did that mean? For a start, I didn't think that was possible. I may have had a lot of ideas in my head, and perhaps a fault lies in that. However, I wasn't feeling any "simpatico" with the folks, and there didn't seem to be any attempt on their part to come to terms with me. I have discussed this with PhD supervisors from other universities, and I think this is definitely part of the truth.

Things came to a head eventually when I was summoned to a meeting with the head of the school. He requested that I give an account of my progress – my ideas and my plans. I prepared a document, which I submitted to him ahead of time. At the meeting, I spoke for about twenty minutes, going through the material, which I was able to do without reading from my notes. I knew it and I understood it. At the end of it, he had no comment. None. The only thing he said was, "I didn't see a schedule in here with dates on it."

That was enough for me. I was out, as of that moment. I said, "I'm done here" and walked out. I resigned from the program and I do not have a PhD. I have come to think that that is okay. I can still say, proudly, that *Human Values and Ethics in the Workplace* is my substitute for a PhD. In 2021, I had a paper published in an academic book, presenting my ideas about what should be taught in business ethics courses. The citation is:

> Martin, G 2021, Rethinking the content of ethics education courses, *Research in Ethical Issues in Organizations*, vol. 24: Educating for ethical survival, pp. 139-145.

I have had more than ten papers published in academic journals, mostly on business ethics. I could say that I am more of a writer than an academic, to be facetious. I have written over fifteen books and I have five volumes of poetry in addition.

Would I be "further along the track" if I had done the PhD? Well, I might, but then again, not necessarily. In 2019, I wrote a book called *A Foundation for Living Ethically*. I structured it as a conversation between two people, question-and-answer style, addressing fundamental questions in ethics. It was intended for "ordinary mortals".

In September 2019 I attended a workshop in Sydney conducted by Nora Bateson, on "Working in the Liminal Zone", about conducting Warm Data Laboratories. No, I won't explain that – it dealt with complexity theory – but it was a rich and rewarding experience. I invited people there to be "early readers" – to take a copy of the draft ethics book and review it for me. I ended up with around a dozen volunteers. I received a generous amount of feedback in many forms. As a result of the feedback, I reworked the book heavily, adding and subtracting content, reordering it, and rewriting many sections.

On the back cover of the final version, I said, "In this book you will find a plausible foundation for living an ethical life, based on five core human values. It begins with the simple idea of ethics as having regard for the well-being of others." Here are some of the comments from my "early readers":

> "I think you have done an amazing job. I liked the Q-and-A conversation format and the short chapters. It made it easier to understand and to see the

critique/teasing out of the implications of the ideas. It covers a lot of ground and doesn't get bogged down in detail or in stodgy explanations of impenetrable philosophers."

"The questions the book asks are really powerful, linking ethics and values. It is a guide for an ethical life. I like the idea of a conversation."

"You have clearly put a lot of deep thought, care and study into your creation. The way you have structured the book—as a conversation between, say, an ethicist and a student—is likely to draw many readers to your work."

I think that if you don't sort out what you think about ethics, you are subject to any temptations and pressures that come along, and you will have no good reason to resist. Unless you can stand upright, and know why you are doing so, you might as well join the scramble for popularity, power and material success. But your victories will most likely be transient, and make you poorer personally.

63 Family history

When I last checked, I was about to talk about family history: "I came back to NanoWrimo in 2016, and the topic this time was family history." For the sake of context (because I said this in my 2016 NanoWrimo exploit), I started exploring family history because I was at my mother's ninetieth birthday lunch (November 2013) and some of my cousins were there, and I realised I could not with certainty name all of her siblings. For my father, who had died in 1967, it was even more uncertain. And I felt that I should know at least this much for certain.

I was also aware that I knew almost nothing about my mother's parents, and nothing at all about my father's parents. And there was the suggestion that my mother knew things that she had not told me, and didn't want to tell anyone. Whilst I respected her feelings, I also felt that it would be good to know about my ancestors, even if it proved to be uncomfortable.

By the time it got to November 2016, I had learned quite a bit. But it was just a station along the road. I had filled in many facts about my parents' parents, but there were still significant gaps that I discovered the truth about later. I suppose that I now have a history of my family history! My first family tree chart was in a template in an Excel spreadsheet, and it dates from February 2014. Later I moved to My Heritage, online.

In the spreadsheet, my mother's parents are correctly listed, with their correct dates of birth and death. I noted there that my mother's mother, Margaret Florence Mackie, was born in Richmond, Victoria. I hadn't known that. I thought both my parents' families had come from the inner suburbs of Sydney, for a long way back. So, there was a story there about Victoria that I didn't yet know.

My father's parents were even more surprising. Yes, his mother was born in the inner suburbs of Sydney, Balmain, but his father was born in some place in northern Victoria called Bethanga. They used to mine gold there. His father died in Lidcombe Hospital in 1955. I had thought he died before I was born. The spreadsheet says his mother died in 1956, and she was buried at Woronora. This is just wrong; I thought I had found her, but it turned out to be someone else.

Needless to say, I had hunted down most of this information myself. My mother had shown me the certificates she had, for example, my father's death certificate. But some information she either did not know, or was not willing to talk about. She was not too resistant to my engaging in the exploration, however.

The Excel spreadsheet goes back as far as my great grandparents, so I knew that my father's father's parents were Thomas Martin, born in Cornwall in 1856, and Philippa Dower, born at The Murray in South Australia (SA) in 1852, although it notes that her birth could also have been at Moomba (SA) in 1859. I knew that my father's mother's parents were Edwin Eaglestone, born 1858 in Oxford, England, and he was a stonemason, and Ellen Elizabeth Lewis, and she was born in 1859 in Sydney (later, I found out that she was not; she was born in Launceston, Tasmania).

On my mother's side, I knew her father's parents were James Archer, born 1858 at Newcastle (he was born at Fullerton Cove; Newcastle was just where the birth was registered) and Alice Neil, born 1862 but I did not know where. I had not yet found James's father, who had been a convict. Alice was born in Sydney, but her parents were Irish.

My mother's mother's parents were George Briggs Mackie and Frances Emily Bulling. I had trouble finding George's birth; I thought it was around 1861. Frances was born in Ballarat in 1865. I thought they got married at Linton, Victoria in 1882. The year turned out to be correct, but it was in Fitzroy, Melbourne. George was born in 1863, I found out later, and probably in Ballarat (there is no birth certificate).

Once I got serious about the quest, I began to purchase certificates of births, deaths and marriages. I now have hundreds. The world of family history online is rife with cheerful conjecture, and I wanted a solid foundation of facts. When I had a good few steps under my feet on this journey, I thought it would be interesting to write about the journey. My NanoWrimo feat came to be a book called *A Modest Quest*.

The chapter headings provide an idea of where I was going:
1. The beginning
2. Rabbit holes and my parents' siblings
3. Certificates, cemeteries and the discovery
4. My mother's home breaks up
5. My father's home breaks up
6. The second horizon
7. Where do occupations come from?
8. Bethanga, Victoria

My family history quest had different stages. At first it was about trying to get my bearings and establish some starting points. After a while it came to be about acquiring certificates, which were not only useful in giving dates and places for events, but they also gave names to parents so I could start the next phase. Once I had a goodly pile of names and places, I started to focus on details of burials. I wanted to be able to visit cemeteries and discover things there that I could not otherwise learn.

You might think that gravestones will not tell you more than a death certificate, but that is not always so. At Woronora, I found the grave of Thomas and Philippa Martin (died 1945 and 1931 respectively). They had eleven children, some of whom died in the Bethanga area, and some in Sydney. It is a large double grave. As well as containing them, it contains two of their children: Norman and William Thomas. The latter is my grandfather.

William Thomas and his wife had seven children. Why does he show up here? One would expect that of a child who died without having a family of their own. In Norman's case, he was married, but his wife died after him and she was cremated; she has a plaque in a wall at Woronora. In William Thomas's case, it left me puzzled. When I purchased his death certificate, I found that it described his marital status as "married". The significance of this was that it meant his wife was still alive in 1955. I had not known that until then.

And so the story goes. I ended the book with the story of Thomas Martin's life, my great great grandfather, 1834 to 1904, for two reasons: (a) I had only recently discovered the story, (b) it was an uplifting story. Thomas Martin (born 1856) had come out from Cornwall as a young child. My great discovery was that he had been the manager of a gold mine at Bethanga for twenty-five years, and he had worked out the process to extract gold from quartz economically. He was obviously much loved in the local community.

What was happening now was that I was finding context for the people I had located as a dry set of facts: births, marriages, deaths, places, dates. I now had a growing history and I was part of it; I was connected. I had ancestors. Also, the book had illustrated the irony of its title: a modest quest. It was clear that the story would keep going, and unearth new treasures. Six years later, this has proven to be very true.

The following year, 2017, I felt bold enough to tackle a book on the journeys of all my direct ancestors to Australia. I called it *They Went to Australia*. I used the following quote in this book: "The history of our family is part of us, and when we hear any secret revealed, our lives are made suddenly clearer to us." This was from *A Chorus of Stones* (1992) by Susan Griffin. I still feel the truth of that quote, every time a door opens up into another part of the family tree.

64 Travel to Asia

Have I travelled? The first answer is "No". I grew up in Sydney; I lived in Mackay for less than two years, I lived in Kyogle for over twenty years, and moved back to Sydney. I had travelled within Australia, as far as Melbourne, Adelaide and Hobart. All of my children have travelled further and wider: England, France, Ireland, Venezuela, South Africa, United States of America, and some other countries I've forgotten. Oh, and my children's partners include people from New Zealand, Zimbabwe, Italy and Argentina.

My children (and other people) encouraged me to travel. I thought about it. At a certain point (2006) I realised there was no reason not to. But where would I go? Once I asked this question, there was a multitude of possibilities. I thought I would go somewhere that wasn't as far as England. Remember, too, that as yet I had no family history reasons to travel. I thought I could go to somewhere in Asia, not for too long, and the condition was that I had to know someone in the countries I was going to.

Fortunately, there were possibilities. Because CCH had outsourced their sub-editing to Malaysia, there were people there that I worked with regularly online. They did the sub-editing on my commentary. They were based in Kuala Lumpur. I could meet up with them. I didn't need to be dependent; I just needed to know that someone was around that I could meet up with.

I also thought about language. My facility with foreign languages is non-existent. However, this was my first visit, and I thought I would mainly visit cities, so I thought I could probably survive with my sole language, English.

I thought it would be nice to visit Hong Kong. Fortunately, a colleague at CCH had left the company and gone to Hong Kong, where he got a job as an editor, then manager, with a British company that produced similar types of publications for professionals. He would be willing to meet me and talk about life in Hong Kong. And, another colleague had left to work in Hanoi with Volunteers Abroad. She was sharing an apartment with two others, and there was a spare room I could use.

Again, I didn't think my lack of language would be too much of a barrier. In Vietnam in particular, people wanted to practise their English. I had one language-based experience when I was walking around Hue, a city in the mountains of Vietnam. I loved it there, but it was an unusual time. A typhoon had been through the city a few days before I arrived, and lots of trees had been blown down, and many places were still covered with water.

I was walking through an outskirts village where the water was still receding from the streets when I came across an elderly gentleman, dressed in clothing best described as flowing, just like his hair and beard. He was sweeping the water off the tiled front steps of his house.

He spoke to me in French, which I had learned many years ago at school and not used since. He asked me, in French, if I spoke French. This was unexpected, but lo, I had an answer: "Je ne parle pas Francois!" (I do not speak French.) We both laughed, and then he said a few things in halting English. I had exhausted my stored hoard of the French language.

My travels lasted for around two weeks. This was, after all, my first trip overseas. If it worked out alright, I could do it again. And yes, I did catch up with my colleagues in each place. It was warm and friendly. The interesting thing about the sub-editors was that there were three groupings of them: Indian, Chinese and Malaysian. Among the sub-editors with whom I had worked, there was one of each. Each of them wanted to show me an aspect of Kuala Lumpur that was traditional for them. Accordingly, I went to an Indian restaurant, a Chinese restaurant, and a temple with a golden statue twenty metres high.

At the temple, which was maybe twenty kilometres out of town, there was a long staircase up the mountain to a cave. On the way up the stairs, we stopped for a rest and to take photos. The lady put down her purse for a moment. Instantly, one of the many monkeys scampering around raced over to it and pulled out a packet of headache tablets and started opening the packet and scoffing the pills. I don't think he'd read the fine print. I don't know how headache tablets affect monkeys.

The Chinese restaurant was in a restaurant district, a pedestrian mall. It was of simple décor: aluminium chairs and Formica tables. The food was excellent. I had the strange feeling, déjà vu, that I had been there before, in the 1970s. It was a vivid feeling. There was nothing in my own life that I could relate it to. I tried to make sense of it. What was I picking up on? But I just had to accept it as an episode without an explanation.

I had some interesting experiences in Hong Kong. I thought I should be sensible and go on a bus tour for a day, since I was only there for a few days, and I had no idea what I should see. The adverse side of this was that it was mostly a set-up for selling. For example, we were taken to a jewellery factory, and we were encouraged to buy jewellery. Since I was a male, I must have a girlfriend: "You buy ring for girlfriend?" "No girlfriend."

I did catch up with my colleague here. We had dinner at a street cafe. It was lively and fun, and the food was great. When he left CCH in Sydney, he did the obligatory exit interview, and he unleashed and told them what he thought of them. Then he went to Hong Kong, satisfied that he had vented, then left the country. But, about a year later, CCH bought up the Hong Kong company. Oh uh!

It was okay. One of the Sydney managers came to visit. The Sydney manager remembered him, but he couldn't have cared less. Some managers manage to skim easily across the surface of life.

While I was on the bus trip, we came down to a harbour, and there was an enormous floating restaurant on the water. It was about four levels high: the "Jumbo Floating Restaurant". It would have seated hundreds. I had the sensation that this restaurant had been in a book I had read when I was about eleven. At that age I was reading novels of all sorts of different genres, and that novel had been about gangsters in Hong Kong. Part of the action had taken place in a huge floating restaurant, and I had visualised it just like this.

65 Vietnam

When I arrived in Hanoi, at 9:30 in the morning, I had a transfer booked on a car into the city, and the road was downright scary. It was about eleven lanes wide, only there were no lanes. There was just a swarm of traffic, and cars moved to the left and the right at apparent random. I had to tell myself that these people were used to this way of driving, and nobody was setting out to kill or get killed. I did arrive safely.

My colleague from Sydney took me to a restaurant for lunch. It was in the old French quarter, and the house was three stories high. We were on the verandah of the top floor. There were many courses, and the meal took about two hours. I love Vietnamese food.

Most of the streets were narrow, and the cars and motor scooters wove in and out among each other. At first, I needed guidance to cross the road, as I couldn't see how that was possible. It wasn't distinct stop-start traffic lights like Sydney; it was a constant flow. I did realise that everything was moving slowly, and that people were conscious of each other. Gradually it became less scary.

I took a plane flight to Hue, about an hour south of Hanoi, then got a bus down to the coast: Hoi An. This had also been hit by the typhoon, but life had resumed. I ordered a tailor-made suit, getting my measurements taken on the first day, and coming back the next morning to get the final alterations done. It was a nice thing to do, and it was a nice suit. I loved Hoi An; it was an old city, where ships used to come to replenish their fresh water, and it had been a trading port for several hundred years.

I went into a restaurant there one day for lunch. I ate Vietnamese food. When I finished, I decided I wanted dessert. The menu said "Fruit Salad". That was what I wanted. This was not the tourist season, so there weren't many people in the restaurant. I saw the girl who had served me leave the restaurant, and about five minutes later she came back with a bag. A few minutes after that I was served my fruit salad. It consisted of a pineapple cut up, just a pineapple, nothing else.

I thought that was amusing, even though it broke my rule: a fruit salad must consist of at least three different kinds of fruit. But the pineapple did taste excellent, very sweet.

Back in Hanoi, I went to the Temple of Literature. It is maybe a thousand years old. You could call it a precursor to universities, or you could say it was the first university. I went to a concert there, of Vietnamese music, which I enjoyed. I remember seeing statues, but I don't remember seeing books or scrolls. But walking around inside those walls, I saw that this was the high end of a culture.

At this stage, I hadn't had the idea of keeping a diary on a trip. However, I had my first digital camera, a Fuji, one megapixel. I also had an extra memory card. This meant, for the first time, I could virtually take as many photos as I wanted. This was a new concept for me. I decided that I would take my camera out as soon as I arrived somewhere, and take photos before I started thinking about it. In the end, I took around 700 photos.

When I came home, I organised them into a folder for each place. Then, when I was trawling through the photos, it was just like walking down the street. One time in Vietnam in the afternoon, I was walking down a street with my camera out, and school had just come out. Suddenly I was surrounded by a crowd of school-children in uniform, grinning and wanting me to take their photo. My camera had a little screen where you could show the photo once you had taken it. I showed the children; they were delighted. It was most excellent. If I went to Vietnam again, I would learn some Vietnamese words.

66 New Zealand

The next time I went overseas, it was to New Zealand. This time, I went to a conference, at which I was a speaker. This was one of those things that I wanted to able to say I had done – to have spoken at an overseas conference! (Note, I did not say "bucket list", because that expression aggravates me.) The conference was at the Auckland University of Technology. It was the Australasian Business Ethics Network Conference, 2-3 December 2011. My paper was called "Human values: A unifying framework for ethics and spirituality".

I had a tube of toothpaste confiscated at Customs in Sydney. I confess, I was going to hold up the pilot and force him to clean his teeth.

At the conference, they discussed ethics and the business world. I said, "The reality of big business is that executives have power, and it is married to both greed and fear. Between themselves they have camaraderie. They are not at all threatened by an intellectual debate about business ethics, because any problems it raises, they will solve it with Public Relations." People tended to describe this as cynical.

I heard Milton Friedman quoted at the conference as if he were credible. His creed is basically "Greed is good" and "Business people are not responsible for ethics". I talked about Ayn Rand (the novelist and "philosopher", with the book *Atlas Shrugged*) as being the spiritual mentor of the greedy brigade. She and they have the delusion that it is they who make the world work, and that it is necessary for the world to be greedy. People tend to describe my criticism as excessively gloomy.

The conference started with Maori tradition, a haka. It was done with a complete absence of pomp, yet it was powerful and moving. We were all in a room, about fifty people meeting one another, when six lads came in. They all looked to be in their late teens, and they were dressed in ordinary street clothes – jeans and tee-shirts. The facilitator explained why they were there, and invited them to take the floor.

As of that moment they became a performance: the fierce chanting, the foot stamping and hand clapping. It was strong and proud. When they had done, they nodded to the audience and the facilitator thanked them for opening the conference. And the lads went on their way. As I say, it was very moving: they had touched something deep.

67 A new book

2011 was the year when I started the PhD work. I had written *The Little Book of Ethics* that year. Ah, I haven't mentioned that. I wrote it after the big book, *Human Values and Ethics in the Workplace*. The Little Book was little – 100 pages as opposed to 300. I liked it a lot. It looks at ethics through the lens of five core human values: honesty, peace, right action, love and insight (later I changed insight to appreciation). It relates these values to the aims of human life, where ethics is united with meaning and purpose. This was how I saw the link between ethics and spirituality.

The message of the Little Book was the same as my first ethics book, but it left out the effort to establish the business context for ethics, and the effort to place my work within the wider literature of business ethics. It was reduced to the essence of the central concepts, and it was designed more as a self-development tool. My paper got a good reception at the conference, and it was subsequently published in a journal.

This was also the month after I had written my third book as part of National Novel Writing Month. It was *To the Bush and Back to Business*. I took it to New Zealand with me on a new device called a Transformer, which was hinged with a keyboard and screen like a laptop, but small for travelling. While I was waiting at the airport to catch the plane to come home, I finally sat and started reading the manuscript.

I felt that it was coherent. It had a theme, and it pursued that through the experiences it described. I thought that what it had to say about business and ethics was passionate and articulate, and my perspective was unique. I also saw, however, that it was primarily about a person's experience, including the marriage of stories and poems with prose. I asked myself whether I thought it would be successful, but this is a moot point, because I never promoted it.

I am able to say these things because on this trip I kept a diary. I had not done this on my Asian trip; I was intrigued with the digital camera then. This time I bought a forty-eight-page exercise book and wrote in it each day. The forty-eight pages were not enough, and I had to buy another one in Rotorua.

I left Auckland and drove north, in search of trees. I stayed at Hokianga, on the edge of the ocean. The ocean was very mild, but I was told it could get wild. I read a Maori story about the place. The original ancestor Kupe came out of the sea and named everything, bringing it into being. When he grew old, he turned again towards the familiar sea, never to return. He asked the people to keep alive the source of the light. He said that Hokianga was the wellspring of the world of light. And so the songs are sung.

I write to remind myself of the source of the light. Most of my life I have been writing, "Not here, not here, not here." What is it we have forgotten when we were so busy learning the ways of technique, the ways of business, and the ways of money? We do not remember what it is we have lost.

It is the completeness, the ecology, the community, the reverence for earth. "When a society loses its soul, it develops neurotic behaviours." So said Thomas Moore. Lines of my poems keep returning to me: "waves wash to listless lapping foam"; "the birds singing always only clear joy".

While I was in New Zealand I thought a lot about my experience as a writer, the books I had written, and their lack of sales success. But someone had given me a quote earlier in the year: "It's better to write for yourself and have no audience than to write for an audience and have no self."

Things I know
It's better to write for yourself and have no audience than to write for an audience and have no self.

68 Tane Mahuta

I went to see a tree: Tane Mahuta. It is the lord of the forest. I walked along a wooden path for a few minutes, and then I heard some people talking, so I looked towards them. They were looking up at a kauri tree. I wondered if this was it, but it didn't seem so much bigger than the surrounding trees. But then I sensed something behind me, and I looked around, and that was when I saw Tane Mahuta. It was massive, with a girth about four times the girth of any big tree I had seen. It is the biggest tee in New Zealand. I think now of the movie "Avatar" and the massive tree in that movie, that could host an entire community.

Tane Mahuta is about two thousand years old. I thought, perhaps a tree is a mind that thinks about the whole earth. If so, this tree has been thinking about the earth for that long. The day before, I had spoken to a lady who said she had visited this tree fifty years ago. Not far from there, you can walk down a track to the Cathedral Grove. Here, standing on a wooden platform, you look down into the gully and the kauri trees are gathered around, a community of minds standing majestically and silently. Surely this was what J.R.R. Tolkein was inferring in his stories about the Ents in *Lord of the Rings*?

I drove south, heading towards Wellington, from where I would fly home. I went to Rotorua, the place where you can see hot mud spewing out of the ground. I come from Australia. My knowing is that the earth is solid. You can rely on it, unquestioningly. But here, not far from the town, I found the earth oozing and sucking and gurgling, with sulphur steam rising in gusts. And nearby was a duckpond, with ducks being oblivious.

There were dozens of these outlets in the park. Some of them were deep, say, two metres in diameter and two metres deep, and others were shallow. Some were just vents for steam, and one was a pile of rocks that let out steam. When I walked near one, I heard it as well: the sound of steam being forced through long vents inside the ground. That brought it into focus, the weirdness of that muddy steam pouring through the earth beneath my feet, and the sound it made. The smell of sulphur was pervasive.

I saw a geyser that spewed jets of water into the air every so often, about three metres high, and clouds of steam issued forth constantly. Some of the mud pools made ever-moving, overlapping circles of mud. Sometimes you could hardly see what was at the bottom of the holes because the air was so full of steam. It was like a proverbial witches' brew. A group of Japanese ladies with pretty umbrellas came to take photos.

It is a different perception, knowing that the earth is not uniformly solid, but is in parts intensely active. One becomes a sailor upon the earth. Later, when I became a family historian, I learned that the ancestors on my father's side came from Cornwall, and they were miners in the earth. And some on my mother's side came from Fife in Scotland, and even though they lived close to the sea, none of them were sailors or fishermen.

The image of ourselves as sailors upon a shifting earth stayed with me. When I wrote *The Big Story Falls Apart* in December 2012, I used an image of the hot mud belching and steaming up from the earth for the front cover.

69 Napier

I visited Napier, on the east coast. To get there, you have to drive through steep mountains, so my impression of Napier was that it was a place at the end of the mountains. It is an unusual place, because most of it was destroyed in 1931 in an earthquake, and it was rebuilt in the style of Art Nouveau. It was a community decision to do this, so most of the buildings reflect that style and they date from the same time.

While in Napier, I gave an English lesson to a Chinese student. It was impromptu. I was sitting in a Chinese restaurant waiting for my take-away dinner to be prepared when he walked up to me and asked me how to say something in English. It was sweet. But I won't tell the story here. I have included it at the end of this book. It is called "The Language Lesson".

On the way to Wellington, I stopped off at the home of a fellow CCH writer. Some of our products contained New Zealand commentary, and this man was responsible for most of it. I had met him once when he came to Sydney. He had invited me to visit him if I ever came to New Zealand. Curiously, he lived in Martinborough: my name. He lived in a beautiful old home that was built in 1911. It was on one hectare of land, and he was growing grapes: Pinot Gris. We enjoyed a lovely lunch of salmon, salad, bread and cheeses, and white wine. We talked about life, business, and our employer. It was warm, mutually respectful, and enjoyable.

I gave him a copy of *The Little Book of Ethics*, although I suspected he might find it a bit too philosophical, idealistic and spiritual. He was a believer in hard economics and "realism". I wrote in my diary: "It is important for me to find the common ground without losing what is the core of my difference, so as to be able to say what is helpful."

70 Echidna

Occasionally, odd things happen, that have no connection to anything else that is happening, yet they seem to be significant. I live in a suburb that is next to the bush, and the bush links up with a national park. But my house is not too near; it would be a kilometre's walk away from the bush. I live in a very old house, maybe one hundred years old, so I work on it from time to time, fixing things, adding things, changing things.

It was October 2008. I had added an end wall to my back verandah, using weather-boards and including a window. I was pleased with this because it created a sense of space on the verandah – the space was visually contained; the verandah didn't just fall off the end. It also stopped the verandah from being a wind tunnel when it was windy.

Next, I decided it would be nice to have a set of shelves there: fixed shelves. It's nice to have shelves to put things on. So, I made them out of nice wood, some of which I bought, and some of which

I repurposed from a piece of pine furniture that was no longer needed.

I was quite pleased with my shelves, and I varnished them with Estapol, three coats. When it had dried, I put a couple of things on the shelves, because it's nice to put things on shelves. The next day I was sitting in the kitchen when I heard movement on the verandah. It was like small-scale blundering. I had a cat then, and cats don't blunder, so I knew it wasn't the cat.

I came out onto the verandah, and there was the cat, sitting and looking at an echidna. I could understand the cat's amazement. I too was amazed. The echidna was bumbling around, in that swaying, rocking echidna-way. It wasn't bothered by the cat. It needn't have been: the cat had a look on its face that said: "I don't know what that is, but I'm not going anywhere near it!"

The echidna wandered all through my shelves. It was as if it was doing an inspection of my recent work. It had come a long way to do it. From the bush, it would have had to wander past about fifty houses. How was that possible? The cat just sat there, eyes wide.

When the inspection was done, and the echidna apparently approved, it wandered down to the other end of the verandah and round the corner of the house. It wandered all the way to the corner of my yard, where there is a stand of bamboo, and then it lost itself among the bamboo. All of this happened slowly enough for me to go and get my camera, so I have photos.

I checked the next morning, but there was no sign of it. I never saw it again.

When I looked at the face of the echidna, it looked like a wise old man. I wonder how we can have an image of what a wise old man looks like? The eyes are important, and the forehead. There is a timelessness about the face, as if it has seen "long time". There is long time, just as there is deep space.

I told a friend that I had seen an echidna in my backyard. She said it is significant when an echidna appears in your life. I hadn't thought of that, and I looked it up. It symbolises resolving issues and learning from them. The echidna is a gentle creature. It seems relaxed as it goes about its business. However, if threatened, it has the ability to erect the spines on its skin. Protection and self-preservation are the spirit messages of the echidna.

Among native peoples, the echidna symbolises tenacity and curiosity. The echidna demonstrates that being wide open, uncovering new wonders every day, is a positive trait of our personality: a child-like approach to life. Their friendliness and awareness can easily open the hearts of other people.

Perhaps it is necessary to say why I do not regard the idea of totems and spirit messages with scorn and derision. Some would argue that there is no science here; these are simply loose, "general" ideas. May I suggest that, instead of adopting a hard, "scientific" stance, that you examine what comes up and consider what is helpful to you. By that I mean, what is helpful to your growth as an individual. Whether we are a scientist or a lover of poetry, we are here to grow and develop, which is to seek to understand our place in the midst of this complex mystery.

Years later, I remember the visit of the echidna, and its wise old face, and its slow, rocking motion as it ambled through my new shelves, inspecting my work. What I learned: the value of being curious, friendly, aware, and fearless.

So, the correct approach is to ask what is helpful, rather than to demand that something be "true", or "real", or "provable". You will be happier and you will grow more deeply into your better self.

Things I know

Ask what is helpful, not what is "real" because it has been "proven".

71 Going to Woodford

I started this book off following chronology, but, having done this before, I can tell you that themes start to come in, and then you have to learn to be more flexible with time. You can see that already; I have ambled, like an echidna, between 2006, 2011, and 2008. It is now necessary to go back to December 2004, because I think it was a hinge point in my history.

What came before? In October 2004, I obtained a divorce from Lady 3. It was the resolution of an unsatisfactory time. Work as a writer and editor continued amiably. I had received my Master of Education (Online Education) (or, MEd) from the University of Southern Queensland, and I was starting to do some work on online courses. I felt confident about what I was doing; I had achieved a level of competency. But I needed to expand my scope.

Within a week, two people said to me, "You should go to the Woodford Folk Festival. You'd really like it." The Woodford Folk Festival is at Woodford in Queensland. It is only a few hours from Kyogle, so the joke was that I had lived in Kyogle for twenty years and had never been. It was like people who have lived in Sydney all their lives and have never been on the Manly Ferry.

The festival had grown out of the hippie days of the 1970s. After thirty years, it was still going. It had gone from strength to strength, even though there had been difficult years, as I heard. It was odd that two people had said this to me in a week; this had never happened before. But it was like two sudden spring showers on a seed that has already decided that it will burst out of its shell.

Once I had been exhorted the second time, I realised that this would be the year I would go to Woodford for the first time. It meant preparation, because I would camp. I had to acquire camping gear. I had been in the Boy Scouts, so the idea of camping did not daunt me. I talked to people who had been to the festival, and they described the environment to me.

I decided I would camp, but not cook. I would have muesli for breakfast, and the only thing I needed a fire for was to make a cup of green tea in the morning. Otherwise, I would eat at the festival for lunch and dinner. I bought a new tent, and a small gas burner. I took an Eski and some ice; I figured I could buy ice there if I decided I needed the Eski.

I had a friend in Sydney whose mother actually lived at Woodford, and he met me on my first day at the festival. He advised me to take my time, slow down, and just enjoy it. The Woodford Festival is six days long, a long time. He said, "There's plenty of time. And most artists play more than once, so just relax. You won't see everything, but you will see more than enough. And make sure you get to the last night: the Fire Ceremony."

I wandered off. The festival is in a big valley, and there are several venues, from small (say, twenty people) to big (say, 100, 200, 500), then there is the amphitheatre at the end of the valley, where there is room on the surrounding hillside for maybe 30,000 people. There is plenty of food, of any preference, and there are stalls to buy clothes and alternative artefacts. It is beautifully colourful.

It was mid-afternoon, and I found a venue and sat on the hillside rather than inside the tent. It was a Celtic band, sweet and melodic. Before long, I was feeling close to tears. I was unwinding; it was me, unwinding. The music flowed into all the parts of me. It said, "There is sadness, but the love is deeper."

And it was as if that was the secret language of Woodford. Over the next few days, much of the time, especially when I was listening to music, I was close to tears. But also, it was a place where I didn't have to explain it or apologise for it. One felt it. It was as if everyone knew.

There was a lot of humour at Woodford, and also, a lot of outlandish behaviour and dress. In the city, there is also humour and outlandishness, but I always felt on guard about it. One always expected a hook or a trap in it. At Woodford, it seemed that the demons were exorcised, and then comes creativity, and creativity's close companion is humour, along with beauty. Even the names of some of the bands give it away: Monsieur Camembert, Fourplay, Stringmansassy, That1Guy.

If I look at the timeline of my life, I think Woodford was a hinge point to the unfolding of creativity. It was in the years after this that I began writing and publishing books. Even to clarify that this was what I wanted to do and was now determined to do, I think was the fruit of Woodford. All those tears – it wasn't as if it was all sadness, it was seeing and hearing that freedom was possible, was nearby, that brought it on.

I have been to Woodford six times now. I went in December of 2004, 2005, 2006, 2007, 2012 and 2017. Each time it was different. Sometimes it was wet, sometimes it was hot, and the music always had a different flavour. Most importantly, that first Woodford taught me that there was still music being created in the world, and it wasn't just re-presenting music from the 1970s. As if to emphasise this point, Missy Higgins was there, only three weeks after I had seen her at the State Theatre. She came onto the big stage at the amphitheatre one night, sat down at the piano, and played, "All For Believing". Then she walked right out to the edge of the stage and peered into the hillside against the glare of the lights. She said, somewhat in awe: "There are so many of you!"

And it must have been awe-inspiring for her, so young and so freshly in the limelight. But she was much-loved. And I thought, "Yes, there is new music, and it is from the heart, and so it is good."

Next: I remember this as being on my first day. It was towards sundown, Queensland sundown in late December, with no Daylight Saving Time. Still wandering, with no plan, I heard music and walked into a tent. It was strange music: strange rhythms, two violins playing, and a vibraphone; no singing. The audience must have been close to five hundred. There were four musicians on stage, and the music was as if to interrupt and transport. It could have been Eastern European, gypsy, or French. Perhaps. The rhythms were sustained but not dominant. It was the melodies that suggested other places where you could be.

What caught my attention then was an assortment of players dressed up in animal costumes, cavorting around the stage among the musicians, as if this was part of the transporting. This went on for an hour or more. There was no silly laughter. It was not like that. It was kind of serious, but immensely uplifting, as if there were different rules when they played. This was Coda. They usually performed as three or four musicians, but the extras were known as the CODAdependents.

It was quite an introduction to Woodford. After it, I felt unhinged from my customary world. It was dark, and I wandered around looking for a meal. I was stunned, and everything was wonderful.

72 New Year's Day

Woodford again. It was New Year's Day. On New Year's Eve, there are lots of concerts, which go quite late, so New Year's Day, especially in the morning, is relatively quiet. But there are still concerts. I went to see Kangaroo Moon. They were mostly instrumental, very rhythmic. I had heard them before, and I liked them. There was the suggestion that their music was a "type of Australian music", if you were searching for a phrase. That's my phrase. There was a hint of deserts, mountains and vastness in their music.

There were not many people in the tent. After all, it was the morning of New Year's Day. But most of the people were dancing; it was that kind of music. And I watched a lady walk in, quite purposefully, put her bag down, and dance. When she had finished doing that, she picked up her bag again and left. I was in awe, so much so that I wrote it down as a story and called it "Dancing with intent". The story is in the section at the end of this book.

73 I Ching reading

At Woodford, you could meet someone on a pathway somewhere in the valley, between one tent and another, and talk. Or you might be sitting on a hillside and someone would come up to you. And instantly you would be talking about something deeply. Connections were easily made.

One time I was sitting on the hillside near a perplexing bamboo sculpture and a lady walked up. She asked me if it was okay to sit down, and it was. Soon we were talking about the I Ching. Then she said, "Do the I Ching for me." I said, "I can't. I don't have anything with me: no coins, no book."

She didn't think that was a sufficient excuse. I tried again: "I don't have the coins with me." She countered with, "We can just use ordinary coins." I continued to resist: "Ordinary coins are money. It's not appropriate."

"Yes, but the Chinese coins were money too. We can just use ordinary coins."

I was losing. But I couldn't do it. "Listen," I said, "there are sixty-four hexagrams. I don't remember all of them. You could throw a hexagram and then I wouldn't be able to interpret it for you." That's a rather solid argument.

Her answer was, "I'm sure you'll be okay. Let's just do it."

It's laughable, isn't it? There is no common sense at Woodford. Her faith in me seemed to require my faith in the universe. We proceeded.

We found three coins of the same size, decided which was yin and which was yang, and she formulated her question. I said, "Don't tell me the question. Then I can be free with what I say about the hexagram, and you can tell me if it makes sense to you."

I took out some paper and a pen, and we made a space where she could throw the coins. I drew the six lines as she threw them. I forget whether there were any moving lines (which means a second hexagram is involved), but in any case, I looked at the two trigrams and as it happened, I knew which hexagram it was. I understand the dynamics between the trigrams and I gave my interpretation of the hexagram for her.

I asked her if it made sense, and she looked pensive. She said that what I said was very relevant to her situation, and helpful. We hugged.

74 The three muses

The Three Muses: at the first Woodford Folk Festival I went to, I took a perfect photo. At night time, when you walked around the streets of the festival, there were travelling vignettes, or I suppose they would be called pop-up artists today. (Oh dear, time changes and even the manner of speaking changes.) You would be walking along the road, along with a crowd of other people, relaxed, and come into a square, and suddenly a group of musicians would arrive and set up and play a few numbers.

Sometimes it would be a hillbilly family band whom you guessed had never been to a city, singing songs from the hills with banjos and washboards. The songs were from long ago. Sometimes it would be one or two giant, beautifully coloured paper mâché figures, lit up from the inside – animals, fairies, dragons, angels, mythical creatures – held and led by attendants.

On such a night I came into a square and there were three maidens high up in the air, gyrating in smooth arcs. They were standing on curved steel poles which were anchored on the ground, and they wore large, fringed frocks. They reminded me of those dolls that girls used to buy at sideshows and circuses when I was young; they were sparkly, and the dolls were princesses in frilled dresses attached to the top of a long stick.

I took a photo, and when I looked at the photo later, the three maidens happened to be positioned (composed) perfectly, looking out on the crowd, lit up serenely, with their arms outstretched to the people below. It was a magical moment. I immediately labelled them the Three Muses, because it just seemed appropriate, regardless of my lack of knowledge of Greek mythology. The muses inspire art and music; what better place for muses to show up than at Woodford?

The aftermath: When I produced my two collections of poetry in 2007, I used photos of Woodford on the covers. The cover of *Love and Armour* shows the photo of the three muses (yes, I did love it). On the cover *of Flames in the Open*, the cover is a photo from the Fire Ceremony. It also has a photo of my Horseshoe Creek house on the back cover.

75 Kate

Kate Miller-Heidke was also at the first Woodford I went to. She came from Brisbane and she was young, twenty-three at the time. I had not heard of her, but I read that she had studied opera and then gone to pop. She wrote her own music. She was playing in the middle of the day in a tent, with maybe five hundred people in the audience. I had never heard operatic prowess put to such extraordinary but pertinent use in pop music. It was exalted. Her songs could be funny, they were intelligent, and were sometimes heartfelt. Near the end, she did an acapella version of someone else's song.

I have heard her do a few of these, and I don't have notes for my visits to Woodford, so it was either "Staying Alive" (Bee Gees) or "Psycho Killer" (David Byrne and Talking Heads). Either way, when she starts, she is in operatic mode, slowed down and melodramatic, and you don't know what the song is until she gets to the chorus, and then it hits you like an explosion.

When she had finished, astounding the crowd, the lady sitting next to me turned to me and looked straight at me, and said, "Every moment of that was a surprise!" It certainly was.

Years later, after Kate had become a big star in Australia, I was back at Woodford and so was she. It was December 2012. In 2009 she had released a song called "Caught in the Crowd". It was a song about bullying, and bullying was becoming a public issue. My goodness, I had written about it in the context of management for CCH. But this wasn't just a song about bullying; it is about the friend of a person who was being bullied. In the song, the person singing the song fails to stand up for the friend: "And I turned my head and walked away".

I think this song is so powerful because this is the behaviour that most people have experienced. Many people have not been bullies, and many people have not been bullied, but I think nearly everyone has been guilty of letting down a friend when they have been in need. So, everyone can relate to that song. It touches hearts. The song came to be used in schools as a conversation-starter with school-children, to talk about bullying.

Kate often told the story on-stage that a boy wrote to her – only because the teacher made all of her class write a letter to Kate – and said that he liked her song, but in it she had rhymed "school" with "school", which is not a rhyme. However, he wished her luck in her future song-writing. The dry humour of a primary-school boy.

So, that's the background. It is December 2012, and Kate's song has been doing the rounds of Australian schools and is part of the conversation about bullying. It was a weekend, and on weekends, a lot of school-children come up to Woodford from Brisbane for the day. For many, it is their first "big day out" as teenagers. The organisers had put Kate in an open-air venue right near the entrance gates, and the concert was on at around mid-day.

I had just arrived there, because I love to see Kate sing. The atmosphere was very loud, because hundreds of teenagers were coming in through the gates, and they were so excited to be at

Woodford. It was quite wonderful to hear the excitement and to know it was a milestone in their growing up. It was sunny, and they were marching onward, just to get in to see what was there, to see what it was like. They hadn't really registered that Kate had just begun a concert right near them.

Then Kate started the song, "Caught in the Crowd", and after a couple of chords, an amazing thing happened. The entire noise level went quieter. It was palpable. All of those teenagers had suddenly registered that Kate was there, and she was playing that song. Many of them stopped in their tracks and looked around to where the stage was. That song touches hearts. But I think Woodford is the only place where I would have seen a reaction like that of the school-kids. It said as much about Woodford as it said about Kate or the song.

Kate also has a wonderful sense of how to shift the mood. After that she played a song that was quite sassy and humorous. I have never seen anybody exude glee the way she does.

In 2019, Kate Miller-Heidke was selected to represent Australia in Eurovision. She did the performance of her song atop the same "bendy poles". One fan said, "It feels like Cirque du Soleil." The steel poles and the aerial gyration were the product of a Melbourne group called Strange Fruit. I thought it was extraordinary to combine both the movement and singing. It was a long arc for me, back to the performance I saw one night at Woodford in December 2004.

76 The Lettering House

The last time I went to Woodford was in December 2017. This year there was a new innovation (for me, but then, I had missed a few years): a postal service. It was called the Lettering House, typically whimsical and ambiguous. It was a crazy idea – you could write a letter to someone else at the festival and the trusty postal officers (yes, there were postal officers on push-bikes, in uniform) would deliver it – "To the woman who was dancing with her child" et cetera.

As crazy as it was, it unleashed a torrent of letter-writing. Dozens of people turned up at the Lettering House each day to sit and write – and decorate – letters to someone, and peg them up on the board to be delivered. It was, like many things at Woodford, a master-stroke of whimsy.

What could I do with this idea? I couldn't see myself writing a letter to the woman who was dancing with her child. I spoke to one of the trusty postal officers, young men and women in jaunty uniforms, who told me enthusiastically of their random but devoted duties. I wanted to do something that reflected my fluid state of mind. I had been to the Lettering House and I noted that there were a number of different Woodford postcards that you could just pick up and use for whatever you wanted.

My version of letter-writing was to write a postcard to all the people of Woodford every day of the festival, and post them on the notice board in the Lettering House. I suppose you could read this as a record of one person's journey through the six-day festival. I have included the text of the postcards in the Stories section of this book. Okay, it is more a series of poems than a story. That's what Woodford does to you.

77 Bob Hawke

Bob Hawke, the ex-Prime Minister, came to Woodford in 2017. I saw him at the opening ceremony at the amphitheatre. I had seen other politicians at Woodford before, especially if it was close to election time. They always seemed uncomfortable, but the ones who would have been absolutely mortified did not come. Bob Hawke had no reason to be uncomfortable: he was retired, and he was friends with Bill Hauritz, the Director of the Woodford organisation.

Bob gave a speech in which he talked about shame, thinking of Australia's history, but his closing words were, "Do the job that needs to be done." He spoke to the best in everyone. And then he did something else: he sang, in a quavering voice, "Waltzing Matilda". I never thought I would be brought to tears by an ex-Prime Minister singing "Waltzing Matilda", but it was not a performance for acclaim, it was a performance with all the sincerity that emerges at Woodford. It stood for so much more than a swagman sitting by the billabong. Or perhaps Bob Hawke saw himself, near the end of his life, as just that, a swagman beside the billabong.

78 Woodford talk

I was a performer at Woodford once. No, I did not sing. In my first year there, I saw that they had a venue for talks: the Greenhouse. The talks were mostly about environmental issues and political action, but there were also talks on alternative medicine and health, and building a wholesome society. I thought there was a place for a talk about ethics, so I applied to speak at the 2006 festival. I was accepted.

My talk was called "Ethics and Aspiration in the Workplace". My first ethics book was close to completion; I had finished a draft, and it was called *Ethics and Aspiration: Human Values in the Workplace*. It was later that I changed the title. It was a good time to take my ideas out in public. I presented some of my ideas, for example, the idea that people operate at different levels, so despite the fact that the language people use to talk about ethics is the same, people operate differently. They also mean different things by what they say. This idea seemed to resonate with the people who came to hear me. It was encouraging.

In my profile I said, "Glenn is a writer on training, human resources and ethics for business publications. His haphazard career spans teaching, managing community-based organisations, community development and living in the bush. He has a B.Bus.(Hons) and M.Ed."

It's hard, trying to be on the outside looking at yourself as well as trying to make sense to the audience in the context for which you are composing it. Nevertheless, I suppose what I said was true. I think the main difference now is that I am not trying to seek other people's approval. I know the value of what I have to say.

79 Chai

Chai. There has always (in my time) been a Chai Tent at Woodford. If you want to meet up with someone, you tell them, "Meet me at the Chai Tent." And when you meet, you have a cup of chai. The chai is prepared in huge aluminium teapots which look as if they came from a Country Women's Association kitchen. The milk is mixed in with it, it is sweetened with honey, and it looks soupy. It is, of course, lovely and satisfying. I seldom drink chai other than at Woodford, because that's how I remember chai tea.

The Chai Tent was also the place where "impromptu" acts would perform. There is a blackboard outside, and you can put your name on the board. You get twenty minutes. Sometimes, artists who are on the program will book themselves into the Chai Tent to do a practice run. You don't get a lot of attention, because people come here to talk. I think the impromptu acts later moved to a new place called the Pineapple Lounge.

There was one act that I saw in the Chai Tent that has stayed with me. It started out with a Japanese couple on two-stringed lutes. They were dressed in formal Japanese attire. It was very traditional and it was lovely. Then, onto the stage came a trio who brought traditional Irish instruments with them: a guitar, fiddle and recorder, ready to join in. I thought, "This is not going to work." But, amazingly, it did work. The different strands of music wove themselves together and became something else. The ambience had changed but it was all harmonious.

Just when I had got used to the idea that these two types of music from two very different worlds could blend together, an Aboriginal youth stalked along the back of the stage with a didgeridoo. He came into the group of musicians and began to play with them. Again I found myself thinking, "This will not work at all." And again, I was surprised. The didgeridoo blended right in and augmented the existing sounds. It was delightful and the music was now straining the walls and roof of the tent.

This wonderful performance showed me something. It was a lesson about the different tribes and nationalities on earth. In the 1970s, in the days of Gough Whitlam's reforms, Member of Parliament Al Grassby had popularised the idea of multiculturalism – different nationalities could learn to live with one another without having to "assimilate", wherein some people would have to lose their existing cultural identity. The performance in the Chai Tent showed that something else was possible: the different cultures could explore how they could blend together, forging what each had into a greater song.

Things I know
The lessons of music are greater than arguments.

80 Fire Ceremony

The Fire Ceremony. The timing of the Woodford Folk Festival is exquisite. It starts the day after Boxing Day and it runs until the first of January. New Year's Eve, as you would expect at a festival, is a big, rhythmic, exciting musical event, with many kinds of performances over the evening. It accommodates all moods. But the big night is the next night, the evening of the first day of the new year.

The Fire Ceremony is a large-scale drama, played out in the space between the big stage and the audience on the hillside of the amphitheatre. The large paper mâché figures that we have seen during the week form part of this spectacle, moving swiftly around the arena to convey a story that reflects on the events of the year, in Australia and the world. Artists have designed the figures, playwrights have written the script. The tale is augmented by the songs of a choir.

Where did a choir come from? We have only been here a week. When you arrive at the festival, you can join the choir. That means you go to practice each day and learn the songs you will be singing at the Fire Ceremony. There are up to five hundred people in the choir, singing four-part harmonies.

The concept is mythological: the idea that the old must be destroyed to make way for the new. The centrepiece of the event is a huge paper-and-stick figure, several stories high, colourful (of course), and thematic. One year it was a stack of cards – symbolic. There were two giant people, who seemed like ordinary people looking at the world thinking, "What is going on?" All the other figures racing around seemed like our mad, modern world.

An Aboriginal man comes into the middle and lights a fire in the traditional way, blowing sparks into a handful of twigs and brush. This is all shown on big screens beside the stage: very modern. The fledgling fire is taken over to the giant structure and it is lit. While the fire blazes up, fireworks go off. The audience is quiet, pensive and engaged.

Tomorrow is really when the new year will begin, and we will begin it anew, with a fresh spirit, hopeful but not naïve, solid, realistic, but urging our artfulness to break out, because the world will be better if we live that way.

81 Nostalgia

I have indulged myself by talking about Woodford at length, but I have also been abstemious. There is so much more that I could have said. It has been appropriate to talk about Woodford extensively, because it has been important in my life. Now I need to talk about the idea of nostalgia. Has this merely been nostalgia?

Nostalgia is defined as a form of melancholia caused by prolonged absence from one's country or home. It derives from the work of a Swiss doctor, Johannes Hofer, who wrote a treatise in 1688 about mercenary soldiers who became homesick. It was seen as a serious medical condition. It is also described as a bittersweet longing for the past, or a wistful or excessively sentimental yearning. So, there is something sweet about it, but it is also something to be wary of falling into too deeply.

I don't think I have been guilty of nostalgia. The past is also the lens by which we view the present, and from that perspective it is useful. We are not disconnected fragments of memory; we are a continuity. Or, more than that, we are the continuity that we weave out of the events we remember, as long as we stand guard against self-delusion.

> "The modern view is that nostalgia is an independent, and even positive, emotion that many people experience often. Nostalgia has been found to have important psychological functions, such as to improve mood, increase social connectedness, enhance positive self-regard, and provide existential meaning" (from an internet source, unnecessary to pursue).

That's fine, too, but it glosses over some possible negative effects, for which we don't need to consult experts. We know the dangers of "living in the past", when one denies the present. We know that people are inclined to cling onto the past if they see the present as difficult. The healthy purpose of delving into the past is to bring back useful insights to the present, so that we may be better people.

Viktor Frankl, a Jewish prisoner in one of Hitler's concentration camps, survived and wrote *Man's Search for Meaning*. He said the dreamers who denied the present were the first to fall apart.

Frankl's point of view is radical. He says, "It did not really matter what we expected from life, but rather, what life expected from us. We needed to stop asking about the meaning of life, but instead to think of ourselves as being questioned by life – daily and hourly" (Pocket Books, 1984, p. 98). There is room for contemplation of other places and times, but not for helpless hankering.

Many people go to Woodford with sorrow. Woodford is not dismissive of sorrow, but nor does it wallow. It says, "There is sadness, but the love is deeper." At least, that is my message from Woodford. I don't speak for others. So, am I nostalgic about Woodford? No. I know this.

Things I know

We are the continuity we weave out of the events of the past, when we realise there is sadness, but the love is deeper.

82 Soup and moonlight

This story is out of sequence, not that I have been very strict about sequence. I tell it because I remember it. I tell it because at one time I was involved in the establishment of a Steiner school up on the far north coast, in the hills – but you know that already. A lot of mothers (and fathers) wanted a Steiner school for their children, as a better way for their children to grow up. I didn't have any children living with me at that time; they had been taken away to the Blue Mountains. Nevertheless, I was interested. Since I had had experience working on constitutions for community-based organisations, they asked me if I would help.

There was a plan for myself and a lady (the midwife who lived in my valley) to visit one of the primary organisers over on the Cawongla Road one night. I suppose we could call her Lady 4, given that I am not divulging names. At the meeting, we were to go over the draft constitution and adapt it. And yes, this organiser was the lady who had been at the lecturer's office at Southern Cross University one day when I happened to have to visit there.

But there was a prior commitment. Lady 4 had an adult education class that night. We would have to go after that, and she said she would be hungry. I think she was teaching massage that night, and perhaps I even organised the class. So, food. Surely I could do that.

I had made a good soup that day, so I thought I would put it in a Thermos and it would be hot. We decided to stop at the lookout to the east of Kyogle that looked down on the town. I had nice bowls and spoons. I think I even had serviettes. What I hadn't counted on was that it was a full moon. Everything was crystal clear and it was beautiful. We had the loveliest meal, and then we set off on our journey to do business. We were both pondering all things: life, the adult education class, what would happen as a result of our work for the proposed Steiner school, perhaps ourselves. It felt rich and it was worth savouring.

Yes, the school was started, and many children enrolled. It still exists (as of 2022); it is called Rainbow Ridge Steiner School. And this is called a "fond memory".

83 A death

I have another memory. This one is about a death. You remember when I started at the Challenge Foundation in Casino, and there was a crisis precipitated by the bank manager who thought he was invincible and he could steal money without repercussions, only he couldn't? In the wake of that, the CEO came up from Sydney, and despite the fact that he had no power over me, he tried to persuade me to sack some of the staff? And I didn't sack them?

I stuck with those staff all the way through, and I had no reason to regret that. Fred was one of those staff. He looked after the supported employment service, and trained clients up to do nursery work, from which they got a lot of satisfaction. But there was a history to Fred. As well as being a mental retardation nurse at Stockton (near Newcastle; yes, he told me he had met Lady 1), he had been in a mental institution for a while, not just any institution, but Chelmsford Private Hospital at Pennant Hills in Sydney.

Fred was subjected to "deep sleep therapy". The chief psychiatrist was Dr Harry Bailey. The hospital conducted its "treatments" between 1962 and 1979. To supposedly cure depression, addiction, blindness and other conditions, he would put patients into a coma for up to thirty-nine days via a cocktail of barbiturates. He would also administer electro-convulsive therapy while they were in a coma — often without patient consent, or anaesthetic, or muscle relaxants — with devastating outcomes. Over twenty patients died; some reports say twenty-six patents died. Mainly because of the barbiturates, fit and healthy patients either died, or left with chronic pneumonia, kidney damage, bowel haemorrhages, deep vein thrombosis, and other ailments.

Fred told me one day that he had been in the hospital and was subjected to "treatment" there. It was now the mid-1980s; a Royal Commission had been held, and the New South Wales Government had held its own investigation. A class action had started, and Fred was mulling over whether he should sign up to it. By this time, Dr Harry Bailey had committed suicide.

I pondered this situation for some time. There were strong arguments to join in. Dr Bailey had done extreme wrong, and extreme harm to many people, with all the conceit that some doctors can muster. But, on the other hand, Fred had got out of the hospital and got a job (the one at Stockton, and then at Casino.) He had brought a friend with him to Casino: Michael, who was one of the few people I know to have come back from heroin. He had a good support network of friends at work, and he was loved. Should he tear himself away from that to go on a righteous quest? Perhaps he would get compensation from it, but what would it cost him, personally? It was likely to leave him bitter, and a victim for the rest of his life.

It depended how committed Fred was to the path of redress. I thought it would cost him personally, and I said so. I said I was expressing my opinion, that's all, but that this was what I felt. He decided to stay. The other thing to say about Fred is that he smoked roll-your-own cigarettes all day. It was constant. Other people smoked, mostly because they enjoyed the ritual of rolling their own cigarettes, but Fred smoked all day.

A couple of years after I left the north coast, someone told me that he had died of lung cancer. By then I was embroiled in Sydney life, and I didn't go up to the funeral. I was sorry about that. He was close to my age, also; it hurt. Fred was one of the good things about the Challenge Foundation in Casino. He was decent. I remember him fondly. I have used his name because he is no longer alive and he had no children; and I haven't used his family name.

84 Another death

There was another death, a client of the supported employment service. (I have told this story before in *The Ten Thousand Things*, but it fits with my train of thought here.)

The client was in her early twenties, but she was not in good health. She died the year after my departure from Casino, and I went to the funeral, in the big Catholic Church there. There were a lot of people attending, because the affection between clients and families was high. Some people were shocked to see me there, but I think they thought it was a good thing, and they were welcoming. Father Relihan (whom I knew from St Mary's) performed a dignified Mass. The interesting thing came at the end.

I was walking down the aisle towards the back of the church to leave, and the man who had been Treasurer on the committee saw me (the doctor who was also the programmer). Isn't it interesting when a doctor goes to a funeral? Normally I would have thought they were too busy, and it's not the sort of thing that doctors do normally. He made eye contact with me and extended his hand. I took it. It was a personal gesture, not a public act. I felt that it was his way of saying that the misunderstandings between us no longer existed. Our handshake was firm and honest. It was a good way to leave that encounter.

85 Professional staff

After I resigned from the hapless PhD, I decided I needed a job, because I had let my number of clients run down while I was trying to make headway on the PhD. It was a sudden thought: "I think I need a job!" A couple of days later, a person I had known several years previously rang me to ask if I knew someone who would be good at developing online courses for a staff training unit at a university. It happened that I knew someone who would be perfect for the job – me! Since I had acquired my MEd (2003), I had not really done justice to the degree, and it was now 2012.

I was over sixty, so I didn't let myself get too optimistic; prejudices can be subtle but persistent. But I went for an interview and I got the job. Then came the interesting part: the job contract. I knew my employment law well, and I had been a contractor for several years, so I was a bit sensitive about the contents of contracts. The clause that I was sensitive about was the one about the university retaining copyright over work I write as an employee. I wasn't complaining about this; it was a standard clause. But I said to the human resources officer, I have written a lot of material prior to arriving here, and I don't want the university claiming ownership over that. You need to protect me as well!

Clearly this was a new thought for her, and an uncomfortable one. She had never faced a potential employee wanting to change the terms of their contract before. I said, I can give you a guide; it doesn't include everything, but this list will be indicative. And I produced a list that covered the books I had written to date, and articles and commentary I had written that wasn't bound by CCH. She was relieved to have a solution, even though I thought it was a bit rough. She incorporated the new clause into the contract.

So, then I started another phase of my working life. I was an instructional designer, and I was sixty-two. Here are the modules I produced during the almost three years I was there:

- Work health and safety (five modules: orientation, risk management, office safety, manual tasks and hazardous chemicals)
- Career development for academics; career development for professionals
- Orientation for new employees
- Inducting your staff (for managers)
- Introduction to performance planning and development.

It was a creditable body of work, and it was all done to a high standard. Some of it also incorporated my knowledge, such as the career development modules. I was wary that the academics might be sensitive about my input (professional staff, as we were called, weren't supposed to "know things" that they deemed to fall within their domain, but they were largely positive. I didn't run into petty jealousies that would have been irksome.

The reason this came to an end was that my manager had a sensitive ego. I was on short-term contracts, usually twelve months, but it was June, and she offered me a five-month contract that would end just before Christmas. I thought this was offensive. I said so – not in offensive terms, but I did say it was not an attractive proposition. She claimed that was all the university would offer at this time.

However, there was a prelude to this. I had upset the manager. How? We were responsible for producing a new orientation module for new staff. Part of this was to get a short interview from the Vice Chancellor recorded. I organised it and got it done, without any problems. I felt pleased, because the unit had been talking about the orientation module for a year without anything having happened. But, my manager heard about it and hit the roof. Apparently, I had no right to do this, and I had stepped on her turf. (The Vice Chancellor hadn't seemed to think so.)

Her ire was so great that she wrote me a 500-word email. Nothing less would have served. But I had gone home for the day. She was still fired up, so she spent twenty minutes berating my colleague. I suppose the five hundred words came in handy. I read this and heard the story the next morning. I guess I am not diplomatic. I wrote her a one-line response which said, "I was just doing my job." She didn't talk to me for a month.

So, the new contract, I think, had its roots in her ire. I had a month to accept the new contract; there was still an expectation that I would accept it. But I had another issue with the contract. It had a clause in it that protected the university from me defaming it after I left their employment, universities being sensitive to social media. Of course, a university is a business, and businesses endeavour to surround themselves with legal protections. But I had history.

After I had been sacked from the Challenge Foundation, one of the more odious people on the committee got together with the editor of the local newspaper, who was another odious person, and they concocted a front-page story about me. It did not directly accuse me, but it clearly left the impression that I was either incompetent, dishonest, or both. I made a complaint to the Press Council, but the reply from the newspaper didn't come until six weeks later, and it was stuck obscurely on about page six.

So, I had a case in point, and from that experience, I wasn't going to let this clause go. I felt that I should have protection against the business (the university) after I was no longer working for it. It was only fair, and contracts were supposed to protect the employee as well as the employer. I persisted. The HR officer hated it. She didn't like the very idea that a contract could be a two-way negotiation. She said she would have to consult the Industrial Relations Team. I said, "Yes, you will need to do that. Get back to me."

86 College

However, something else happened. Another job came up. It was for a similar job, and it was in the college that the university ran for young students who were not successful in getting into university at first try. They could go to the college and do a preliminary course, and then go into second year at university. The job seemed perfect. I applied for the job on condition that they did not discuss it with my current employer. I had never done this before, but I know that many people apply for new jobs while they have a bad situation going on with their current manager, so I'm sure I wasn't the first person to make this stipulation. They said they wouldn't, and I believe they kept their word.

I got to the interview stage: my second job interview after the age of sixty. It was a panel, so, numerous people, many of whom, I could tell, knew very little about what I would be doing. The important thing was, I had found out what the job was about. The college wanted to run an introductory course for engineering students. I thought, this is going a long way back, but I think I can swing it. I pulled out the transcript of my University of New South Wales Engineering Degree. I had only completed two years of study, in 1968 and 1969, but my results were excellent, and I didn't care about the time lapse.

I did enough photocopies of the transcript for everyone in the room to have a copy, and I took them along. I kept them in my folder. The interview was long; there are always so many questions when there is a panel. But eventually they got to it: was I confident to handle engineering material? I said, "I have something to show you," and I took my time taking the photocopies out of the folder and passing them around. They would be able to see the dates on it, and they might laugh. It was over forty years ago.

However, I said, "I am not pretending that my knowledge of engineering is up to date, but I can tell you that I am familiar with engineering material. That doesn't leave you."

They gave me the job. The next week, before I had left the staff training unit at the university, my manager asked me why I had not signed the contact yet. Mind you, I was still waiting for a response from the Industrial Relations Team. That was when I told her two things: first, the Industrial Relations Team had not responded to me, and second, I was leaving the job – I had got another job.

For a while, I was happy enough in the new job. I wasn't all that interested in engineering: there was a reason why I left it over forty years ago. However, I was in charge of my work, and the real challenge was to create a learning environment online. My manager was out of his depth with it, so he left me alone.

I worked there for four and a half years. I left on the last day of January 2019. When I left, I said my resignation could be construed as retirement, and I subsequently described myself as being in quasi-retirement. I can tell good stories about the college, and bad ones.

On the first of February 2019, I held a book launch. The timing was symbolic. I was a writer now, not an employee. I had just finished *The Search for Edward Lewis*, a mammoth effort of 434 pages. The book was about Sarah Crosby and Edward Lewis. Edward got the title of the book because I was looking for him. I had already found Sarah. They are my great great grandparents on my father's side. I had known nothing about my father's family. Sarah and Edward were both convicts; Edward was transported as a child in 1845, and Sarah came out in 1850, still less than twenty. They were both sent to Hobart, and they met there and married. They were close in age.

As of writing, I still haven't found Edward's death. I am fairly certain I have found the story of the last twenty years of his life, but I have not found his death. There seems to be no death certificate and I still have not found a grave. I found Sarah, miraculously. I was looking for one of their children at Rookwood, and suddenly there she was: her gravestone was staring at me. She died on 4th September 1897.

I have written many books since leaving the university. The period of my "quasi-retirement" has been very productive. A book of poems was finalised in May 2019, called *That Was Then*, which was my first book of poems since 2017. It was also intended to be my first poetry book, because it contains a selection of my early poems. I sub-titled it *The Early Poems Project*. In February 2020 I published the ethics book, *A Foundation for Living Ethically*. Covid was in full sway and there was no book launch.

I did manage to go to Tasmania in October 2019, while there was a brief respite in Covid. Subsequently I wrote a book about it: *The Quilt Approach: A Tasmanian Patchwork*. It referred to my first visit there in December 1973, alone and hitch-hiking. It also referred to family history because I couldn't go to Tasmania and not look for traces of Sarah and Edward. The trip itself, in 2019, was about going on a walk in the Tarkine area of north-west Tasmania with a small group and two guides. It was a lovely experience, energetic but not too exhausting.

As well as all this, I met up with some family. Their ancestors had been the grandparents of William Archer, who was my great great grandfather (on my mother's side), so, a long way back. William Archer was a convict; their ancestors were well-to-do, and they were keepers of convicts. For all that, their ancestors seemed to have treated their convicts well. They lived in the north of Tasmania, just south of Launceston. I like to make the point that not all ancestors were savages.

87 Four pillars

After I finished writing *A Foundation for Living Ethically*, I started to think about what I hadn't said in that book. It was, after all, a book on ethics, not the whole of life. I had been trying to articulate what was important in an ethical point of view. But the question remained: what are the things that are important if we were looking at all of life? I was thinking about the assertion of the poet John Keats in "Ode on a Grecian Urn": "'Beauty is truth, truth beauty,'—that is all ye know on earth, and all ye need to know."

I can see that there is truth in beauty, and there is beauty in truth, but it doesn't quite answer my concerns. If you wanted to name some fundamental categories of life, that were wide enough to embrace all that you thought was important, what would they be? Of course, morality would be one of them, but morality does not stretch to cover all that we think is important in life. I was thinking very broadly, although I was not interested in summoning up a multitude of things. I felt there had to be a short list that was broad enough.

Part of my interest in this question was because of family history. When you are exploring an ancestor, you have certain things in mind: what were the things in life that were important to them? So, that became my context. These categories, could I see them in relation to my ancestors' lives? That would be a good test.

So, after a while, I came up with four categories – what is important in life? I called them "the four pillars". They are: Competence + Morality + Beauty + Love.

The thinking was this: when we start out in life, we are on a progression towards competence. We learn how to look after ourselves, feed ourselves, dress ourselves and so on. We learn to talk and read and write, and many other tasks, even sporting activities are part of our competence. Competence is basic to our self-image. When we grow up, we generally learn an occupation, a craft or profession, and that becomes a big part of our self-image as an adult. Many of my ancestors were artisans: carpenters, miners, stonemasons, painters, plasterers, dressmakers.

Morality is a fundamental part of life. There is no human community without it. Care for one's family and neighbours, honesty, responsibility, fairness, are all aspects of morality. Among my ancestors I see many signs of their commitment to morality. Their lives seem to have been imbued with it.

Beauty is the third pillar. This is to say, it is not enough to be competent. There is also an urge to make things that are beautiful. Keats would approve. I see this also in the work that my ancestors did, that there seemed to be a quest for aesthetics in their work. And in our lives, we may see that it permeates everything, from the littlest things, like tidying objects on a table and putting them in order, to the biggest things.

And the fourth pillar is love. It is not necessarily romantic love, but it includes that. It is a broad appreciation of everything in life. Without love, there is no joy.

There are other aspects that I would call "outputs", such as happiness and joy. My four pillars I would describe as "inputs", the things you should focus on. Happiness may come, but so too will sorrow. Focusing on happiness does not guarantee happiness, and will likely interfere with it. Focusing on Competence, Morality, Beauty and Love will give you a full heart. Striving to be "happy" will then not matter so much.

I think Viktor Frankl would approve. I think my ancestors would also approve.

I also think that William Irwin Thompson would approve. We would both agree that his diagrams are saying something different: Headman, Shaman, Hunter and Clown, and their society-based counterparts, are roles you consider once you accept the idea of competence.

88 Staying home

The coming of covid was opportune for me. It coincided with my retreat to home. It coincided with my decision to stay at my current house, and not follow the aged people's path of relinquishing their familiar surroundings for something smaller, and no doubt, more modern. I had been here twenty years when I realised that this was the longest time I had lived anywhere. I had been at Greenacre for nineteen years, and at Horseshoe Creek for nineteen years. Surely this was the time to reconsider my abode?

I believe my house at Cherrybrook is close to one hundred years old. It has gone through "incarnations", the latest of which was in the 1980s. I love living in an old house. It has a past, the same as a family does. I didn't have anywhere else I was hankering to be. Yes, it would be nice to be somewhere other than the city. I always thought that the city was a place where you lived because you had a need – a job, for example, or a passion for opera. And when you no longer had the need, it didn't make sense to stay.

However, I didn't have anywhere else I strongly felt the need to be – not in any country town, and not in the bush. That was my Horseshoe Creek days. I can make use of the city. I can go to concerts. I can go to the State Archives and other places to do family history research. I can get on a bus, a train or a ferry. And most of my children and all of my grandchildren are within reach. It seems like a good bargain.

Once I decided to stay, that is, after twelve months thinking about it, I got some renovations done on the house: the functional areas – kitchen, bathroom and laundry. It was a bit difficult, because people were telling me I needed something modern and "fresh". I could cope with "fresh"; I wasn't comfortable with modern. But people tell me they think what I've done is great. I am happy with it all. No regrets.

I got a new deck and a carport too, and solar heating. That satisfies me, and I deem myself to be satisfactorily, sufficiently, modern. So, in the first big year of covid, 2020, I finished three books. I've mentioned *A Foundation for Living Ethically* and *The Quilt Approach*. The third one was called *Future*. The subtitle was *The Spiritual Story of Humanity*. It was a bold subtitle, but it said what I wanted it to. I had acquired a number of books on the history of humanity. That's a great story, and one that is changing all the time, as new discoveries are made.

I was interested in the perspective of the writers. What was their overall belief about the story of humanity over time, all several thousand years of it? Most of them were excited about "progress", particularly the story of technology over the last three hundred years. Yet if progress is so definitive, why are we in the middle of a climate crisis? What would the story look like from a spiritual perspective?

I didn't presume that I could answer this question, but I did think I could say a few pertinent, provocative and perhaps useful things about it. And I thought a history of humanity should explore our violence, cruelty, greed, hierarchical societies and unregulated economics. We tend to believe that we will prevail because we are so big and so technological, but there are stories about societies that have died out that should be a lesson in caution and humility.

I do not have a plan to save the world. The problem with such plans is that they then have to be implemented, which would seem to reinforce all the object lessons about hierarchies and dictators. Instead, I said we should start with the self, remembering that we are "of spirit". Accordingly, we will see our past differently, and perhaps there is wisdom in our past that we have not yet tapped into.

On the cover of the book, I used someone else's image. It was the first time I had done so. I usually use one of my own photos. When I went to Tasmania, in Hobart at the Salamanca Markets I had seen some pictures by a local artist, and one in particular intrigued me for this book. It was a girl in a meadow, and she was releasing a white bird. I thought, "This is the way we should approach the future: as if we were the girl in the meadow releasing a bird." There is no violence or conquest in this image, and it is hopeful. It looks like a good future.

I sometimes wonder if my life is schizophrenic. I have a perfectly functional life writing books and producing them in print. Technology has been kind to self-publishing authors. But there is little audience for the books. Occasionally someone will buy a book, and occasionally someone will comment on a book they have read. But, "it is better to write for yourself and have no audience than to write for an audience and have no self".

And, fulfilment is to carry out one's duty.

89 Library

The other attraction for staying at my current home is the library. I have mentioned it before. It has fourteen sets of shelves, up to 2.5 metres tall. The total shelf length is around 70 metres. It has an aisle, and two living spaces, one for a desk, computer and table, and one for two lounge chairs. This doesn't include the shelves in the house, which are mostly for fiction, travel books, nature and humour. But yes, I do consider them to be part of the library. And they consist of over twenty shelf-metres of books.

I wonder if it will expand beyond my capacity to manage it. Since I came back to Sydney, I have discovered book fairs, and realised they may contain excellent treasures at a modest price. I am not interested in "collecting books", and I am not interested in first editions or books of that ilk. My books are intended to be functional, and within my purposes and interests.

Sometimes I cannot resist a book, for example, *Mary Reiby, the Woman on the $20 Note*. My great great grandfather on my mother's side, William Archer, the convict, did what many convicts dreamed of: he went home to England, just as Mary Reiby did. And when she came back, she could say that she came here as a free settler. William Archer was likewise "cleansed", and my mother could say, "There are no convicts in our family." I am quite sure she did not know the truth. And yet my mother occasionally said teasing things to me, like: "Keep looking, you never know what you will find." Did she realise that the past could not hurt her now?

Also, I found *Hall's Ireland* by Mr and Mrs Hall, first published in 1843 (before the Irish famine) and published in 1984 as a boxed set of two decoratively bound paperbacks. My great great grandmother, Sarah Crosby, comes from Waterford. The Halls are not flattering about Waterford. They describe it as "perhaps the least interesting and certainly the least picturesque of the counties of Ireland". Yet, they offer comprehensive descriptions, and their descriptions elicited some affection from me. I would like to go there to compare notes with them. Their account was meant to attract visitors to Ireland.

Sarah was probably born in May 1833. Something must have happened to her family in the famine in 1845-1846. They may have both died. After this, Sarah went to England. She would have been only around thirteen, illiterate and malnourished. For two years she moved around England, first working at a big house in Bath, then going to London. She was homeless there, and desperate. Things came to a head when she attacked a policeman who tried to remove her from a Refuge for the Homeless. The newspapers were kind: they agreed that she was desperate. She was gaoled and transported to Van Diemen's Land. The picture of Waterford that the Halls carefully portray is sombre against the backdrop of what happened to Sarah.

At the same time, I am here because Sarah survived. And it is good to remember all this.

Life sucks in air, already triumphant against the windy, broad-scale tide of decay, of tearing things down, of wearing them out. Sarah survived where many convicts didn't.

90 Career progression

Have I done more than make fragmentary attempts at a career path? Have I approached something concrete and significant? I have been a long time approaching. I guess that by now the goal is not fame. Do I feel that I am approaching something?

I was the first in the wider family (that is, among cousins, I suppose) to go to university, so it was important in the family. It was difficult for me to leave engineering because, apart from resolving my own issues, there was the family to consider. Had I failed to find my way into the new social possibilities?

I did manage to complete my teaching course, although it was only one year, and I went into teaching as "two-year trained". In terms of the family, that was good enough and that was all that was expected. A degree would have been nice, but at least I had moved beyond the trades. And now, knowing so much about my ancestors, I can see that I really was the first person to move beyond the trades. It is difficult to draw the boundary around a family. On my mother's side, back among the relatives, there was a lady who became a nurse, and then became the matron of Darwin Hospital. She was there in 1974, in charge of the hospital's work with the wounded after Cyclone Tracy.

And I failed at my second attempt at a degree. When I left the University of Sydney, I had completed two years of a Bachelor of Arts, studying Philosophy and Education. I never felt the impulse to go back. I didn't feel any attraction from the cerebral brigade there. I loved ideas, but I had had my motorcycle accident, and it brought me back into my body. I wanted connection with nature, and I wanted to live in a healthy way. That was more important than a scholarly life in pursuit of some elusive and contestable ideals.

I am being harsh in saying that I failed at university. I didn't fail, and I made a point of not failing, so that no one could hold it against me. I left! I could say the system failed me, but that too is ridiculous. I had my own life to work out: the "system" was not responsible for that. So, do I have regrets about the educational phase of my life?

How could I have any regrets, when I went back to university twenty-five years later and triumphed? I left with a Bachelor of Business degree, First Class Honours and the University Medal. It was a feat to rival my performance at school, where I ended as Dux of my final year. My name is engraved on the notice board.

Is there a shape to my haphazard career? It may be problematic from the family point of view. There may have been expectations, or at least opinions among aunts and uncles. Yet, in my experience, my family was never a forum for the opinions of aunts and uncles. I still like the profile I wrote for the Woodford

Folk Festival: "His haphazard career spans teaching, managing community-based organisations, community development and living in the bush." I think that sums it up well, except for one thing: I am a writer. Perhaps I didn't realise it then, but I know it now: everything is fulfilled.

There were times when I thought I was going to be put back into the academic route. When I studied for my Master of Education (MEd) degree, I enjoyed it, and I think I am more of a student than anything else in life. But I was always pragmatic, and I knew that you had to engage in some activity where people would pay you money. I knew there was nothing attractive about poverty.

The MEd was, however, intended to be practical. It was just when online learning was taking off. Financially it was a huge win for employers. Instead of paying a trainer to train groups of, say, twenty at a time, one could create one online course and plug it in. The employees could watch it whenever it was convenient, and hundreds of employees could be trained at little to no cost. Oops! I said "watch" it. Well, I thought I would like to design courses, and online courses were coming into demand.

CCH was developing an online learning unit and I applied for a position with it. I didn't get the position. I was amazed, given that I was obviously the best possible person for the job, but I realised that my manager had blocked me. She didn't want to lose me from her team. By now I was at a time of life where such machinations were laughable. It took me a couple of years, but I left CCH.

91 A public role

As an external contractor, I began looking for other opportunities. I did not want to be a "dependent contractor", which would have been to be a de facto employee. During this time, I had become involved in the Australian Institute of Training and Development. It was turbulent, with fights, accusations, and people leaving. I thought that I might provide a steadying hand. I was given the position of National President in the middle of the turbulence.

It was a month before a national conference and the CEO had left suddenly. It left things very uncertain, and if the conference was a financial failure, it could have ruined the organisation. Someone on the board suggested that we get an event manager, and said he thought he knew someone.

So it was that I met an Irish lass who had not been long in Australia. She had come out here working on the Olympic Games in Sydney. She seemed driven, but more than that, she seemed clear, and I felt that I could work with her. She started taking over the reins for the arrangements for the conference. So many things were murky, non-existent or unsatisfactory, but we worked through them. Sometimes we were on the phone for two hours a day, working through details. Nothing was left vague.

The conference was a success, in terms of the number of delegates, the quality of the program, and last of all, the financial outcome. Many people were surprised and grateful. I had been put into the position of having to speak for the organisation, having to represent it. I could do this competently enough, but I was too aware of the swirl of politics and opinions that constantly surrounds leaders. I had no wish to extend my time in the President role.

I ended the conference on good terms with the Irish lady. Perhaps I should call her Lady 5. We respected each other. I worked as a volunteer on some street festivals she organised, such as the Glebe Street Fair. She introduced me to a role at the Department of Planning, designing an online training course. Lady 5 and I remain good friends.

On the side, something interesting happened. Because the CEO had left in a hurry, there was an edition of the organisation's magazine that had not been prepared. I stepped in to fill the void. But, after the dust from the conference had settled and things were settling down for a while, there was the question of getting an editor for the magazine. I knew one.

The other business of the organisation was less than satisfactory. There was the quest to find a new CEO. We went through a search process with a recruitment company, and there was a man who seemed okay, and we employed him. Then there was a succession of events that suggested he might not have a clue about how to fulfil the role of CEO, and that he didn't feel the need to take it all that seriously. As I usually did in difficult situations, I did my homework. I checked out his background.

What I discovered was that his main referee was a fraud. It was a friend who had been put up to giving the reference, and the information provided, overall, could be described as cavalier. The recruitment company had been remiss in not realising this – one of their presumed core competencies. I had had enough. I wanted him out.

I took it to the board, and there was agreement. They also had not been impressed with the CEO. One of the board members was going to fly up from Melbourne, and he and I would conduct the termination interview. The other man would lead the interview because, he said, he was experienced in HR. So, we started the interview, and my good friend wanted to conduct the termination on the basis that the CEO had gone against a direct order.

I was thinking, "Who does that? It's such a fragile basis for termination. People often fight in the workplace, and say things they regret. It often doesn't lead to termination. And he is the CEO, so he should be presumed to have some latitude! Why are we doing this when we have a clear case of fraud and deception, and if we wanted to, we could take it to the police?"

In a muddy kind of way, that train of thought eventually entered into the conversation, but from my perspective it was unsatisfactory. I would have been much better off conducting the interview alone. But my colleague finished with quite a good opinion of himself. Well, at least the deed was done. Not what I regard as a satisfying day's work. He had turned a clear moral issue into a contest of power between him and the CEO. It could have turned out messy.

92 Magazine editor

The thing that did interest me was the organisation's magazine. I was familiar with it, and I thought we could do better. After a while, I got myself off the board. The lady who took over as President was a decent, feet-on-the-ground person, whose ego was not disturbed by the title. I tended to the magazine. I think I did good things. I took the number of pages from thirty-two to forty-eight, and the quality of the content was high. Previously, many of the articles were vanity pieces rather than helpful information and insights about training and the working environment.

Since I had a background with CCH of attending seminars and conventions and reporting on them, I started to do the same for our events. I would go back to the presenter when I had written it up, to make sure they approved, and that was what was printed. I had some people say, "You made me sound better than I do." That was pleasing. The truth was, I was expressing them, but I just had a clear flow of thought.

I also started visiting people and interviewing them, people who were well-known in the field. We reported on developments in the field, such as when a new training package was released, with comments from someone prominent. We followed themes, like influence, organisational change, and the use of stories in training. We looked at broader issues too, like climate change, and strategy. I also did occasional articles on the history of the organisation.

We did some themed issues too, such as online learning, and discussed the different approaches being tried. I carried out this role for five years. I enjoyed it, but the role was still being treated as if it were the 32-page simple fluff piece that it had been five years previously. I decided I couldn't keep working for the minimal pay and I didn't need to, so I left. It was April 2010. They were upset and angry. I saw this as a simple consequence of their attitude. I was free. I was slowly realising that I was not in anyone's power.

2010 was the year that I published *The Ten Thousand Things*. It is interesting to look back at these dates. It would seem that once I had written my own story, I could not be held any longer in the magazine editor role.

93 Academia

However, we go through some trials in order that we can go through other trials. It was the PhD episode that followed, most certainly a situation of powerlessness. My explanation is that I was tempted by an old dream. I should have known by now that the PhD was not necessary, but when you start producing books, you get lured by that idea of seeing it on the title page: "Dr Glenn Martin". I suppose the dream goes back to juvenile wishing. I would not just be the first person in the larger family to go to university, I would be Doctor Martin.

I should have known to leave it alone also because I had had enough sense to avoid academia up to this point. My experiences at universities had not been warm and fuzzy or uplifting. First there was the alien, industrial environment of the engineering degree, then the chaos of the Bachelor of Arts years. At CCH, I occasionally had to liaise with academics, who were invited to write chapters of books, usually on human resources.

For the most part, I did not have a happy experience with academics. (There were exceptions, whom I remember fondly.) For the most part, they did not have the virtue of being clear, or knowing exactly what it was they wanted to say. The worst were those who had long ago forgotten that it is always necessary to address these questions. It is what keeps you honest, and may in time enable you to be competent. In contrast, we also had to work with solicitors, who wrote commentary on employment law. They were invariably excellent, exactly what you would want – clear, comprehensive, well-informed, logical, articulate. Their commentary could be relied upon to be a helpful resource.

It was an interesting contrast. So, yes, I learned my unnecessary lesson. I accept that there are pockets of excellence in academia, and some people have this experience. However, my experience was largely negative. I think we have to be guided by our experiences and passions. They were taking me elsewhere.

94 Young, Living, Firm Ground

I produced a book of poems in 2020. I had an approach from a publisher in India. It seemed that I could not be hurt by this venture, so I proceeded. I had no expectation of making money. I hadn't earned any money from my poetry in Australia; there was no reason to believe it would happen in India. But it was interesting how this came together so quickly. I had the idea of three parts: Young, Living and Firm Ground. I chose the poems to fit into each part. For the front cover, I chose a photo from my travels in Vietnam in 2006, although that was many years ago. I don't know why it came to me.

The title of the book was *The Way Is Open*. The photo was of a gateway in the Temple of Literature in Hanoi. I was thinking of the expression in the *Tao Te Ching*. The Way is the path you are on. It is nameless, but it is always coming into being.

After I finished with the ill-fated PhD, I ended up at a university, but, ironically or appropriately, not as an academic. Mostly our team were dealing with professional staff training, but sometimes we were approached to offer services to academics.

I had worked for around fifteen years on the CCH publication, *Managing Training and Development*, by which time I had written or rewritten most of its 1,600 pages. I felt competent to talk about any aspect of training and its management. I also felt that I had a good grasp of the underlying principles of learning. But I was asking myself, where was I in my life: Young, Living, or Firm Ground? I was certainly beyond Young, but that was no problem. Was I in the "Living" phase of my life, or was I on "Firm Ground"?

I think it shows in my reactions to things. When the manager castigated me for approaching the Vice Chancellor's office directly, was I mortified? I was not. It was her problem, and I didn't have to own it. We had managed to have some decent conversations. I told her I was exploring my family's history and she was interested. She told me that her mother lived in Sydney, but she was getting older. Her mother had come over from China, and the whole village had burned down. There were no family history records. Perhaps that was in the troubles that led to the establishment of China in 1949. I was sympathetic.

I was on Firm Ground. I wasn't to be shaken by an act of petulance.

I had written a poem a few years earlier: "I live in the city". It said, I live in the city, but at night I hear the sound of the mopoke, just as I did in Horseshoe Creek. I live in the city, but it is an abode, it is not my real home. But I am not one of those who see the city as a prison. I am not hungering for release. When the traffic stops at night there is silence, and it is the same silence that I listened to at Horseshoe Creek. I light a candle and the flame burns. It burns oxygen and travail equally.

I put that poem in *The Way Is Open*. I put it in the "Living" section. If that is how you live, eventually you will end up on firm ground. What am I approaching? Firm Ground.

95 Death of a publication

It was ironic that I ended up in a university, after resisting it for so long. Not long after I started there, the manager at CCH rang me up to tell me that there was no more work for me. It was December

2013. They had discontinued updates for the products I had been working on, and they were discontinuing *Managing Training and Development*, the product I had worked on ever since I started at CCH in November 1997. I thought I had done well to maintain the number of customers for this long.

The product was devised in the early 1990s in response to federal government legislation requiring companies to conduct training for their employees. It was a Paul Keating initiative (the Prime Minister at the time). CCH figured that companies might need guidance on how to provide training. So, as well as legal commentary (minimal), it included information on how to run training programs, how to design training programs, and how to manage the training function in a company. The legislation was ended when John Howard came to power in 1996.

I worked on all these aspects of the commentary, keeping it up to date and adding new topics to keep it "fresh". It was a most useful resource. The writer in New Zealand used to write for it as well. Realistically, the product should have been retired in the mid-1990s. It was impressive that it kept going for so long. I had used it myself when I was doing my Master of Education. It was the best commentary I knew on the practicalities of training and learning.

Now that it was gone, it was as if part of me had disappeared. It wasn't just the fact that I was no longer working on it; it had ceased to exist. There was no longer any sign of the work I had built up over the last fifteen years.

But, I had encountered this before. When I was sacked from the Challenge Foundation in Casino, I was devastated by the fact that all I had built up over the previous six years was being pulled apart, and I had put my heart into it. What I eventually learned was that you can't count on leaving a legacy behind you. I had done good things; now they were subject to the local environment. They could not depend on me, and I had no part in their future.

Many years later, I visited Casino, and I went out to the plant nursery we had established. It was still there, and it looked alive and well. That was good. It meant that the spirit of the plant nursery had lived on, despite the ructions of some greedy, power-hungry and destructive adults. They were nowhere to be found now.

The *Tao Te Ching* says that everything is change, and we must not expect things to persist. They are subject to the wheel of change. In the midst, there is life, the unchanging, the eternal. It is wise to take your focus off the monuments you wish to create. And what are books, but monuments?

96 Travel to England and Ireland

I had thoughts of talking about my trip to Ireland and England in 2018. I suppose it was significant because it happened the year before covid, in which case I would not have gone. This time I kept a diary, but perhaps people will feel that it is silly, despite the wonderful things that happened there. I am not a travel writer.

I arrived in London at seven a.m., in the rain. Then it took two hours to get through customs, so that someone could ask me what I was doing in England and then commend me to enjoy myself. There were about a thousand people lined up, and just five people on the desk.

When I came out to connect with my transfer to the hotel, no one was there. They had gone. I found a man from the company, and he said they only wait an hour and a half. I could wait for two hours for another car. Poor show; I was tired.

I went to the British Tourism counter and they organised a car for me, for which I paid (again). My driver was a black man with dreadlocks and a nice suit. The car was a Jaguar. He was polite and friendly, and pointed out areas as we passed. He told me the history of blacks in England.

When we arrived at the hotel, there was a fire engine outside with lights flashing. That was amusing. However, the crisis seemed to be over. I went inside. There were ten steps up to the reception area, so everyone with bags had to get them up the steps. Mystifying. My room wasn't ready, so I left my suitcase at the cloak room and went walking for a couple of hours. I just walked around the neighbourhood in a big circle. I walked past the British Museum. It wasn't raining much, just drizzle, although it was even more amorphous than that. There are lots of nice shops in the little streets around the museum.

I didn't go inside places. I wasn't ready to do that. I just walked around outside. I saw streets of houses, uniform for an entire block. I saw a statue of Mahatma Gandhi in Tavistock Square. I came across the building for the Quakers, the Society of Friends. I saw a fantastically frivolous building that I think was a hotel, circa late 1800s. I found some food stalls outside a place called the American Church, which was a church building, now with alternative predilections. I had a nice felafel roll, Lebanese.

You see? Travellers' stories.

Then, this odd encounter. I went out to get some dinner at 8.30 p.m.. I found a Korean restaurant in one of the little streets around the British Museum. It was nice to eat some normal (for me) food – rice, tofu and vegetables.

Walking back towards my hotel, I was approached by a man carrying a large carry bag. He was polite. He asked for my help. He was homeless in London, with a wife and little girl. He had found a place to stay but needed 40 pounds to obtain the place. He had been looking for a place all day, and his wife and child were at the place. He had gone back to get the bag, which was at a church nearby, which turned out to be the American Church where I had had lunch.

He was Irish, from Cork, which I guessed from his accent because of my Irish friend, and he confirmed it. What work could he get in London? He was a plasterer. He invited me to walk with him to the place, which was twenty-five minutes away. I said I was tired and didn't want to walk all that way. He said he could confirm with me. He had a case worker, Roy Mitchell. His own name was

Danny Clarke. He gave me a phone number, which I could ring in about an hour and he would get Roy to talk to me.

I gave him the money because he was a homeless Irish in London, as was Sarah Crosby in 1850. How could I judge that he was genuine? I could accept that he was, but of course he could have been a cad. So I gave the money for Sarah, an offering to the universe. I was tired, and didn't remember to call back later, but that would probably only have called up more questions about verification.

So, my first night in London, and the highlight is a homeless Irishman and my donation to him. You see? So many people would call me stupid or gullible. But it's not their business.

My time in London included museums and art galleries. It was all good, but you probably don't need my opinions about Picasso or modern art. When I went to the Picasso exhibition, the most intriguing thing was the man taking photos of the people looking at the Picasso paintings.

I went to Westminster Abbey. Yes, it's impressive, but we were kind of rushed through, and you are not allowed to take photos in there. I could have taken many! But I found this quote inscribed in the floor: "Thou art the journey and the journey's end."

The author was Michael Mayne, who was the Dean of Westminster from 1986 to 1996. His ashes, of course, lie in the Abbey. I love the quote, because while it may be true that we should focus on the journey, not the destination, the journey doesn't make any sense unless there is a destination, and we must not forget that. Thank you, Michael.

Things I know
Enjoy the journey; don't lose sight of the end.

97 Ireland and Cork

After that I went to Ireland: to Dublin and Cork. In Dublin I saw Christ Church Cathedral, which was dignified and impressive, and I saw plaques in a park for famous Irish authors, such as Oscar Wilde, George Bernard Shaw, W.B. Yeats, and James Joyce. I saw the statue of Molly Malone with her cart, selling cockles and mussels. I ate at a vegan restaurant where my daughter had eaten when she lived in Dublin about fifteen years ago. I saw an exhibition of the Book of Kells at Trinity college. There was much to love.

After my fill of Dublin, I got on a bus and went west, to Castletownbere in County Cork. My Irish friend in Sydney (Lady 5) came from here, and she was actually visiting now, seeing her mother. There was a second reason too. A friend at work happened to come from this same town, and I wanted to visit his father.

I spent some grand days there, involved in local activities and mixing with Lady 5's family and my work friend's father. It was a shift from places of renown to places of groundedness and love. We went on a walk up Hungry Hill in the mist and felt immersed in that boggy landscape as the mists drifted around and made hills and lakes appear and disappear at whim.

I enjoyed the life of a Bed-and-Breakfast in a lively garden, with flowers everywhere. With Lady 5, I visited an artist and musician, Timothy Goulding, who lived in the hills further west. One night we went to a concert in Castletownbere by Liam O'Maonlai. He was in a group called the Hothouse Flowers in the 1990s. He was extraordinary. Usually, artists will do a sad number towards the end of the concert. No, he made the audience cry in the first ten minutes. It was a playlist that traversed all the emotions. He was a wonderful musician and larger than life.

I went on a memorable day-trip with my work friend's father. I could tell he loved his son, and that he wanted to show me significant things. There seems to be an undercurrent of sad events in Ireland, and quests for the spiritual. We went to the town Dingle, because he had been born there. When we arrived it was boisterous, because there was a festival on today. There were hundreds of people, and cars everywhere. But he knew exactly what to do: he drove into a side street and then into a private property. I was puzzled, but we got out of the car and he went over to the house and tapped on the wall, and said, "This is the house I was born in." And he owned it now.

We went to the church where his family used to go. He genuflected as we entered, naturally, habitually. There was a grotto outside the church with an exalted Mary of Fatima. Along the trip back we stopped to look at an ancient (2,000 BC) site of stone walls and beehive-shaped shelters, the Fahan Group, still looking very solid after all this time. It was quite an extensive maze of stonework across the hillside; it suggested an established way of life. It seemed isolated, but I guess that assumes there is somewhere else that is the centre of things.

Along the side of the road at one point there was a grotto, a set of statues, all in white stone, with Jesus on the cross and people looking up to him. I am told this is common in Ireland. It is part of the fabric of life. And amidst that, there is the striving to break free of the religious cultural bonds. It does not seem to be resolved. My work friend's father genuflects when he enters a church, and he lives an honourable life.

98 About Cornwall

I also went to Cornwall. I saw many interesting places. Yet, it is the encounters that stick. I caught a taxi in London to Blackfriars Station. I told the driver I had been to Cornwall, and he said he was born at Hayle, the next town around the coast from St Ives. He was about sixty, and had grown up there, and it had been very much the country life, catching fish and rabbits, and some kids also made money breeding dogs. When the blackberries were in season, they used to take buckets and collect them. Life was very much in the outdoors, and not about what you could buy, nor about watching television. He still goes back there to visit family every year, and so do his two children.

He said the township of Hayle had two ends – one was more about the digging of ore (tin and copper, as the case may be), and the other end was more about the processing of the ore. The town kept some kind of balance between mining, fishing and farming. Nowadays there is talk about opening the mine again because prices have changed and it may become viable again. There is a mineral that is used in lithium batteries for mobile phones etc. (My son invests in lithium mines.)

He said social media wasn't breeding tolerance; quite the opposite. He said you can hear it in the language people use – it is about hate and divisiveness. He was against Brexit, and said that people who were for it were impervious to facts. When they heard a fact, they dismissed it and carried on. Leaders like Donald Trump and people of the same ilk in Britain and other countries were capitalising on it by telling people what they wanted to hear, with no regard for the truth.

The taxi driver looked like my father. The Cornish roots show.

99 Railway interlude

Another day in London, I was on the Underground, competently changing lines from the Circle line to the Central line at Liverpool Street Station when a very Chinese lady, young, dressed ever so elegantly, asked me for help. I was staring at the sign to see what platform I had to get to. I thought, "This is amusing. Do you have any idea how ignorant I am?" And then I thought: older man with grey hair, looks sane, hopefully is helpful.

So I said, "You want me to help you?" (Emphasis in the right places, and I had a smile as an accompaniment.) Her story was, in stilted English, that she had just got off a plane from Tong Cheng in China. (I had not heard of Tong Chen.)

She loved art and she wanted to be in London to experience it. She wanted to go to Bethnal Green. She had a large suitcase that she needed help with, getting up the stairs. It was like being on the hillside at Woodford and being asked to do the I Ching without my books or coins. Would I know the answer? Well, I was going to Bethnal Green, so in fact I did.

Bear in mind, it was peak hour, and the trains were crowded. We let one train go; it was too crowded, and tried for the next one. She got on, and then grabbed my arm and dragged me in to make sure I got on too, and she wasn't marooned alone. We got to Bethnal Green and I helped her up the stairs with her suitcase.

Once we were on the footpath and could relax, she said, "I have to take photo of you, because you are nice man." She told me her name was Baowon (phonetically), meaning wind over water (the I Ching understands that: it is 59 Huan, Dispersion). She got out her phone and got her directions from Google Maps and off she went.

I couldn't find Tong Chen on the map of China, but I was struggling with her accent. She said it was a big city in the southwest of China, and it was the capital of the province. So, it may have been Chengdu, capital of the Sichuan province. She was in London to experience the art world.

100 Cornwall and London

I was in Cornwall. I caught the train there from London, picked up a hire-car and stayed for a week. One day I drove to the St Ives Archive, about a mile up the road from the guest house where I was staying. I was a bit early, so I thought I would walk down to the beach at Carbis Bay. There was a walking track between the houses. After about a hundred metres I came to a T-intersection, and I was puzzling about which side to take when a man walked up the path towards me. He asked me if I was lost, and if I was alright. I said I was lost, but he took this to be a joke. He said, smiling, "No, you're not lost. I've seen you around here before." That was a bit unusual.

Off he went, and I found my way to the beach. It was beautiful, and like St Ives, there was a train station and a train line running parallel with the beach. An idyllic place. There are lots of modern houses around here, not grand, but comfortable suburban houses with land around them.

I went to the St Ives Archive. It was odd in the sense that they didn't seem to be expecting visitors. There was a big office and a reading room with books and folders. I told the man my situation and I showed him my book: *They Went to Australia*. He was sympathetic but he said they didn't really do family history. They do local history. I told him about my experience on the pathway down to the beach. He looked me up and down carefully, and then said, "You know, you wouldn't look out of place in a line-up of Cornish gentlemen!" and we both laughed about it. It had been 161 years since the older Thomas Martin with his wife and his young son had left Cornwall for Australia.

The day I left Cornwall to travel back to London on the train, Saturday 19th May 2018, was the day of the Royal Wedding: Prince Harry and Miss Meghan Markle. When I arrived at London and got out to walk around, there were picnics in the parks everywhere. It was festive and people were happy. There were picnic baskets and picnic blankets and clean, casual clothing. There was picnic food, animated conversations and laughter. It was memorable. It felt nice to be there, when conviviality seemed to have blossomed so universally.

I went to Kew Gardens one day. It was delightful, a very rich experience. The strangest looking tree I saw was the Monkey Puzzle tree. While I was looking at it, two couples walked up, and one of the ladies asked me how to grow them from seed. I gave her instructions. So, I look like a guy that knows how to grow Monkey Puzzle trees.

I went to the Tate Britain gallery. It's on the riverbank of the Thames. I knew there was a monument to Millbank Prison somewhere near there. Millbank Prison was where Sarah Crosby was held before being transported to Australia in December 1949. The prison was here between about 1816 and 1890. I asked the guide at the Information desk of the gallery for directions. He said, "Yes, it's a bit further down the road, and Henry Moore did a sculpture to commemorate the prison."

I found it, and I put my hand on the stone that had been at the prison gate where convicts were loaded onto the ships that would take them to Australia. Sarah went on the *St Vincent*. Henry Moore's sculpture was nearby.

101 Office decorations

That's more than enough about my trip. When I came home and went back to work, my office was festooned like a Royal Wedding picnic. There were flags, pictures, a magazine of the Royal Wedding, and a picnic basket with picnic food just like I had seen in the parks in London. There was also a mock family tree on one wall, which charted my supposed connections to Aston Martin, Dean Martin and a bunch of other famous people with "Martin" in their names. This was a tradition that had grown up for when someone returned from a holiday. It was inventive and humorous, and a sign of our mutual affection.

Perhaps we travel far in order to come home. But that could be such a trite, nothing sort of statement. Perhaps better to say this: we try to make sense of things, we try to bring order to things, and we are teased by inexplicable incidents, like the man on the pathway at Carbis Bay. Had he seen me before? Or someone like me? Did it occur on another plane, as dreams do? Is there some part of me that still lives in Cornwall, and is happy there, like the taxi driver in London who was born in Hayle and remembers his wholesome childhood fondly?

102 Disengaging

I gradually disengaged from work. It was like when I was the editor of the training magazine. It served a purpose for some time. It allowed me to exercise my talents on composing and putting together all the content of a magazine, and then being able to do this regularly to a consistently high standard. Not that this was ever seriously appreciated, not consciously, anyway. But eventually I realised I was not "home". I was not where I belonged.

When I quit from the magazine, I received an email from one of the staff. She said she was sorry to see me go, and it was "the end of an error". I had to agree, although I found it difficult to see how a person in marketing would lack the language skills to distinguish "error" and "era".

With the job at the college, I similarly realised I was not "home" and I could not continue much longer. There were some big conflicts, not on my part, but there were people there who felt they had licence to abuse others, and that stopped at my door. Their conceit continued, but my principle was simple, not sophisticated: I require respect. I even consulted the university's policies to discover if there was, in fact, a policy about respect. There was: I was on firm ground.

At one point I had a girl in her twenties, a new employee, attempt to force me to carry out a task for her that was her responsibility. "No," I said, "I will not be doing that. You will be doing it yourself." It was reported to me that she cried. This was presented to me as an argument against me. Oh dear! The upshot was that I did not have to do any work for her or anyone else in her team. It was not a sensible solution. The solution was simple: respect.

But, it was not my mission in life to enforce principles like respect in errant workplaces. And in terms of work, I had done some good things. We had devised an online training course for teachers to train them to teach online. We created some resource materials they could access and digest by themselves, and then there were some zoom sessions that we ran, during which they carried out practice exercises. It was respectable material, nicely conceived and well-executed. But what more was I going to do at the college? From here on it would become trivial.

I could be home. And I know I have said it is not my home, it is just my abode, somewhere to be for the duration. But I have loved my home, and it has become a nurturing place. I think I love my home the way parents love children. It is as simple as it is, and whole.

Some people retire and are still restless. They look for part-time work. I had no second thoughts. Once I had accepted that I could survive financially, always with a view to modesty, I made the move. It was as if I had removed a whole lot of clutter and now had room to bring some big ideas into fruition. There was nothing to interfere with my time or energy. You could say: this was what I had been a long time approaching.

103 Four pillars: Competence

It could be asked: where do I stand in relation to the four pillars? It's a fair question. Competence. We go through stages. Let's say, three stages: Dependence, Independence, Interdependence. And competence can relate to all aspects of life, not just the area of work. It can relate to your whole perception of how you are travelling through life. The Dependence stage is where you rely on others and follow social conventions. When you move beyond this, you can be more of an architect of your own destiny, making your own decisions, relying on your own judgement, developing your own style; this is what Independence looks like.

So, what is Interdependence? Why would you want it?

If we just talk about work, and just talk about the place I progressed to, that is, being a writer, I understand what dependence is and what independence means.

What is it to be a writer? It is something more than wanting to be seen as a writer. You need to understand what it takes to write. Words are not so easy to manage; they are like sheep that roam the paddock and are not interested in being rounded up and pushed through a particular gate. To be a writer you have to be the sheepdog that can round up thirty or forty sheep and usher them through that gate. And in the case of words, they have to be in a particular order.

At the publishing company I had a new employee working for me once. I had not employed him, but he was given to me to supervise. I gave him a story to write. It wasn't hard. He had the transcript of a court case that was about 3,000 words long, and he had to write a summary of about 600 words from it. I gave him plenty of time. When he brought it to me, I read it and he had missed the point. It was full of "He said this and she said that", but it missed the lesson of the court case, the one that readers would want to know.

I tried again. I found a case that was deliberately simple, and asked him to produce a summary. I asked him to look for the critical point, then to write the story in a way that would interest the reader and explain the point. I gave him some examples to read. But he couldn't do it. He didn't seem to get the idea of the critical point, and the essential structure of a story. I told him we couldn't keep him, and to look for a job that he could do.

So, writing is tough because the goal can be elusive. But if you have been doing it for a while, do you develop? I think you develop confidence, as long as you remember there are traps in that as well. And there is the untameable aspect of it. It is not only about technique; it is about having something unique to say. The counter-model is the author of Mills & Boon romances; you can spin them out forever by mixing up the ingredients a bit differently each time (just as you can spin out endless PhD theses for subjects with shirts of a different colour). But the stories will all take place within the same continuum.

My concept of independence embraces development to the point of having cultivated your technical skill (people have said to me, "The writing in the book was beautiful"; my mother said, "You always did have a good way with words"). But also, it embraces the cultivation of your individual voice, and your eternal quest for having something vital to say.

So, the question again: what is Interdependence? I think it evolves out of the quests that occur at the stage of independence. The quest of an individual voice is achieved, so it is no longer the great goal. But the need to have something vital to say looms larger. Yet, interdependence implies another party with whom we are interdependent. Some people seek to personalise this – God, a spirit, a force – but I think that is to reduce its vastness.

The Tao accepts that the heart of being is vast and nameless. We are confronted by it, beyond the confines of any religious terms, in the present moment. The only learning is to practise awareness of it, beyond mere intellect. We proceed beyond Independence to Interdependence.

What is my view of competence now, as a writer? I think the core of it is that you are trying to say something, to put something into words. There is a feeling or an idea that has not yet been expressed, and when you have written it down you will know if you have expressed it appropriately, or adequately. Failure is a high possibility. But sometimes the fire is lit; sometimes the water is hauled up from the well. There are moments like that. So, in a way, you are trying to express what you don't know, not what you know. You are in touch with the fire and you are not burned. At the beginning there is wonder, and on good days, it is there at the end.

104 Morality

The second pillar is Morality. You could say there are three stages here as well. However, another perspective is that there are five core human values, so it is a question of how you see yourself against those values. I name them as: truth, peace, right action, love (or deep respect) and appreciation.

I do not think it is appropriate to purport to score yourself and assert your innocence in life. Life is dirty, and so are we. I could see that, palpably, in the crowd's reaction at Woodford to Kate Miller-Heidke's song, appropriately called "Caught in the Crowd". We know the guilt we bear. What we come to very quickly, when we consider our failings and shortcomings, are two things as the causes: our lack of courage, and our failure to see what was important at the appropriate time.

I think that if you are committed to continually correcting yourself, then that is the way to live. Then you will be more and more in tune with what life requires of us, as Viktor Frankl argued.

And that is all there is to be said here on morality. The book, *A Foundation for Living Ethically*, provides the framework for the five core human values by which you may live a worthwhile life.

105 Beauty

The third pillar is Beauty. It seems to me that beauty is in contest with struggle. When we start out in life, we are inexperienced and so we encounter struggle. Accordingly, we focus on survival, and we develop an attitude of "This will do." And there is wisdom in that. Indeed, in the circumstances of the time, it probably was exactly what would do. I would never be scornful about that.

However, one develops competence, and even mastery, and then the question arises again: what is the best you could do, after you have satisfied necessary concerns? You discover that you still have strength to do a little bit more. So, your work gets better. It even becomes excellent. It gets admired. And this is the goal. We always want beauty; the question is merely whether we have the capacity to produce it. Some people learn to fake it. We live in a world of promises, so people get used to faking it, to producing tricks and effects.

In the I Ching, there is a hexagram called Adornment (22). But the message of the hexagram is that beauty must come from the inner core, not merely be pasted on the outside, like jewels and make-up. Alfred Huang says, "Beauty helps the people to act in accordance with the proper time and proper situation. Thus, humanity is adorned."

Beauty, whether natural or human-created, reminds us of perfection, and how we long for it. And, reminded of it, we act more like we should, humbled and appreciative of all life. I have tried to make my book covers aesthetic. I have also sought to make my house attractive. I am getting there.

106 Love

The fourth pillar is love. I figured this question was coming. The last time I went to Woodford (December 2017), I went to see a palm-reader. I was curious: I had never done that before, and besides, I was at Woodford. He remarked about the shape of my hand. He said it indicated a practical person who likes to be able to do things for himself. Trades people have such hands. He was surprised that my endeavours are intellectual, but he said it can be applicable in that sphere.

My hands probably look like those of many men in Cornwall. However, it is true of my adult life. I made an effort, especially at

Horseshoe Creek, to learn how to do things for myself so I was not dependent on others.

He asked me if I still worked, and he asked me why. He asked me about travelling and whether I had done much, and he suggested I would find much joy in travel. I told him I was writing about family history, and he took this to be a hobby, but he said I could combine it with travel. Six months later I went to England and Ireland. A little over twelve months later, I left work.

Then, he asked me if I was in a relationship, and he was surprised when I said I wasn't, because the line indicated activity. He said I should think about attracting someone, and how I had to be of the right vibration, or I would be invisible. It was an interesting experience.

So, I must have thoughts on relationships and love. Lady 1, Lady 2, Lady 3…. Has there been anyone else? Have I been trying to attract someone? There have been phases, and adventures that have not gone well. I know the psychological opinions about being in a partnership as you get older; they say there are statistics: those who are in relationships live longer and are healthier.

Our society has become rather fond of statistics, as if the circumstances of individual cases did not matter at all.

Things I know
Humans are repositories of opinions, usually other people's.

107 Love and marriage and me

Nevertheless, it's not a simple case of arranging for a woman to fill a space. Lists of attributes may work on dating apps, but life is a little more subtle than that.

I have had helpful offers, but I have met women who talk the same language but come from a different planet. I read Elizabeth

Gilbert's book, *Committed*, the one she wrote after *Eat, Pray, Love*. I liked the book; she talked about the reasons for marriage. But then, she was still young at the time.

I also read what Hua-Ching Ni had to say about marriage. He is the author of a translation of the I Ching. He had a different perspective, as an older man, and as someone who had an identity as a spiritual teacher.

So, having weighed all this up, I wrote an article about it: "Love and Marriage and Me". It was published in *Living Now* magazine in 2020. I have included it in the Stories section. No need to repeat it all here. I still find what I wrote salient and persuasive.

A further point: If you were to apply the three-stages perspective, the third stage would be where love opens up to include everyone and everything in life. It is not confined to romantic love between two persons.

108 Finish

I'd like to finish now. It is a memoir of sorts. It is incomplete in many ways – rightly so, purposely so. It is an idea, a thread through my life that may make some kind of sense – the journey has been a long-time approach. Some people might have liked less, and some might have liked more. That's as it may be. I have kept names out of it for the most part, because I have been illuminating the lessons of my life, not setting out to expose other individuals. Perhaps this is not how other people do things, but the point of living is to arrive at the way you do things, not how other people do them.

This book is part of my whole body of work, and a writer should not repeat what he has already written, so I have pointed to my other books where the fuller story of particular episodes or themes is located.

I do not know what comes next. One needs to draw breath first.

If I had to say how to live, I will put it this way:

"First, be contented. Then, use all of your capacities to make the most of your life: your intelligence, make peace with your emotions, and be awake to what is happening around you in the present moment (always be ready for transformation)."

Enjoy.

Stories

The Language Lesson

A story from a few years ago about an incident in a restaurant while I was waiting for take-away.

I was travelling in New Zealand, just one week driving around the north island (December 2011). This day I had driven from Lake Taupo to the small city of Napier, on the east coast. It was a quaint place, which was particularly gratifying since most of the town was destroyed in an earthquake in 1931. You would expect the architecture to be post-earthquake homogeneous and utilitarian, but in fact it is an art deco delight, a deliberate decision of the city fathers at the time.

I had booked a bed-and-breakfast place to stay at, and I had found it, in a quiet nook near the top of a hill. It was an enchanting old weatherboard house with a small courtyard, modernised for the comfort of travelling folk. I decided it would be nicer to buy take-way food and bring it back here rather than eat in town.

I went to town and looked around. It was all very pleasant. My only jarring experience was the discovery that the beach did not have sand; it was all granite pebbles. My definition of beach includes sand as an essential ingredient, so this was messing terribly with my understanding of the concept of 'beach'. But I guess that's why they say travel broadens the mind.

I decided on a restaurant for my take-away meal. It was in the middle of town, an old-fashioned-looking Singapore restaurant. When you walked in the door, there were piles of goods all around you. Turn right for the restaurant, and go straight ahead for the take-away counter, in among the groceries and fridges.

A waitress was ready to receive me. She was tall, and elegantly dressed in red silk with a lace trim – something my mother would have been pleased to have made. Other family members – a mother, and a cousin perhaps – were going to and from the kitchen. The mother was wearing a half-apron in floral.

I ordered dinner – tofu and vegetables, Lor Han style (it is home-style Chinese cooking). There is a stool for me to sit on, in front of the fridge and close to the people bringing food from the kitchen.

I am sitting, waiting, and listening to the chatter of Chinese people in the restaurant, all pleasant and animated, when a young Chinese man, in a suit, appears. He's come from a table in the restaurant, so I hadn't seen him before. He must have seen me when I walked in.

He addresses me. He says, "Please, can you help, how you say in English?"

I stand up so that we are closer, and he continues, "I want to say, in English, what is it, when someone has done you big favour?"

I try "Grateful".

He says, "Yes, but there is word to say 'feeling'." He puts his hand on his heart.

I try "Appreciate" but I know that's not it. He's heard the words he wants to say, but he can't recall them. But then he says, as a question, "Move?"

"Ah", I say, "You mean, 'I am moved'". I spell it for him: "M-o-v-e-d." With the 'd'.

He is not quite satisfied yet. He touches his heart again, and then I get it. "You mean, 'I am deeply moved'?"

And that's it. He says it: "I am deeply moved by your...."

I nod happily, saying, "Yes, that's it!"

And he grins and he says, "Thank you!" Then he adds, laughing, "I am deeply moved." We both laugh.

He goes back to his group, and I hear him say it to someone, and there is the sound of appreciation. Then he is explaining it, and saying it again, and someone else is saying it and there is happy laughter.

When my meal is ready, the elegant waitress smiles and thanks me for being patient with the young man. I smile too.

Dancing with Intent

An experience at Woodford Folk Festival, December 2006.

She came into the tent where the band was playing, bag in hand, purposeful step. There was space for dancing – it was late morning on New Year's Day and few of the new-year revellers had surfaced yet.

The band was performing with practised design, creating sweet landscapes of sound. This was a band that had been carving out its own space for over ten years. It knew its mastery of that space, swinging from grand to frolic, summoning trickle, flow and storm from guitar and fiddle, didgeridoo, piano, drums.

Song was high and rhythm established. The woman barely looked around. Barefoot, she entered the space and moved, picking up the time, tuning body to sound.

People dance to give heed to music and the occasion of gathering with others. Or they dance to acknowledge the excitement of the music. Most often they dance in habitual moves, and with one eye on the censor, who is a shadow in the back row, ever-critical.

The censor says you must be careful not to look foolish, and the most cautious way to ensure this is to watch others and copy them. And when we are all in synchrony with that projected image, we have ground down our patterns to doggerel steps. We have a small repertoire of moves we all know, and we can look at each other and know we are at least safe.

The woman is not interested in safety. She does not dance to prove she is like others. Her feet and her body tell a story, and it is her own.

The band is above this. If they have a pact with dancers or with the audience, it is secret. They keep to their score, and the places it takes them. They soar, moan, laugh and affirm, they lilt, lament and beguile. They do it loud to shake the thin canvas of the tent, and they take moments into softness to suffuse the tent with gentle magic.

And the woman stomps her feet. Not heavy, but with firmness. Not clumsily; rather, with grace. Her feet are making a statement. What is it about? She stomps, and her feet meet the earth of the tent's floor. Stomp.

Around her there is the scattered flurry of other dancers. A young man on a backpacker's holiday from Europe, with wild, bright clothes purchased only this week. A young mother and her two-year-old daughter, sharing new adventures and whirling for fun. A woman in her forties taking her respite from corporate life and trying to remember what is worthwhile.

In among this, a tribal ceremony without precedent, a woman alone in a ritual of reconnection. Stomp on the earth, the earth that is our mother, the earth that gives birth to trees standing tall, the earth that bears our food and lies underneath as we sleep at night.

This was a dance of affirmation, of joy in feet meeting the solidity of earth, of gratefulness for each footfall and its answering thud. The strength is in her now, in her stomach, in her heart as she too whirls, carving an arc between other bodies and tracing the air with lightness.

Late-morning stragglers wander in and assume seats, enjoying the music's journey as they continue waking. The sun vies for attention as the heat rises.

In her soundless ritual, the dancer wears the heat with delicacy, perspiration at her throat and through her blouse. The meaning is in the movement as the band's story comes to completion. She arches her body with arms reaching out and up.

We know that trees live out of the earth's strength. We know that they sink their roots deep and wide, and build on that to climb through their trunk to the sky. We know that the branches of trees speak the glory of possibility, and the roar of leaves is deafening when the wind is wild.

There was no saying of this in words. There was the music, the longing of song, and the woman's feet beating out rhythm on earth. There was the quiet certainty in her performance. This was the renewal, allowing the strength of earth to enter her body, to find herself come again into grace and unafraid.

Then the going forth again.

The last song, the sporadic clapping of a hot, late-morning tent at a music festival, warm sentiments (fantastic, magnificent) and bags collected. The woman picks up her bag from the chair and is quickly away.

Postcards from Woodford

The Lettering House was a crazy idea – the idea that you could write a letter to someone else at the festival and the trusty postal officers (yes, there were postal officers on push-bikes, in uniform) would deliver it – "To the woman who was dancing with her child" et cetera.

As crazy as it was, it unleashed a torrent of letter-writing. Dozens of people turned up at the Lettering House each day to sit and write – and decorate – letters to someone, and peg them up on the board to be delivered. It was, like most things at Woodford, a master stroke of whimsy.

My version was to write a postcard to all the people of Woodford every day of the festival, and post it on the notice board in the Lettering House.

Postcard, Day 1: Wed 27 Dec 2017

Is it only a thought if it lands somewhere?
Some things just need to be said (after a while, and while it is still salient).
Stand up straight.
Play nice.
Be kind.
Enjoy.
In adversity, repeat.

Postcard, Day 2: Thur 28 Dec 2017

Yesterday was all advice.
Yes, yes, of course.
Today we unwind.
Because I was not expecting Bob Hawke to sing Waltzing Matilda.

And I was amazed once again at the beautiful minds of the Welcome Ceremony.

Home, for a while.

Thank you. It's music, and free, and love, and then, there it is: joy. Included.

Postcard, Day 3: Fri 29 Dec 2017

The survey asked: "What is it?" – in one word.

But I would use many words: light, lovely, frenzy-from-the-outside-but-harmonious-from-within, cohesive and in colour, nothing is a bonus because it is all included.

The bucket descends into the well and arises drenching.

Bob Hawke talked about shame, but he said, "Do the job that needs to be done."

And rest in plenty.

I don't think I have to try. It is already okay. It has always been becoming so.

Postcard, Day 4: Sat 30 Dec 2017

Day 4 goes down as well as up. Started out with good expectation, good intention.

After time, disappointments. After events, annoyances.

Fatigue (they say).

Recovery? What would words do anyway? They would have to be big words.

"I don't care!" "Go to hell!"

I use my biggest word: "Nevertheless."

Look, I have brought you a smile. I may only be saying, but this is what I am saying.

Postcard, Day 5: Sun 31 Dec 2017

Weather Report: It is hot and muggy.
This morning I learned that most males think 9.30 a.m. is the best time to have a shower. I think 4.30 p.m. is the best time while at Woodford (tell no one), but I wanted a shower this morning because of Sentence 1.
I have been listening to people – catches of conversations. It's good to listen without judging but also without giving up on my understandings.
I observe good times (enjoyment), unhappiness and irritation.
I think (today, anyway) the core guidance for living well is to have good will.
So.

Postcard, Day 6: Mon 1 Jan 2018

I am putting out the fire and scattering the ashes. We have to think of the road now, and the weather vying for our attention.
I have packed away moments and encounters, music that is entirely new, or old and worth remembering.
To say we danced may seem taunting to those who were not here. We have been in the belly of the whale, and now it will vomit us out.
But we will open our mouths and birds will fly out.

Love and marriage and me

An article on relationships, for Living Now magazine, June 2020.

When we say "relationship", we are often talking about a one-to-one relationship between two persons, intended to be long-term, maybe lifelong. Let's accept this. What is to be said about such relationships?

I once met a happy couple who had five young children and a chaotic but snug household. I was travelling to pick up my children for the holidays, casualties of a broken marriage (my first). My car had broken down on the road – in the dark, in the bush – and they stopped for me. He was a mechanic. I drove my car to their house and he fixed my car.

Their wisdom? All first marriages are a mistake, and why wouldn't they be? Both people are too young, too headstrong, and too ignorant about life. Second marriages are second chances to get it right. A bit harsh, perhaps, but essentially optimistic.

I read a book by a Tai Chi master. His view was that marriage is about creating a safe context for children to grow up in. "You are looking at maybe twenty-five years of your life", he said. "Don't get married and have children unless you understand that this is the commitment you are making." He went on to say, "After this it doesn't matter. You don't need to be married for life, and in twenty-five years you have both probably changed a lot. You probably want different things." (This was Hua-Ching Ni, author of a translation of the I Ching.)

I also read, in Richard Wilhelm's translation of the I Ching, that there are two ingredients to marriage – affection and tact. I liked this; it seemed to have yin and yang in it, a balance. However, my wife of the time (my first marriage) didn't like it. She thought that affection was a weak form of passion, and she thought that passion should last. She was also offended by the suggestion of the need for tact.

Let it be said that Richard Wilhelm was a married man as well as a student of the I Ching, many years into his relationship with both. I thought about that; I liked it. I'm not going to explain what I understand by affection and tact, but I had never read that sentiment before, and it seemed like a real insight. I still think so.

Many years on, I am not "in a relationship". Finally, I feel okay about this. As Hua-Ching Ni said, marriage is primarily for bringing children up, and those days, for me, are long over. I am not against being married for life, but I don't think it works out that way very often. Many long-term marriages I see consist of two people who have learned ways to tolerate each other: "I'll put up with your foibles if you put up with mine."

"Foibles" is an extreme way to talk about the need for tact. If we accept Wilhelm's perspective then we accept the need for tact, but if the essence of a marriage is toleration, then I would give Hua-Ching Ni's idea consideration – do you really need to be married? Is it only for dependence? Or is it just a habit?

Recently I read Elizabeth Gilbert's book, *Committed*, the one she wrote after *Eat, Pray, Love*. Suddenly, she and Felipe have to commit to formal betrothal, for immigration reasons. They had both been passionate resisters of a legal marriage – given their respective first-marriage experiences. I still have the image of that couple in the hills behind Coffs Harbour, in their modest house full of kids, each other and happiness. Late at night, the mechanic working on my car in his garage, and me in the kitchen discussing marriage with his wife while the kids played and laughed.

In the end, perhaps, it is not about solid, logical arguments, but impressions; real life as it occurs. And love, conscious love – the awareness of this.

Elizabeth Gilbert. I thought it was strange to be reading a book on marriage at the age of seventy, having forgone all of that. Having had too many repetitively bad experiences. (Yes, you could say it was me. My response is that my greatest sin was bad choosing. At this point, it is no longer relevant.) I enjoyed Elizabeth's book. She was no longer an adolescent; she was an adult who could think about all the various perspectives on marriage.

The idea that stuck, after all the details, was that there are three reasons for marriage. One, historically the most important, is property. Not that the wife is property, although that was often part of it too, but the idea that marriage is about protecting property. It is an orderly way of passing property onto the next generation.

The second reason for marriage is convention. I am not claiming that Gilbert said this, but this is how it sits in my mental framework. There is much weight in social convention. You grow up. What do you do? You get married. Male or female. That's what you do. Through it you get acceptance and belonging, and you know all the things you have to do, day by day, year by year. It is quite difficult to live apart from, or outside of, social convention. To do so, you have to grow into your individuality. You have to be robust and self-confident. Do you know many people like that?

The third reason for marriage is romance, the love that two people have for each other. Love, passion, affection – sometimes there is no need to unwind them, and sometimes there is. I'll leave that to the reader. In many respects this is a modern idea, except for the rich and powerful. There has always been a certain licence that was extended to them. Nowadays romance is theoretically open to all of us.

Elizabeth Gilbert and Felipe sorted out their stance. They juggled property and romance. They found a way. In the end, the immigration issue was sorted out, she had bought a house that had been a church, and they got married in that house. Kinda perfect, don't you think?

I trust they are living well. I remember Richard Bach, he of *Jonathan Living Seagull*, the book that inspired millions. And then there were other books he wrote, and in them was a woman that he swore love to. But, after one of those books was published, stories came out about how he had left her for someone else. Of course, life moves on, but promises are promises, and people didn't like it. After that, Richard Bach's books lost their gloss.

So you have to ask, what is love? And what does it mean to promise forever?

Life is seldom picture-book perfect. But there are words and there are feelings, not always in synch. It's so hard to keep things in synch. In relationships, there is so much that you have to work out – you, the other person, and the space between us, which is my space and your space. But there are moments when you touch, in the light of the beyond. In the morning sun, do not reach far. Bask in the warmth. And that's what you do: you keep renewing the promise.

Other books by Glenn Martin

Stories/Reflections on experience
The Ten Thousand Things (2010)
Sustenance (2011)
To the Bush and Back to Business (2012)
The Big Story Falls Apart (2014)
The Quilt Approach: A Tasmanian Patchwork (2020)

Books on ethics and life
Human Values and Ethics in the Workplace (2010)
The Little Book of Ethics: A Human Values Approach (2011)
The Concise Book of Ethics (2012)
A Foundation for Living Ethically (2020)
Future: The Spiritual Story of Humanity (2020)

Books on family history
A Modest Quest (2017)
The Search for Edward Lewis (2018)
They Went to Australia (2019)
No Gold in Melbourne: A Scottish Family in Australia (2021)
All the Rivers Come Together: Tracing Family (2022)

Poetry collections
Flames in the Open (2007)
Love and Armour (2007)
Volume 4: I in the Stream (2017)
Volume 3: That Was Then: The Early Poems Project (2019)
The Way Is Open (2020)

Local histories
Places in the Bush: A History of Kyogle Shire (1988)
The Kyogle Public School Centenary Book (1995)

www.ingramcontent.com/pod-product-compliance
Lightning Source LLC
Chambersburg PA
CBHW070725160426
43192CB00009B/1317